"Survival was often linked to the sacrifice of someone else. Indeed, the underlying interrogation of this work is embedded in the questions that can only be pondered, never answered: *What would you have done?* . . . Schwartz's journey is more about life than death, and her book is a small monument to the uncounted victims who did not die in the Holocaust. With self-revealing prose she reminds us that the deepest suffering, if not the greatest, rests with those who survived."

    Prairie Schooner

"A fascinating picture. . . . It is a measure of [Schwartz's] nuanced approach and refusal to settle for pat, simplistic answers that her book finds and genuinely values a rare point of light in that darkest of times without ever exaggerating its overall significance."

    Washington Times

"Unlike profiles of Oskar Schindler and Raul Wallenberg, those well-known righteous gentiles who saved Jews through a combination of money, power, and bravery, Schwartz focuses on the everyday kindnesses practiced on a small scale, neighbor to neighbor . . . [from] 'The barber cut Jewish hair under the sign NO JEWS ALLOWED HERE' to 'Christians paid back debts to Jews even though the law said they didn't have to.' . . . These may be 'small acts of defiance,' Schwartz concludes, but 'decency is so often such a solitary act; it's evil that draws a noisy crowd.'"

    JBooks.com

"Schwartz's tone is gentle, her prose brilliantly clear and her insights keen."

    Kirkus Reviews

"This book of moments and little stories surprises and horrifies, soothes and disturbs. But it is, above all, a beautiful read by a charming writer."

Wilson Quarterly

"Whether or not one can, or should, move on from the Holocaust is central to Schwartz's many important themes. . . . *Good Neighbors, Bad Times* gives evidence of the need to connect, to honor, to fight against the obliteration of lives with which one has some unchosen connection."

America

"Mimi Schwartz has written an engaging account of her journey into her family's German-Jewish past. But *Good Neighbors, Bad Times* is much more than that: it is also a shrewd and insightful meditation on how our collective histories are discovered, constructed, revised, and debated—and how, finally, we learn to live with them."

Michael Walzer
author of *Just and Unjust Wars*

"*Good Neighbors, Bad Times* is utterly riveting. It reintroduces, one story at a time, the kind of human complexity to our understanding of 'the perpetrators' so often lacking when we confront the devastation of the Holocaust. Mimi Schwartz bravely takes us along on her journey to re-create the ethos of a particular village, its surprises, uncertainties, contradictions, provocations, and shares with us her humbling conviction that—no matter how inhuman the orders that come from above—there is no such thing as a monolith when it comes to the reactions of individuals. Her book casts a ray of light into the darkness, which was not so absolute as it has often seemed."

Rosellen Brown
author of *Before and After* and *Half a Heart*

"A thoughtful, elegantly written memoir. . . . Through the author's voice, we hear the voices of a dwindling group of survivors—Jewish and Christian—whose perspective and remembering are as complex as they are insightful. This is a Holocaust memoir that is as much about *then*, as it is about *now*. *Good Neighbors, Bad Times* will make you smile, but it will also make you think. I highly recommend it."

> Carol Rittner
> coauthor of *The Courage to Care:*
> *Rescuers of Jews During the Holocaust*

"Mimi Schwartz has found a fresh way to write about the unspeakable loss of the Holocaust: her humor, warm humanity and honesty, her appetite for contradiction and irony, sparkle on every page. The result is both deeply affecting and full of surprises."

> Phillip Lopate
> author of *Getting Personal* and *The Art of the Personal Essay*

GOOD NEIGHBORS, BAD TIMES

Echoes of My Father's German Village

M I M I S C H W A R T Z

Mimi Schwartz
September, 2012

University of Nebraska Press | Lincoln and London

Source acknowledgments for previously published
material appear on page 260.

Library of Congress Cataloging-in-Publication Data
Schwartz, Mimi.
Good neighbors, bad times: echoes of my father's
German village / Mimi Schwartz.
    p. cm.
ISBN 978-0-8032-2640-1 (paper: alk. paper)
    1. Black Forest (Germany) — Ethnic relations —
History — 20th century. 2. Jews — Germany —
Black Forest — History — 20th century. 3. Christians
— Germany — Black Forest — History — 20th
century. 4. Black Forest (Germany) — History,
Local. 5. City and town life — Germany— Black
Forest — History — 20th century. 6. Kristallnacht,
1938 — Germany — Black Forest. 7. National
socialism — Social aspects — Germany — Black
Forest — History. 8. Schwartz, Mimi — Family.
9. Immigrants — United States — Biography.
10. Assimilation (Sociology) — United States.
I. Title.
DD801.B64S298 2009
305.892'404346 — dc22
[B]   2009033094

Set in Scala and Base Nine.
Designed by A. Shahan.

For My Father

There is a place that existed before you
came to it, closed with the secrets and
complexities of history; and there is
the place you experience in the present.

EAVAN BOLAND

Unfortunately, for historians, the vast
majority of humans have disappeared
into the past without leaving a trace
of their existence. What remains amounts
to nothing more than a tiny fragment
of human experience, even though
the components of that fragment could
fill so many archival boxes that you
couldn't get a statistically significant
sample of them if you read for centuries.

ROBERT DARNTON

CONTENTS

ILLUSTRATIONS

a few are newcomers (Protestant and Muslim). Some are well educated; many more did not go beyond the eight years of the local *Volksschule*. There is a Jewish survivor of several concentration camps; a schoolteacher with a Nazi father and grandfather; a Jewish daughter who escaped to America but could not get her mother out; a Catholic boy who was in Hitler's army and now spends his retirement years doing research on local Jewish history. And many others, people neither heroic nor evil, whose stories allowed me to reenter my father's old world and walk around for a while with you, my reader—as if it were ours.

Mimi Schwartz

GOOD NEIGHBORS, BAD TIMES

PART ONE | CLOSE TO HOME

1 | TREADMILL TO THE PAST

Fragile black lines on shades of green. A handful of tilting houses, a church bell tower, rolling meadow, forest. This little watercolor hanging above my father's side of the bed in Queens, New York, was like his reading lamp to me: nondescript. I put it in the same category as the four-poster bed and the dark mahogany armoire: old and German. It now hangs on the third floor of my house because I needed to fill a bare wall, a bare, cracked wall—and because my mother was moving to a smaller apartment in Manhattan. The village scene was surplus.

In fact, my mother said the tiny village may not be Benheim, as I had always thought; it may be any Schwarzwald scene, made up, anonymous. No matter. In the world framed in chipped gold leaf above my treadmill, I imagine my father herding his father's German cows, a piece of fresh-baked linzertorte wrapped in his pocket. I hear his stories about growing up here before Hitler (*Did I ever tell you how we had to walk five kilometers to high school in Dorn, one way? Rain or shine?*) as I fast walk daily, three miles per hour in fifty minutes, rain or shine. Beneath the motor's hum is the echo of a past I pushed aside in my busy American life, a past I now run to catch up with before everyone who knew that world is gone.

His village is tucked into a hillside of a narrow valley at the edge of the Schwarzwald forest southwest of Stuttgart. When my father was born in 1898, this tiny farming community of 1,200 was made up of Catholics and Jews (only three Protestant families in those days). Facts like that used to wash over me, but now I can tell you much more: how, in 1645, the Order of the Knights of St. John allowed two Jews fleeing Poland to settle on their lands in the village of Benheim. And how the arrangement was this: if the Jews paid protection money and three pounds of sugar yearly—and brought a goose to the festival of St. Martin's Day—they could stay and trade cattle, leather, and small household goods, door to door.

The arrangement must have worked, because despite ups and downs with unreasonable rulers, two Jews became 10, 18, 50, 150, 250. . . . By the time my father was born, half the village was Jewish. They had been granted citizenship in the 1850s; and after that they were allowed to own homes, build a new synagogue, and start a Jewish school. "It was the best place for Jews!" my father used to say in Queens many years later. The Jews felt so comfortably German that half of Benheim's volunteers in World War I were Jewish, including my seventeen-year-old father and his older brother Sol. After the war ended in 1918, many left village life for the big city, and Jewish populations often dropped in half, but not in Benheim. Despite the wild inflation of the 1920s and rising anti-Semitism elsewhere in Germany, Benheim Jews continued to feel safe in their little village. A few young roughnecks joined the Nazi Party in 1933, but most people—Jews and Christians—felt that "the crazy house painter from Austria" would soon disappear, leaving the amiable balance of this village as it had been for generations.

No Allied bombs fell on Benheim during World War II, so you can still see my great-grandfather's house and the other fifty or so steeply pitched houses of the Lower Village. You can see the bell tower of the Catholic church rising above them, and the *Volksschule* where everyone went to school, and the two *Gasthäuser* where everyone drank beer (a third has become a home for political refugees from Turkey, Kurdistan, and Afghanistan). You can see the old stone tower of the Order of St. John (the palace has been torn down). And the synagogue (now the Protestant

Evangelical Church). And the switchback road still leading to the Upper Village with its medieval farmhouses of thatched roofs and tiny doorways, some four feet high. Many houses now have satellite dishes and new casement windows, but the view across the valley is still dense forest that the child in me calls Hansel and Gretel woods. The villagers call it the Schwarzwald, or Black Forest, because something in the air, long before air pollution, makes the giant green conifers look black at a distance.

You can still see the Jewish cemetery, which is up the dirt road that climbs a hill leading to a stone gate, deep in the woods. The old graves are still intact, 946 of them. And from there, you can see over the old red rooftops to new condominiums built where my father once herded cows in the days when Jews still lived in Benheim.

I knew none of this for most of my life. All I knew were some faded stories that I'd been allergic to as a kid in Queens, born in 1940, three years after my family arrived in New York's harbor. I'm an American, I'd mutter whenever my father started with his *In Benheim this, In Benheim that* . . . usually when he thought my sister and I didn't behave nicely. *In Benheim, everyone behaved!* Or when we fought over the best seat in the car. *In Benheim, we all got along!* To prove it, I never studied German, never looked through my parents' mildewed albums (now in my attic), and never wondered about the Schwarzwald watercolor with tilting houses and a bell tower. Or about the pastel, also in my house, of a tiny horse and wagon racing through the dense forests to somewhere.

Not my world, I kept thinking, until forty years later, in midlife, I saw an old Benheim Torah that was 1,800 miles from its Schwarzwald home. An old man in shorts and a kibbutz cap, who knew my father, was showing me around Oleh Zion,* a vil-

*Like the names Benheim and Dorn, this village name has been changed to honor requests for individual privacy.

lage in Israel founded by a group of Benheim Jews in 1937, the same year my family came to America. I had no tape recorder, took no notes (didn't know then that I was starting a quest), but I still hear the old man saying: "*Ja*, the Christians of Benheim rescued the Torah for us during Kristallnacht." He patted the case that holds the ancient scrolls and said proudly: "The Nazis had brought in a truckload of hoodlums from outside, from Sulz, to destroy the synagogue like they did everywhere in Germany that night. But these people, Nazi orders or no, decided to save what they could for the Jews. They buried things outside the gate of the Jewish cemetery, deep in the woods, and after all the craziness ended, they sent the Torah here to us. And we have it still!"

I was surprised. I never thought of ordinary Germans rescuing a Torah or anything else Jewish back then. My images were of black boots marching across the Hollywood movies I grew up watching at the Queens Midway Theater, ones full of Nazis I hated and feared. I looked at the old Torah, almost four feet in length, and wondered who grabbed it from the fire and why? And how many helped to carry it, a heavy thing, to safety? And did neighbors see them? And were they denounced? Echoes of my father's nostalgia came back. *In Benheim we all got along!* But he had meant a boyhood before Hitler, not during Nazi times.

The old man guided me to the Memorial Wall of names carved into stone beside the Torah. "They were *not* saved," he said softly. I looked at the list of eighty-seven Benheimers who died in concentration camps, almost one-third of the Jews of the village, their names lifted from shadow by an electric flame. Gideon, Weinberger, Strauss, Loew, Ettinger. . . . No one in my family, because my father had led our clan, thirty-five in all, out of Germany, like Moses. Or so the story goes, the one I had loved to hear. For if he was the hero, then I was the hero's daughter and would know how to be as brave and savvy as he was.

I bowed my head to honor the dead, but kept thinking about the Torah's rescue, the story I didn't expect. Was it true—or an old man's wishful memory? Did the Christians really do that? If so, Benheim was more interesting than I had thought, maybe even special, an idea I felt obliged to resist. *Is this man even from Benheim?* I wished my father were still alive. I was ready for his stories now, but he had died in 1973, and his brothers and sister soon after. Only my mother was left to remember, and she came from the city, Stuttgart. "Another world!" she liked to tell me.

My eyes moved back to the Torah scrolls, partly unrolled to reveal a passage from the Five Books of Moses in tiny handwritten Hebrew. I thought of how these words had been chanted around the world, the same portion on the same day, for three thousand years. They looked secure between the two heavy wooden handles, even with a charred edge and one slash mark, the remnants of that Nazi night of burning synagogues.

"Too bad the villagers only saved a Torah!" I said.

"What else could they do?" said the old man, his blue eyes darkening. "Many Gentiles were decent, but we were all helpless. It was terrible times, terrible. You can't imagine. . . ." His defense of "the Gentiles" surprised me, because we were not talking about life before Hitler when decency was easy and six million Jews hadn't been killed. I expected more anger from him, less empathy. "*Na ja,*" he sighed, and we were silent.

We walked into Mediterranean sunlight, and I could hear the sea waves hitting the rocks on the shoreline. "Would you like to come to my house for some *gute schwäbische Maultaschen?*" my host asked, a twinkle in his eyes—as if he were already tasting this liver dumpling specialty transplanted from the Schwarzwald along with the forty or so families who rebuilt their lives beside this sea. My aunts in Queens had also made those liver dumplings, served in hot chicken broth. Delicious.

"My wife makes them the best! Her grandmother's recipe!" His blue eyes danced with the comfort of old delicacies.

"Thanks, I'd love that," I said, hungry for a dish I'd forgotten and also for the way bright eyes can keep changing like a watched flame. My father's eyes also did that, flickering between nostalgia, loss, and anger, depending on the memory. And he too loved those dumplings. I could feel his yes in mine.

2 | ANONYMOUS TRANSLATION

In Benheim, the goose liver was never eaten at home because one could sell it in the city, ½ a kilo would buy 2 ½ kilos of beef. Only with great difficulty—and a butcher's bill from Frankfurt—could I convince my father to keep a little goose liver in the pantry for big city visitors like me.

From a German article about Benheim, translated

I read these words in an old folder that my mother found in her closet—and hear my father speaking. He's been dead almost twenty years, yet here's his goose liver story on page 2 of a hand-typed article tucked between mostly German documents, a language we didn't speak at home. The heading reads "English Translation of *Dorfleben in Benheim*" (Village Life in Benheim) and there's no byline, but I know my father wrote it. I recognize the narrator from our Sunday morning walks long ago in Queens when he'd tell me how, after moving to Frankfurt, he'd try to educate his country bumpkin father on the ways of the big city. Dad was *my* country bumpkin, so this story was a favorite, much better than the ones about his unspoiled, farm boyhood "with no fancy houses and fancy lawns like here." He'd always point to the neatly landscaped homes from 110th Street to Yellowstone Boulevard, six to a block, as if I were missing something.

8

Work Hard, Be Charitable, Be Loyal, Be Strong. These were the values my father grew up with—and wanted to pass on to me in Queens. The article's prose is formal, but I hear the man who loved his old blue chair, and sour green apples, and debating world politics (even with an eleven-year-old daughter), and holding tribal get-togethers every Sunday afternoon so the men could plan business strategies while the women gossiped and we children whispered, cursed, and watched the clock tick our weekend plans away.

I hear the man who made regular rounds, family in tow, to every sick relative within a two-hour drive—*In Benheim, people always brought food to those in need.* One week we'd bring recuperative cakes like my mother's *Apfeltorte* to Aunt Johannah, who lived in two dark rooms in a house with a rickety black elevator. Another week to Uncle Herman, the Fuller Brush man, whose rosy cheeks and huge belly defied my father's pronouncement that he "was never quite right" after he came to America. We visited "poor Mr. Lindman" who shook all over, and the Neumeyers who lost both children in Auschwitz and hugged me so hard I got scared. Every week I'd plead to go to the Saturday movie matinee with my friends, but it was mostly "out of the question." I had to pay my respects.

I hear the man who told how his father would not spend five pfennigs to buy a pretzel treat, but spent thousands of marks on a relative who was in difficulty. "It was self-understood!" my father used to say. The phrase resonates when I read in the article about the village code for helping neighbors that says:

Whoever might fall off a roof, or get sick, or have a death or birth to deal with, could rely on the neighbors to stoke the coal, heat the water, feed the chickens, and milk the cows.

I think of the Torah rescued on Kristallnacht, and whether whoever did it thought: "It was self-understood." Is that why they took a chance? I've been telling the Torah story for over a year now because everyone likes it, the unexpected decency. People want to know more about the details of this village life, but I didn't know more—not until this article appeared. Yes, that's the word: appeared. Like a messenger saying, *It is time.*

On page 3 I read about Solomon, the "biggest giver of them all," and remember my father's lectures about selfishness: *In Benheim we were generous. We let no one go hungry.* But I also hear his ambivalence, a feeling that maybe Solomon overdid it:

> Solomon Strassburger was so filled with desire to offer charity, even obsessed by it, that he took in every wanderer who came through. He gave them clothing, shelter, and food even though it meant that he had to walk around in ragged pants. His wife, who tried unsuccessfully to lead him down other paths, eventually left him, and at the end of his life, Solomon was so poor that he had to be supported by relatives and by his community.

My father was too practical to be a Solomon. Families were to be cared for, and ragged pants were for Sundays at home. That pragmatism made him choose the security of America over his dream to be a pioneer in Israel, driving a tractor through melon fields. He loved that self-image, and also the one of him as a young idealist, traveling for weeks by boat to witness the opening ceremonies of Hebrew University in Jerusalem in 1925, a symbol for him of a new Jewish secular pride. The photo of his eighth-of-an-inch face among the thousands on Mount Scopus hangs in my study. He almost stayed, he'd remind me regularly, and *almost* stayed again on a visit in 1933. But his young wife got sick, and Franco took over Spain, and he knew a world war was coming. "Only America was safe!" he'd say in Queens. So instead of a kibbutz tractor, my father drove a navy blue Buick, bumper-to-bumper, through the Midtown Tunnel to Manhattan. He did put up the money to help other German Jews escape Hitler and resettle wherever they could. And he spent hours on the phone convincing others to do the same, saying, "It should be self-understood."

My father left his village, if not its values, at seventeen. "Ran away" is the term I remember—to enlist in the Kaiser's army and see the world beyond Benheim. The same traditions that he praised also drove him away; for he didn't want to be like generations of Loewengarts before him, buying cows from one farmer and selling them to another two hundred kilometers away, Sunday through Friday, year after year. The predictability felt claustrophobic.

Not only did Benheim Jews have to fatten the goose for goose liver and marry well—values shared with the Christians—but the men had to lay *tefillin*, winding leather thongs around their head and arms, to pray daily wherever they traveled for a living. It's in the article:

> Every Monday morning one car of the train from Dorn to Pforzheim was transformed into a chapel, much to the astonishment of Christian travelers. No one shied away from laying *tefillin*; one prayed as if one were in a synagogue.

And every Jew was expected to keep kosher, wherever he was. I read that Benheim had two kosher butchers (the whole village used them) and three Jewish *Gasthäuser*, so keeping kosher at home was easy. But on the road, eating was meager:

> During the week the men, staying in farmhouses, ate only cheese and eggs—unless they brought kosher smoked meat and sausage from Benheim. If one didn't have enough chickens at home, one bought them from farmers and carried them home to be made kosher. The bag of chickens slung over the shoulder or stuffed under the seat in the train compartment was a piece of "baggage" by which one could recognize the Jews returning for Shabbat.

Any Jew who dared to light a lamp during Shabbat, or ride home after sundown on Friday, or eat in a nonkosher *Gasthaus*, was vilified in conversation. For a wayward secularist like my father, a boy who preferred the woods to afternoons of Torah study, the gossip was oppressive. "Everyone knew what was cooking in everyone's pot!" he'd tell my mother, his "big city girl" who spoke French and had been to Switzerland as a girl. She was his ticket out of a parochialism he admired only after he left it—while sitting in a busy Frankfurt café, eating goose liver.

Big scandals, especially involving love affairs, intermarriages, and conversions, could ruin a family, and the offenders were not welcome in a village with clear social boundaries. They had to leave, as the narrator of the article makes clear on page 6:

> I only knew of a single conversion, and he was a young man who had joined the Salvation Army. He was treated like an outcast in Benheim. Nobody wanted to be with him, but I think he never stopped feeling Jewish. Later, when he was sent as a missionary to Palestine, he was the first to come and offer help to his former neighbors. He brought them a cow. Despite his baptism, his connection with his fellow Benheim Jews was never lost.

My father also moved away: first to Frankfurt, at age twenty-one, to learn a new business (actually, not so new—he dealt in cowhides instead of cows); then a continent away to America at age thirty-five. But still his village came along with him—not as excess baggage, but as a moral compass. He converted to American life and made his mother tongue English, yet where he was going always stayed connected to where he had been.

It was that connection that convinced him to leave Germany when most other Jews kept hoping Hitler would just go away. I always wondered how he knew. I'd heard a thousand times how, with his "Aryan" blue eyes and Prussian boldness, my father went to a Hitler rally in 1933, where thousands rose in unison—*Sieg Heil! Sieg Heil!*—in a moment so charged that he forgot for a second that he was Jewish and rose up, too. And how, that same night, he told my mother they were leaving Germany, that Hitler was too dangerous. And how, over the next three years, he and his brothers smuggled out enough money to get visas and restart life in America. Their main scheme was to tape envelopes of cash behind toilet seats of trains going to Switzerland. They devised a code using the price of leather hides in their business to inform whichever brother was waiting across the Swiss border on which train and in which car the money could be found. Six or seven times my father or his brother Sol traveled from Frankfurt to Basle to retrieve the money, and luck was on their side. But the last time, they heard later, the Gestapo searched the train soon after my father walked away with thousands of marks.

A satisfying tale, full of drama and intrigue, but it hinged on one moment of insight: my father attending that Hitler rally. Were there no earlier signs, ones that I should look for? The article says there were. Fifteen years before, as a teenage soldier in World War I, my father who felt so German saw the misery of East European Jews as a warning:

> In Russia we saw what could happen to Jews . . . the bent backs, the subservient manner, the need to suffer humiliations under the Czar without being able to defend themselves. The Jews greeted the German army as liberators, but they were quickly disappointed and so were we. The German soldiers had more sympathy for the Russian peasant than for the better educated but poor Russian Jew. We young German-Jewish soldiers, self-assured and with no inferiority complex from living in a ghetto, were amazed. For the first time I realized that what I saw could happen to Jewish people everywhere, and that impression never disappeared. It was the reason I knew right away to leave Hitler's Germany.

I wonder what lesson this past should teach me, a girl who grew up on milk shakes and ham sandwiches with no yoke of Jewish orthodoxy to throw off. What signs should I be watching for on the Nightly News? Or should I just relax, believing in the America I grew up on, where everybody—Protestant, Catholic, Baptist, Jew, whatever the skin color—was supposed to be ready to jump into the Melting Pot and blend together like the beige carpeting that my best friend had.

Now *that* was American, not like our ugly Oriental carpets carted from a darker, foreign world. Get rid of them! Let the past go! I'd tell my parents regularly, until I left for a carpet-free dorm room at the University of Michigan, a thousand miles away. Let the past go, I'd tell myself, as I dated Paul, a Polish poet, and Nicky from Italy, and even Otto from Austria, once. And again when my dorm mates, Addie and Dennie from Gross Pointe, Michigan, asked me one night, as we sat in our pajamas drinking beer, if Jews had horns. They'd never met one before me. This was trust, I assured myself. Their parents would never have dared to ask. Let the past go, I said again, when my husband and I bought a house from a bulletin-board notice (just the ranch we'd been looking for) because our realtor—who knew the house—had never mentioned it. She didn't think we would "want to live in an integrated neighborhood," one that was one-third black, two-thirds white (just like the Jewish/Christian ratio of Benheim, 1930s).

My parents' Oriental rugs are now in my living room and dining room. Like the framed Schwarzwald scenes, they covered the bareness of the 1902 Colonial we had bought just when my parents were selling their house for a fully carpeted apartment. I have my father's pragmatism, so I decided to like his rugs with the red and blue swirls I once thought were snakes, especially at night. Besides, our neighbors (sixth-generation American) have similar rugs. We go over there for an annual Christmas event of delicious eggnog, meringue chocolate-chip kisses, and wood-carved Schwarzwald nutcracker soldiers guarding the

Christmas tree (our host's heirloom from German Lutheran grandparents), while fat red and green candles glow around the room, making everyone, Jews included, feel cozy.

My father is buried in the sands of Israel, the wind from the Mediterranean blowing over his grave, not far from the rescued Torah of Benheim. Avocados grow in the field beyond the cemetery, and roses, thousands of them, in reds, whites, and yellows, bloom in the field beyond that. Such a tiny cemetery, so exposed, with barely a shade tree for its thirty or so graves, yet here he chose to lie. Not in Benheim, beside his ancestors buried deep in the woods above the village. Not in Cedar Lawn Cemetery, off the Garden State Parkway in New Jersey, next to his brothers and sister and his small daughter Hannah, who died of strep throat soon after they arrived in America.

I wonder what boundaries my father needed to recross before his soul could rest in such a new, old world. When he wrote the anonymous article (my mother has confirmed it was his), he was halfway through his life, my age, and looking back to assess, as I am now, what shouldn't be forgotten. Maybe writing about Solomon rekindled some idealism that only four Israeli gravediggers in khaki shorts and blue kibbutz caps could satisfy. When they shoveled the sand onto my father's plain, pine coffin, I remember feeling his smile even as I cried, the Solomon part of him getting its due.

I wonder what boundaries I need to recross. What else I carry from Benheim besides a love of linzertorte, and crusty black bread, and waking up at 5:00 a.m., "a farmer's daughter," as my husband likes to tease. These are private pleasures, easy to keep—not like laying *tefillin* on a public train or lighting menorahs in unshaded windows. I miss none of that. Nor did my dad, I was sure, until the day he died, when I found out he was to be buried in Oleh Zion, among his former Benheim neighbors. He wanted to be where someone would surely chant the *Kaddish* prayer for him every year, or so he told my surprised mother the month before his heart failed him. "It would be self-understood."

I flip through the rest of the old folder, so full of a life I wasn't part of: letters in German from 1934 to 1939, written from Stuttgart, Amsterdam, Copenhagen, New York, by my aunt, my grandmother, my uncle, my parents. *How scattered they were before reconnecting in Queens!* There's a German newspaper clipping about Oleh Zion and a booklet about Benheim's Jews, published by a church group in Benheim. *Who did that?* A passport from 1926, stamped "Persia." *Is that when he bought the Oriental rugs?* And three yellowed pages of names that sound familiar—Gideon, Pressburger, Marx, Weinberger—with addresses and phone numbers in New York, Florida, Israel, Switzerland, Vermont. Sixty-three in all, neatly typed in columns with the heading "Jews from Benheim." Plus, a page with two names—Herr Adolf Stolle, Frau Anna Rieber—both with addresses in Benheim. *Are they the ones who saved the Torah—or do they know who did?* I shut the folder, already late to teach my autobiography class at my college. I put the list of names next to the telephone. Next week, maybe, after grades are in, I might make some calls. . . .

3 | AT THE *NACHMITTAG*

Today I am meeting the people who used to pinch my cheek and say, "*Lieber Gott*, how you have grown!" —as if I weren't supposed to. Most were probably younger than I am now, but when I was a child at these *Nachmittage*, or afternoon gatherings, everyone seemed ancient and scary, speaking German nonstop. I hid whenever I could, despite my parents' urgings to "Smile and be nice! They've had hard lives!"

I cross the George Washington Bridge from New Jersey, turn left, then right to 187th Street, and find them, as instructed, in the basement room of the Mount Sinai Jewish Center in Washington Heights. It is an old stone building covered with half-successful attempts to erase "Fuck you!" and "Viva Zapata" soaked into its stone pores. I can see from the store signs in Chinese, Arabic, and Spanish that the German butcher with the "Glatt" sign for kosher now shares this neighborhood, once the heart of German-Jewish refugee culture. Except for those anxious to assimilate, like my family, who headed for Queens five miles away. Or to Great Neck if they had the money.

Down a dozen dark steps and through an even darker hall, I enter a room of twenty-five or so old people, chatting away in German. Frail men and women with wispy hair, walkers, wheelchairs, and canes sit around a horseshoe table, sipping coffee out of Styrofoam cups and eating thinly sliced pound cake from paper plates. More little plates of cake, neatly spaced a foot apart, encircle the room on an unbroken chain of tables pushed against the wall.

Ah, the cakes! I remember such a wealth of them at the *Nachmittage* of my childhood: linzertorte, *Apfelkuchen*, poppy seed strudel, macaroons, and marzipan tortes, all full of wonders designed to make each baker shine and each belly bulge. These events were held all over Washington Heights, Brooklyn, and the Bronx, but I went only to those at Aunt Thea and Uncle Julius's house in Jamaica, Queens. Once a year they'd invite all the Benheimers (often, seventy-five showed up) for a "day in the country"—aka Queens—to sit in a backyard, look at trees, drink thick coffee, and eat dozens of cakes, while schmoozing in German about everything and everyone they knew.

I had skipped lunch today in anticipation of these rich, home-baked cakes, cookies, and tarts—the best thing about Benheim as far as I was concerned—so these pale, store-bought slivers are a shock. They are, I find out later, much better than they look, but my first impulse is to skip the calories.

Before I left home, my husband advised me to bring pictures of my father and his house in Benheim so people would know who I was. "Are you kidding? They'll know everything about me before I step through the door. They've been on the phone for days talking about me." Driving here I imagined the *Lieber Gotts* and pinches closing in immediately, but instead everyone just looks up, stops talking, and stares. An energetic redhead, somewhere in her seventies, appears with a broad smile and a handshake. "I'm Hannah Zimmer. We talked on the phone," she says. "Welcome to our *Nachmittag*." I had gotten Hannah's name from someone on the Benheim list who told me that if anyone could help me get information about Benheim, it was Hannah.

Everyone here seems nearing eighty or older, and only Hannah in her emerald green suit looks robust and daring enough to reenter the past with gusto, taking me along. The men are dressed in dark suits and ties; the women favor black or navy blue dresses, just as I remember from long ago. Hannah leads me to the center of the horseshoe and announces: "This is

Mimi, Arthur Loewengart's daughter." I hear "Ooohs!" and see nods of recognition, and then the same broad grins I remember appear on faces that have both sharpened and blurred since I saw them last. Hannah moves me closer to the table. "You don't remember me," says a woman with a gray perm and owl glasses, her face as close as Tante Yetta's, the chief cheek-pincher of long ago. She grabs my hand in pleasure. "I went to school with your Uncle Max. Gretl Dorfman, nee Gould."

Gretl is next to a stooped man who must be over ninety with a round face and the same balding head and big belly of my dad and uncles. "I used to brush the tail of your grandfather Rubin's horse," he smiles, touching my arm. "I'm your father's second cousin, my mother was a Schultzman. We lived next to your Tante Rosa." I nod, not knowing who Tante Rosa is—or anyone else named so far. I was never good at the genealogy game, glazing over whenever the litany begins. Hannah pulls me away, pointing to a stern-looking woman with thin, feathery white hair. She is in a wheelchair. "Mrs. Weiss would like to say hello to you. You remember her and her husband Felix? He died last year." Hannah immediately sees that I don't. "Her husband did bookkeeping for your father when they first arrived." We walk over to greet her.

"So Mimile." She holds out her hand, thin and blue-veined and full of tremor from Parkinson's. "And how is your gracious mother? You look just like her. Please send her my best." Now, in fact, I do remember her, especially her two kids with sad smiles, to whom I was supposed to be extra nice. Ely, the son, taller but still solemn, is standing next to his mother. I smile and say hello, feeling my mother's pressure to say more—and my old churlishness not to.

Ten people later I have been assured that "You look just like your aunt Kaethe!" "You are the image of your father!" "The replica of your grandmother!" "A definite Loewengart!" Then the meeting is called to order. It is a more official *Nachmittag*, sponsored by the Benheim Benevolent Society, formed in New

York in the 1940s to help Benheimers in distress. Ironically, no Benheimer has ever asked for money because, as Hannah puts it, "these uneducated farmers somehow managed to make it in America on their own." They started as janitors, factory workers, nannies, Fuller Brush men, and sausage salesmen, door to door, and they sent their children to school to do better. And they did, more or less—but the Society still collects money, just in case.

My father had a hand in starting the Society, I find out much to my surprise. I always think of him reminiscing about Benheim from a distance. Up close, he was all for assimilation. Yet Hannah says he helped draft the bylaws, and later when I read them I hear echoes of his Solomon story about generosity and sharing:

ARTICLE TWO

To promote the friendship of its Members, to inculcate in them a high sense of loyalty to each other and their common background. . . .

To aid, assist, and care for sick, feeble and needy Members on a voluntary basis. . . .

To maintain and preserve the grounds, graves, and monuments of the old Jewish Cemetery in Benheim, Germany. . . .

I have come today to ask for volunteers to talk to me about Benheim: what it was like growing up there, what friendships they had, what leaving was like, and what living in America was, and is, like. But before "New Business" (that's me), Hannah, the group's secretary for years, reads last year's minutes and praises Mrs. Gideon, last year's treasurer. Everyone applauds. I get such a kick out of calling her Hannah. All of these people were always "old Mr. and Mrs. X" to me. But this lively, self-assured older woman, newly met, is someone I could be friendly with. She is Hannah, I am Mimi, part of the same adult world.

Hannah, who is also treasurer this year, gives a rundown of how last year's funds were spent: $850 to UJA, $400 to maintain the cemetery in Benheim, $1,000 for the synagogue wing of Oleh Zion in Israel, and $200 for the Benheim memorial in Cedar Park Cemetery in New Jersey. Everyone applauds again.*

"Maybe we could give a stipend to a needy Benheimer," someone calls out.

Silence. Is it from shame? Or is no one needy?

"Maybe we could put up a plaque honoring Benheim over the door of this room." It is a silver-haired man, very dapper in a bowtie, who suggests this. The room buzzes with this possibility. Cake is eaten, coffee sipped, as the idea of leaving their mark above the doorway takes hold. "It would cost $500," he says. Silence.

"We pay this Jewish Center $50 to hold a meeting, plus $30 for the janitor. That's enough," says Mrs. Weiss from her wheelchair. Everyone but the plaque's sponsor nods. Voted down. *In Benheim we never wasted money.*

My turn comes. I tell them how my father always told me stories about Benheim and I didn't write them down. Now I want to—and I need their help. I'd like to come to their houses to interview them.

"Why us?"

"Talk to the Israelis!" They are referring to the Benheimers who settled in Oleh Zion.

"Yah, they are the brave ones, the ones who have the interesting lives, right, Sophie?" They look at Mrs. Weiss, who left Oleh

---

*This society is rather unique, I am told. Jewish refugees from large towns and cities had them, but not little villages of 1,200. Benheim's code for helping each other, "Whoever fell off the roof . . . could count on neighbors . . . ," evidently traveled with this group to America.

Zion for America soon after Israel's War of Independence in 1948. She doesn't respond.

"We are simple people," says a woman in a black dress and tiny lace collar. "We did nothing special." Nods of agreement while small conversations flare.

I tell them that I live in a town of Gentiles and Jews, not unlike Benheim, and that we all get along, the way my father said he used to with his neighbors. Now everyone is alert. I tell them I want to know how their Benheim life was like, or not like, my life in Princeton. Silence. "Whatever you remember would be wonderful . . . about school, family, holidays, funny or sad incidents. I'm not looking for big stories! *Kleine Geschichten*," I say, dredging up my skimpy German to lighten the moment.

I feel a stone wall behind their smiles and think, "That's it! I flopped!" until Hannah jumps in, announcing the names of those she has already arranged for me to meet in groups. The group leaders, also prearranged, give me their phone numbers. I am to call and set up the time and place, Hannah says. I will be going to Riverdale to interview her and Gretl Dorfman and Lotte Pressman. I will be going to Brooklyn to interview Mr. Marx and the Gilder sisters—she points to two half-familiar faces grinning on the other side of the horseshoe. I never thought of group meetings, assuming that one-on-one interviews would uncover more, but maybe collective memory is a good start. I return Hannah's smile.

The meeting is over. Four people offer me "a little good cake from the bakery on 169th Street," which I take politely, only to have another eagerly offered as soon as I finish the first. The chocolate with raspberry jam is not bad. There's a tug on my sleeve. "My aunt was a good friend of your Tante Hilde and knew your father, too. He was a wonderful dancer. Wonderful." Dancing in Benheim? My father dancing? He never mentioned that. A little silver-haired woman hands me a paper with her name, address, and phone number. "I'd be happy to talk to you."

"I'll call you tomorrow," I say after years of indifference—not only to Benheim, but to old people. They always seemed to move so slowly as I whizzed by, so except for my mother and her sister, I never made time to talk to them, find out who they are. "We'll make a date," I say, smiling with good intention. I put on my coat, say my goodbyes, and hear a dozen "Please come again! And bring your mother! And your sister next time!" I can imagine that I will, we will, even as I hear my mother and sister saying: *Benheim is not our world.*

Walking back to the car, I pass a window of red chili peppers and garlic hanging in the Spanish bodega and two dozen bratwurst and salami hanging in the kosher butcher. The sidewalks are cracked, broken beer bottles line the curb, and the day is darkening. Few people are around, and I half-listen for footsteps behind me. But I am not afraid, as if I had already conquered something lurking in the alleys of my childhood.

I start thinking about the greenness of Princeton, New Jersey, where I have lived for nearly thirty years. And the boat launching on Lake Carnegie, where I am supposed to be in an hour. One of our neighbors, whose family of ministers dates back to the Mayflower days, has built a fourteen-foot replica of a 1900 New England ship. He has invited friends and neighbors to see if the boat, to be called *The Replica*, will sink or float after a christening with a nonpolluting bottle made of sugar. Sweet shards on a dock. Broken glass under my feet. Kristallnacht, the Night of Broken Glass. Somehow they seem to be coming together, but I don't yet know how.

4 ▮ KAFFEEKLATSCH

I am sitting on a curved white couch, listening to three women discuss "being thirsty." I feel in a time warp, as if back in Queens listening to my aunts discuss the fine points of their favorite subject: being "too fat" or "too thin." Their "too" was more secular in focus, but the rhythm of talk is the same.

"You know, Hannah," says Gretl, "your look says you think I am *too* religious to eat or drink in your house. But that has nothing to do with it. Believe me!"
"Nooo? Are you really *that* religious?" Hannah looks amazed.
"I'm just really *not* thirsty!"
"You're really *not* thirsty? Good, don't drink then!"
Lotte chimes in. "How can you drink if you are *not* thirsty?"
Gretl's frown disappears. "You can't!" she beams.
And all is well.

It's a conversation I imagine in Benheim eighty years ago: at an afternoon kaffeeklatsch in a garden or living room of women whose families have known each other forever. Today it takes place in Riverdale, New York, in a sturdy, middle-class, 1950s high-rise built between the Henry Hudson Parkway and the Hudson River.

The apartment is full of sunlight, like Hannah's big hello.

She has invited me to her home to meet Gretl and Lotte, all of whom fled Benheim in the 1930s while the Jews still could. Hannah, fresh from the hairdresser and wearing a stylish pantsuit, could be sixty, not seventy-eight. Gretl, the "not-thirsty" one, looks in her mid-eighties. Dressed in a dark blue suit, she has tightly curled white hair, intense black eyes, and a strong grip that pumps my hand as she says, "How *are* you?" Her square jaw and bulging eyes remind me of my uncle Fred and some Benheim cousins I've met at weddings and funerals. Too much intermarriage, my mother used to say to explain the lookalikes. In a small village where marital choices were slim, the taboos against marrying cousins didn't hold as they did in cities like her Stuttgart.

Lotte, the cheerful mediator who soothed Gretl with "You can't drink if you're not thirsty!" is the youngest in manner—with cherry cheeks and untamed white hair. In a pink T-shirt half in and half out of her jean skirt, she looks like my kind of woman: a rebel amid Benheim propriety.

I sense old forces at work, shaping the intimacy of these three. I am right, I find out later. Gretl, the "not-thirsty," comes from the most religious Benheim family, one that sent her brother to a yeshiva in Poland! "Unheard of!" Hannah tells me the next day when I call to thank her for arranging the afternoon. Hannah comes from the most worldly family in Benheim, according to Gretl (whom I also call). Hannah's mother finished high school and spoke French. "The family even traveled to Holland to visit cousins. Unheard of!" she tells me. And laidback Lotte was from the least orthodox family. She lived "among the Gentiles, up the hill," according to Gretl, and "even had a little boy friend next door, a *goy*! Unheard of!"

But even Lotte keeps a strict kosher home, which my family never did. "Religion is absolutely in our nature," says Hannah, as we sit on the white sofa, the blinds raised for full light. Gretl and Lotte agree. Hannah's son is a rabbi, and two of Gretl's sons teach in a yeshiva school. I am surprised. I thought the American generation would be like me, celebrating major holidays mostly as an excuse for family gatherings. But many of their children not only keep kosher but also light Sabbath candles every Friday night and send their children to Jewish schools.

Talk drifts to the Jewish holidays in Benheim, which everyone remembers as powerful family moments. "How I loved *Erev Pesach!*" says Gretl, her eyes widening like a child's. "I can still see my father holding a candle, a dustpan, and a long goose feather, going from one room to another. He'd be looking for some unnoticed *chometz* to remove before Passover, and, of course, he always found some—my mother purposely put breadcrumbs on a window sill in every room!"

I know Pesach means Passover, but I ask what chometz is. "Did you not learn that at home?" Hannah asks, her eyebrows rising. "It's anything with leavened bread in it!" There's no malice, but I can hear the three of them thinking: So this is what happens to the daughter of a man who left Benheim at seventeen, stopped being an observant Jew, and married that worldly Stuttgart girl. They are right. My father, on Yom Kippur, would fast for twenty-four hours and play a record of Jan Pierce singing Kol Nidre, but didn't go to synagogue, preferring more solitary talk with God, he'd say.

Gretl continues with her magical night before Passover. "How carefully my father would sweep the crumbs onto his dustpan and wrap up everything, including the goose feather, to throw into the chometz fire the next morning."

"Ooooh, I remember those fires!" Lotte jumps in, clapping her hands in delight. "It was sooo mysterious. We'd go to a place in the middle of the woods, like a fireplace cut into the mountain. The teacher took us. Everyone went!"

I am beginning to see advantages to a group interview. I had not realized how easily one memory triggers another, turning generic descriptions of "happiness" into images of dustpans, goose feathers, and pyres that remove all traces of leavened bread, a luxury the Jews had no time for, fleeing the Pharaoh before the bread could rise. Hence, the matzo. The Exodus story I do remember, even if those of Esther, Joshua, and the Maccabees blur from only one year of Sunday school. No one forced me, so I had no bat mitzvah at thirteen, nor did most of my close friends. Being Jewish in our house was about supporting the new state of Israel and its promise of "Never Again!" Religion took a back seat to that.

"Did only Jews go to the chometz fire?" I ask trying to find out how much Jewish-Christian interaction really took place. Was friendship involved or just economic interdependence?

"Sometimes the other children came, too," says Hannah. But Gretl says, "No, never!" and folds her arms across her ample chest. "The Goy only came to weddings and funerals." Her eyes blaze with certainty.

"Remember the weddings—with all the men in black top hats?" Lotte asks to defuse Gretl's intensity again. "*Ach*, to me they all looked like Fred Astaire!"

They laugh, and I'm wondering how they knew about Fred Astaire in 1920s Benheim, which certainly had no movie theater within miles. Top hats lead to Mayor Kinkele's top hat, worn every Sunday to church! "He was a great friend of the Jews," Hannah says, "and so were his uncle and grandfather before him. All were mayors of Benheim and all were good to the Jews."

"The last Mayor Kinkele was always over by Ilsa Loew, visiting with her father, who was blind and had a radio. Kinkele would come over to listen and talk politics with him."

"He did not!" says Gretl.

"*Ja*, he did. They lived by us," Lotte says, "so we knew." She smoothes her shirt.

"Mayor Kinkele was also a good friend of. . . ." Hannah stops. "Mimi, please turn off the tape recorder." I click it off. ". . . of Ellie. They were close."

Gretl sits up. "I didn't know *that!*"

"She had the keys to his house!"

Lotte leans forward. "I didn't know *that!*"

I lean forward. A scandal in straight-laced Benheim? Dad, are you listening? *In Benheim everyone behaved.* "So what happened? Did they marry?" I ask.

Hannah chuckles. "*Ach*, no. She was sent to the United States. She now owns a fancy dress shop in Cleveland, I hear."

I am asked to turn off the tape recorder for several more transgressions: someone copied someone else's hat design, someone's house was not so neat, someone had a small dowry. Young women were lost, they assure me, if they didn't have a dowry trunk filled with finely embroidered tablecloths, sheets, and pillowcases representing years of careful work. They could never marry well.

I am delighted to have avoided such a life. Worth based on handiwork and baking is not good for someone like me who hates sewing (my grandmother did that), doesn't knit (my mother did that), and loves buying bread in the French bakery two blocks from my house. The women start to debate whose tablecloths had the finest stitching—Hannah's mother's? Or the nuns'?—and I tune out the way I did when my mother and aunts would knit together while I held up my arms like posts as they wound their yarn around them. I'd have to sit still, but in my mind I was always galloping Sultan (the horse I rode in Forest Park) across the Great Plains, a real American cowgirl.

Lotte starts describing how hard her mother's life was, coming to Benheim from a smaller village. *Is there such a place?* "She had to manage with three sisters-in-law and a husband who kept criticizing her. And the worst was baking challah for Shabbat," says Lotte, softly. "You prepared the dough at home and took it to Otto the baker who had a tremendous oven and, when he was sober, baked beautiful bread. He would line all the challah up on display and my mother's was always pale and flat, my three aunts' gorgeously round and golden. Then my poor mother would have to march through the street with her flat bread and everyone would see."

I imagine myself walking beside her mother—with even flatter bread. Lotte is also with us, but not Hannah or Gretl or my mother or aunts. They are all ahead, out in front, their loaves gorgeous and golden.

"*Na ja*," says Hannah softly. "When the political changes occurred, who could afford such pettiness? Once you had to go someplace else, who could afford to take it with you?" I hear the hum of the tape, some sighs. Hannah stands up and shepherds us to her dining room table. Time to eat.

A homemade linzertorte sits high on a stemmed cake platter in the middle of the table, as we four sit around it. The dark, raspberry-filled nut cake is flanked by sliced pineapple, ripe strawberries, and small clusters of perfect red grapes. A tiny dish of gold toothpicks sits beside it, ready as spears. There's also some rugalach that look home-baked, but defrosted. I imagine a Hannah of younger days, having everything fresh-baked, but I may be fantasizing again. After all, Hannah worked in a factory for twenty-five years while raising her three children.

I place my tape recorder on Hannah's embroidered tablecloth with tiny yellow flowers—"It's still beautiful, don't you think?"—and my vote definitely goes to her grandmother. The tiny details are exquisite, much finer than any of my mother's linen from her father's Stuttgart linen store. Gretl and Lotte begin arguing about high school in Dorn—No girls went. *Ja*, my sister went. We didn't mind. *Ja*, I minded—and I remind everyone to speak one at a time so voices don't blend together on the tape recorder. But Gretl keeps jumping in, insisting on her version of history, which makes the others interrupt to contradict her. "You didn't write reality," Lotte tells her finally, but with good cheer. "You saw the world through rose-colored glasses." She is referring to the memories that Gretl wrote down and sent to everyone. Hannah has a copy in her desk and gets it for me. Its heading is "Benheim as I remember it" and begins:

When I think back at the years of my youth . . . a wonderful warm glow fills my heart. I see a tight-knit community unique in her ways, and untouched by outside events. . . . We lived our lives in the old traditional way as had been passed on from father to son. And though we were not learned people, most were religious and our faith in tradition was strong. It had governed our lives from birth to death—from holiday to holiday.

And it's that happy life preparing for—and awaiting our holidays—which most warmly sticks in my mind. . . .

"You write only the good side," says Lotte. She wants more grit, like the major fight her father had with Herr Lemberger about the rainspout.

"Well . . . *your* story is not true!" Gretl retorts. She's referring to Lotte's account of Kristallnacht that was in a local newspaper. "My Simon was the *only* Jew who watched the synagogue burn," she adds, crossing her arms again. "He was in the fire brigade."

"Really?" says Hannah. "I heard many Jewish men were there."

"It was just my Simon."

"My father *was* there," Lotte says, coffee cup in midair. "I remember sneaking down along by Tante Rosa's fence and when I saw him, I said, 'Papa, Papa!'" She sounds breathless. "He said, 'Geh heim! Geh heim!'" She looks at me. "Go home," she translates. She laughs nervously, "To me it was an event! I was thirteen, so what did I know?"

"But, but, my Simon . . . ," says Gretl, until Hannah interrupts her with a plate of pineapple with toothpick spears. And then the rugalach, the little Danish stuffed with raisins or apricots, make its rounds.

Fragments, bits and pieces, no one story to hang onto, no one True version of when Benheim's synagogue was burned on Kristallnacht. There is Gretl's version as a young wife with a hero husband. There's Lotte's version as an adventurous thirteen-year-old who says, "What did I know?" There's Hannah's version as a nanny in America who heard the story from her mother, who was still in Benheim. And the old man's version that I heard in Israel, the one of the rescue that led me to these women whose memories are tied to who they were and who they need to be. Others, too, will tell me about who was there, who did or didn't see a thing, and no one will agree—except on the big pieces of story: That it was outsiders, not people from Benheim, who torched the synagogue. That it was "the Gentiles" who saved the Torah. And that after Kristallnacht even Benheim was unsafe for the Jews.

It was a shock. Jews like Lotte's father had been sure they could ride Nazism out. "He had felt so proudly German," says Lotte, "with his soldier medals and saber from World War I. And our Christian neighbors kept saying, 'Stay, stay, you'll be fine!'" There'd been no beatings or public humiliations in Benheim, "a few children beaten up in the alleys, yes," but no village support for that. In a community with only one radio, the menacing speeches and events seemed far enough away. Until they saw the ruined synagogue.

"You have to remember that the synagogue was our mainstay," says Hannah. "Take away the synagogue, take away the community." The others nod vigorously. No quibbles about that. Or about how the Jewish men, including Simon and Lotte's father, were rounded up the next day and put into jail, a closet-like room in the Rathaus (town hall) never used much, except to sober up an occasional drunk. When the policeman, Hannah thinks his name was Krupps, brought in the tenth Jew, one of the men (Gretl was sure it was Simon) said, "Now, at least, we have a minyan!" All three smile at this agreed-upon humor in the midst of nightmare. Ten men, a minyan, are needed to hold a Jewish service, Hannah explains. I knew that.

Lotte tells about trying to bring a suitcase with chocolate cake to her father in jail.

"Weren't you afraid?" asks Gretl.

"I was thirteen. What did I know?" Lotte says again. "But when he came home from Dachau* three months later. . . ." She shakes her head, her childlike aura gone. "He was so thin, his head shaved. My strong father, like a boy. He was a broken man." Luckily, Lotte's mother—who was never in denial and had been begging her husband to leave for years—had gotten visas behind his back. So Lotte's family made the last boat to leave Germany before the war started.

Gretl says her family left as soon as Simon was released from Dachau. All the Benheim men, in fact, came home from Dachau by March 1939. Unlike many of their urban counterparts who died in that bitterly cold winter, barely fed, in unheated barracks, these Benheim farmers were used to a harsh outdoor life. It got them through.

I never realized that Jews sent to concentration camps were ever released until American soldiers set them free. Yes, Gretl explains, "In 1938 the Nazi policy was not yet to kill Jews—that came later. It was to terrify us into emigration." It worked in Benheim. Those with money or connections abroad left as soon as plans could be finalized. Lotte's uncle in Cleveland sponsored her family. Hannah, already in New York, borrowed the $1,000 needed to sponsor her mother's escape to America. And Gretl's family left for Palestine. Gretl had sold their furniture for cash, they already had visas, and so as soon as they packed up, they took a train to Holland and a boat from there to Haifa.

I like these stories of escape and survival, like my parents'. It is the dark stories—of murder, sadism, Mengele, ovens—that I have avoided since a childhood of bad dreams. Skeletal faces, hollowed eyes, they stared in through the screens of black sum-

---

*Dachau, a few hours from Benheim, was the first Nazi concentration camp. In the early 1930s it was used mainly for political prisoners, but after Kristallnacht in November 1938, ten thousand Jewish men were interned there. Unlike in later roundups, most of these men were released.

mer nights in Queens, children like me still lost in terrors my family had escaped. Could I ever feel safe?

Gretl continues, more softly. "But Simon's parents, we could not take them with us." She looks down. "They couldn't get a visa, and we couldn't wait any longer. We had two small children. What else could we do?" She looks up in pain. "We thought we could get them out later. . . ."

"It was the same with so many," Hannah says quietly. "We thought they would be saved." Her ready smile is gone. Everyone is silent. And then Hannah starts offering more linzertorte, as if its thick raspberry jam will sweeten the bitterness that has landed on the table. Hannah's grandparents and Simon's parents were four of the eighty-nine Jews who, trapped in Benheim, were deported to concentration camps in 1940 and 1941. All but two were murdered.

When I replay the tape, I hear the silence filled with the clatter of silverware, the sips of coffee, the chewing. But when their voices take over again, they are strong and distinct. I recognize them all. Hannah asks if my mother still makes linzertorte. Lotte asks how old my children are and what I teach at my college. Gretl asks where everyone is going for Passover. She leaves tomorrow for a kosher hotel in the Catskills because, at eighty-six, she has no energy to clean out all the chometz and cook everything at home. Three of Lotte's children are coming to her with families. Twenty-four in all, she says proudly. Hannah will attend the local synagogue dinner, and I say I'm having my mother, my two children, and my brother-in-law and family. They beam.

"You are?"

"That's good!"

"What will you cook?"

I tell them brisket, and that my mother makes matzo ball dumplings that weigh a ton but taste great. A recipe from my Tante Hilde.

"Hilde Loewengart?" Lotte asks.

"Sure, you remember Walter's cousin," says Hannah.

"*Ach*, I lived across the street from her!" Gretl says.

They are pleased that I am celebrating, and I'm pleased to please. Passover is the one Jewish holiday I truly enjoy: a celebration of freedom while eating. The bad guys, like the Pharaoh, lose; the good guys win; and lucky people gather around tables in a new world, singing together.

5 | JOIE DE VIVRE

"We inevitably select what we remember from the past in order to have the courage to face the future."

Eva Gossman, Good Beyond Evil

"Look for an old Victorian house with statues on the lawn!" Lotte told me yesterday when I called. And here it is: on an island of single-family houses in the Bronx surrounded by apartment houses already lit up for Christmas. Two white headless torsos flank the driveway and another is tucked into the arms of an old oak tree. *Not* your conventional Benheimer, I think, delighted. The message from this front lawn is "We are who we are."

Familiar, untamed white hair greets me. "Hallo, Hallo . . . " —and Lotte, whom I liked so much at Hannah's, leads me up the worn wooden steps. No heavy Victorian drapes inside, no tiny nineteenth-century drawing rooms. Walls have been taken down to create a giant space, full of windows that encircle an ancient stove that stands, like a throne, in the middle of the room. Furniture is spare, floors creak, and a prop of wood is holding up the mantelpiece; but the look seems a statement of choice, not of chance. We are who we are.

A small man with a navy beret and tweed jacket sits before the stove on a bench that looks like an old church pew. He nods. "This is my husband," Lotte says. "And this is my son, the one who does the sculptures." A lanky man, taller, nods too. And then she and I are climbing stairs that wind and tilt like the Fun House at Great Adventure to "a place where we can talk better." It's a small room, a converted closet, really, lined top to bottom with books. Here, Lotte says, is where she retreated from her seven children to study for her classes. "Seven children?" I ask, amazed.

"*Ja*, they are all grown now." I wait for a litany of accomplishments, the whipping out of photos, but get only, "And I have fifteen grandchildren. You should see us on the holidays. It's good we have a big room downstairs!" She laughs. "We will be thirty-four tomorrow night—and not all are coming, thank God."

I love her eyes, full of the same upbeat energy that has drawn me to all these Benheim women who have made "old" seem young to me. But especially Lotte with those smooth red cheeks—and her favorite words: "joie de vivre." The phrase, joy of life, comes from her three years in Paris in the late 1940s while her young husband was studying to be a doctor. "Right after the war, everyone felt so blessed," she says. "It was like after a spring rain. You could start all over again . . . such wonderful years. We all had joie de vivre."

That feeling, she says, started long before, as a child in 1920s Benheim where "everyone knew me and my family for centuries. I felt so free, wandering through the meadows and woods, in and out of shops, feeling safe and welcomed by everyone—Jew and Gentile alike."

More than the other Benheimers, Lotte's memories are rich with "the Gentiles," especially the shopkeepers like Otto the baker. "I could sit and watch him forever, fascinated by the way he would sweep the oven out, getting it ready for the challah. And there was a carver who did wood carvings of cuckoo clocks and Jesus on the cross, very artistically done. He'd have tools, very sharp tools and would let me carve a little. *Ach*, wherever we went, we were welcome. No one would throw you out."

Lotte even remembers Catholic holidays fondly, recalling

pageants when the children would go with chalices and flowers behind priests dressed in white gowns. Just lovely, she says, like Christmas here. She would go with neighbors to see the crèche with baby Jesus in the manger and be delighted. "It had nothing to do with religion. It was just pretty to look at. And then for *Succot*, when we Jews collected branches to build a *sukkah*, the Christians would celebrate as much as we did. They knew when our holidays were and everything had a place and time. We were all one big family!"

Which is why coming to New York was such a shocker. High buildings, hemmed-in streets, unknown people, dangerous. How different from the cozy innocence she was used to. Her family had arrived penniless, and her father was depressed because "he was no longer who he thought he was: a German war hero with a saber. Respected." But Lotte had joie de vivre. While her father drudged as an usher at Loews Movie Theater, Lotte transformed herself from a "German country bumpkin" into an American teenager. That meant learning English in three months and getting rid of her Benheim look: "I was very robust, a country girl. And I saw these American girls, *Ach*, such gorgeous complexions, and so slim, you know, and they had such nice coats on. I said I want to be like that. The first thing I did was to stop eating, and I had a tremendous appetite. I loved to eat. But I lost lots of weight and I earned enough money to get rid of the *schmatta* clothing that we brought from Germany—I couldn't even look at them. You know you had to be American. I always envied their clear skin and thought it must be the orange juice that they drink. In Germany, who drinks orange juice?"

We laugh, and I tell her how, at fifteen, I did the same dieting thing—minus the orange juice. And how everyone in my family was either pronounced too fat or too thin. She nods, knowing exactly, and we laugh again. I am having too good a time, I realize, thinking we should be more serious. Talking to Lotte is like talking to my friends.

I wonder what would have happened if this lively nonconformist had not had to flee Benheim. Would she, as an adult, have felt as free? Or claustrophobic, like my dad, who bridled against so many rules and traditions? As a mother of seven, she would never have started college at age forty-eight, a feat considering her education ended in an all-one-class elementary school with a teacher who beat her with a cane because she was left-handed. And she would never have completed a BA degree in history at age sixty, marching side by side at graduation with her youngest daughter, age twenty-two.

"So what subject did you like best in college?" I ask, with an eye on the floor-to-ceiling bookshelves.

"*Ach*, everything. History, geography, philosophy, politics, I sopped all of it up like a sponge." School, she says, was her special luxury: "Someone was finally giving something to me!" Of course, she still had a big house to take care of, cooking, shopping, so she would go to sleep very early and get up around two in the morning to do her reading in a quiet house. She pulls down a book on geography, which she declares her very favorite subject, and shows me pages of yellow highlighted passages. Her sons showed her how to read like that and take notes; her husband helped her write her papers; so her graduation was a family event for a family enterprise. She pauses, smiling broadly and says, "Not bad for a Benheim girl from the *Volksschule*. Am I right?"

"Absolutely!" I mean it. Many Benheim women, intimidated by their meager schooling, have said to me, "I'm an uneducated woman. What do I know?" Most, like Lotte, didn't go to high school (a town away). Only a few, like Hannah, were sent away to secretarial school for a year or so. The norm was to marry early and raise well-behaved children, keep a proper house, and make great sauerbraten and linzertorte.

Lotte looks at her watch. She says she must stop our interview early to get ready for Hanukkah tomorrow. No problem, I say, surprised that it is so early this year. I stopped paying attention after my children left for college, leaving the ritual to my husband, who likes saying the prayers and lighting the meno-rah. I never seem to get inspired. Even as a kid, an oil lamp burning for eight days didn't seem like much of a miracle, not like the baby-in-the-manger story and three wise men following the star.

I ask Lotte if we can continue our talks after Hanukkah is over. "Of course," she says, "my pleasure!"

"Are you making potato latkes for thirty-four people?" I ask, as we wind down the stairs. "You must grate a lot of potatoes."

"We manage," she says, laughing, and then I am through the tilted screen door, walking past the headless torsos as she calls "Happy Hanukkah!" and keeps waving.

◊ ◊ ◊

"Hiding. That's what the Jewish children would do when the Christians held their Winter Pageant, carrying the cross," Lotte says bitterly. We are back in her study after the holidays. *Is this the same Benheim? Is this the same woman?* I had expected more about Otto the baker, and the fun she'd had "going house-to-house for eight nights of Hanukkah parties." Instead, I hear how "the cross reminded the Gentiles of what they learned every day in church and school: that the Jews killed not just Jesus, but *our* Jesus. And so should be damned, burn in Hell, and good riddance. When they carried the cross for twelve stations, you never knew what could happen, even in Benheim."

"But last time I came you said how nice the Christian holi-days were!" I am as edgy as Lotte, because there's a "Go home" feeling in the air, as if joie de vivre has been used up and what's left is unmined, dangerous. Lotte signals as much with a story about how depressed a friend of hers became after the Red Cross helped her reconnect to a family she'd known in Yugoslavia fifty years ago. Her friend couldn't sleep for nights. "It was a terrible agony, making her wish she had left the past alone."

"Would you like to stop the interview?" I ask, not wanting

to unleash emotions she can't handle. But Lotte shakes her head, "No, no . . . please!" and puts her hand on mine. We continue, the conversation filled with pauses. I tell myself this is her choice, not mine, but still feel like a scavenger of misery. I worry about my responsibility after I leave: what if she, like her friend, can no longer sleep?

Lotte tells me about one Shabbat dinner soon after Hitler came to power in 1933. The table was aglitter with candles and her mother's good dishes when there was a knock on the door. Three men wearing brown shirts, strangers, came in looking for guns and ammunition. They turned the house upside down and took her father's sword from World War I, saying no weapons are allowed for Jews anymore. "At least they didn't take him away as they did Fritz Weiss, who had a revolver because he traveled at night." *Didn't she say, last time, that nothing bad happened in the early years?* "And at least they didn't pull the tablecloth out from under everything the way they did at Gretl's house. . . ."

"What? Gretl never mentioned that to me!"

"No? It happened right after their honeymoon. 'Look at the Jews, how fancy they live!' the thugs had said, laughing as new dishes and glasses crashed across the floor."

"Who did this? Were they from Benheim?" I ask. Lotte doesn't think so. Were they the same people who burned the synagogue on Kristallnacht? She doesn't think so. "But I was a child, remember. I knew only what the adults said." Now *I* can't wait to go home. Benheim is beginning to sound like every other place in Nazi Germany.

Lotte tells me about taking a train by herself to visit her father who was in the hospital in Tübingen in 1937. It was an hour away, and across the aisle sat two buxom German women who kept eyeing her, and then one said to the other: "Look at the *typisches deutsches Maedel* (typical German girl)! Look at her fine blond hair, her ruddy cheeks! What good health our German girls have! How strong and smart those blue eyes are!" The women beamed and Lotte smiled back, knowing enough to keep quiet.

Lotte delights in this irony—until she remembers the Nazi flags draped in the Tübingen doorways and the great fear she felt walking past them. She hadn't felt that danger in Benheim—"at least not before Kristallnacht, and the arrests . . . and the broken windows."

"What broken windows?"

"They smashed the Jewish windows."

"Who did?"

"The Nazis. And the neighbors could do nothing." She sighs, then brightens. "But the next day they came and repaired all of them. Our neighbor was a cabinetmaker, and he and his sons worked for days to fix everything. Good people. But for that, they were punished. Both sons were shipped to the front a few days later and never came back. They were cannon fodder."

So here it is again: the refrain of Christian neighbors doing what they could. More support for why Benheim Jews say "Decent people, decent people," even as authoritative books such as Daniel Goldhagen's *Hitler's Willing Executioners* condemn all Germans, saying they *all* knew what was going on and should have done more.

"We *all* just pretended," says Lotte, sadly. "We *all* ignored the signs. It was as if the big swastika on the hill wasn't even there."

"What big swastika?" No one has mentioned any of these stories.

"In the meadow above the village. The new mayor—the one the Nazis appointed after they threw out good Mayor Kinkele—ordered it built. All the villagers grumbled, especially when they were taxed for the ugly thing."

"You mean the white cross?" I'd seen it on a postcard, mounted on its pedestal overlooking the whole village.

"No, not that. I mean the *Hakenkreuz*, the black swastika," Lotte says impatiently. "The white cross came later."

Now I'm really baffled. "How could you feel safe with a swastika looking down on you?" I snap in spite of myself.

"We didn't *really* notice it," Lotte says, with her familiar casualness. "This wasn't Berlin or Frankfurt. We knew everyone, and with them not that much changed."

"You were in denial."

"Yes, of course, looking back, yes . . . But back then Benheim was *not* so bad," she insists. "It wasn't like Tübingen—or Nagold where my cousin worked. Plenty of Nazis there. But here, when she came home to say goodbye in 1936 before leaving for America, I heard people, not just my father, say she shouldn't go, that Hitler will pass. Of course, my mother shuddered. She knew better."

I marvel at the contradictions that refuse a neat labeling. The Jews felt safe, but there was a giant swastika. Some Gentiles smashed windows, but others fixed them. No simple tale of guilt and blame here. No way to appease my need for "all good" or "all bad" that brought me into these homes.

In the film *Life is Beautiful*, the father keeps trying to mix joy into their living nightmare so that his son can survive the concentration camp. A bit of song, a game, a funny imitation to feed the spirit, if only for a moment. Lotte mixes the same survival brew to handle the nightmares of memory, and it has worked, although imperfectly. Grief catches her off guard, she says, especially every Hanukkah when she remembers the pain of those weeks after Kristallnacht when her father was still in a concentration camp. "I would never tell my family that." She looks so sad. "For them it's a happy time of presents and cooking good things, but I feel only the loss of childish hope. You know the Hanukkah story, of how the oil burned for eight nights—a miracle—and how the Maccabees were the victors, the Jews were freed, and everything went back to the usual way? I had so much hope the same thing would happen that year. But it didn't. My father stayed in Dachau, and we were in Benheim living from one day to the next, never knowing what would happen. But every night we had faith. We would light the candles and sing "Maor Zu" (Rock of Ages). It was so pitiful. You didn't know what would happen."

"We kindle these lights on account of miracles, the deliverances . . . " my husband said last week as he lit the menorah every night. I had pictured a joyful Lotte in her big room with her family of thirty-four, and I thought: This *is* worth celebrating. This *is* deliverance! A burning oil lamp *is* enough of a miracle. But now I find that Lotte had no joie de vivre, only its pretense so her children wouldn't know the grief she cannot shake. I ask Lotte what she had hoped would happen on that Hanukkah in 1938. "That the Bad would all go away, go away." Her voice is flat. "That things would go back to how they were. Hitler would be overthrown. They would change their minds."

◊ ◊ ◊

We enter Lotte's house through a side porch I don't remember, and her living room has more furniture than I remember. The giant stove is off to the side, not a throne in the center at all. "Was this room always like this?" I ask, disoriented.

"Oh, we always change things around," Lotte says cheerfully. I feel less like Alice in Wonderland, but am still wary. If my four-month-old memories, propped by notes and taped transcripts, are so fragile, what about her memories, sixty years old?

Accuracy aside, there's a relaxed feeling to this third visit. We talk about her son's sculptures, now *in* the living room. I recognize the headless torsos that were outside, but there are some new ones, too: a beaver hugging a tree and a woman's head (the first head I've seen) rising out of a marble slab, half smiling, half sad.

I've come back to Lotte's to decide which emotion holds sway: the joie de vivre of visit one or the pain and disillusionment of visit two. They seem, today, to coexist more easily. Lotte explains that the swastika on the hill wasn't seen as a symbol of destruction, because in the 1930s no one could imagine what lay ahead.

I can't imagine that—until I remember the wooden cross on a lawn near my house and how last week an American flag had been nailed to it. I had passed by that cross so often, for years, and thought: No problem in a free country. But what if more crosses with flags appeared—and everywhere? What symbol would they become?

Lotte talks of how she used to climb up to the meadow on that hill to pick flowers, lie in the sun, and listen to the sounds of the village: "It was so wonderful! I'd hear voices from the village and the sound of the anvil, the smithy made such a wonderful sound that would echo in my ears. The crowing, the mooing of the cows, and the sense of belonging . . . that this was my place." And then she talks of the Nazi festivities that were held under the swastika: "They would congregate at night and make a huge fire. You'd hear crowds yelling, torches swaying. It was very frightening to us. And they'd sing Nazi songs and shout anti-Semitic propaganda."

Day and night in the exact same spot—but is it? I think of the red leaf maple outside my bedroom window in Queens and how, on windy nights, it became a monster scratching the glass panes to enter. Until, in sunshine, it became my lovely tree again.

"Did you know the people who went to those bonfires?" I ask. "Were they out-of-towners or Benheimers?"

"Some were Benheimers . . . There was one, the son of the letter carrier, and the father wanted nothing to do with him. Another family nearby was also Nazi, but most were very supportive of the Jews."

"What percentage took part in these events?"

"Small. The others were ashamed."

"Would you say under 10 percent?" I'm thinking that wouldn't be so bad. Her faith in decency would hold.

"Many came from neighboring towns. You know all the young people had to go to the bonfires. It was compulsory." Lotte shrugs. "Everyone said it couldn't last forever. The Allies won't permit it. The government will fall and everything will be like before." She smiles. "You can't minimize the illusions that people live under."

The illusions were nurtured, she says, not only by optimistic neighbors but by fear of starting new somewhere else, of not having enough money to leave, of having an old parent who wouldn't be able to get a visa. Whatever the reasons, when the Jewish schoolmaster warned in 1934 that the Jews would be slaughtered like sheep, the whole community—Jew and Gentile—turned against him. "He was fired and had to leave the village," says Lotte. "People said it was because he was too old and too severe with children like me, beating us. But I don't think it was that."

The illusion lasted until the day after Kristallnacht. Only then did neighbors no longer dare to say hello in public ("Yet still brought food at night"). And children began to throw stones more openly ("Even so, their parents disapproved"). And the constant barrage of anti-Semitic propaganda had its effect ("When you are pounded with how terrible these Jews are, even I, after a while, began to feel like a bad person").

Even in 1939, right before she left, Bad is trumped by Good in Lotte's memory. The image of the swastika never overpowers her belief in communal decency prevailing over random violence: "The Benheimers weren't animals—*that* wouldn't go in our village. They didn't beat up anybody, or harm anybody. Even if they arrested someone, they were civil. You couldn't just beat up anybody because you felt like beating up. There was a code still maintained, a code of civility."

"Was that true in other small villages?" I ask.

Lotte didn't know for sure. "Many did not have so many Jews."*

*Benheim with its 350 Jews—30 percent of the population—had among the highest percentages of Jews in Germany in 1933. Cities such as Berlin, Frankfurt, and Hamburg, where most of Germany's 505,000 Jews lived, had between 4 and 8 percent.

Benheim's village code is still central to her values. It makes Lotte civil to a "German non-Jew" who has lived next door for the last thirty years. They talk, they exchange books, she gives her *The Economist*, "but we can never be close," Lotte says. The woman came to America after the war.

"What's her story?" I ask, thinking it may be worth pursuing.

"I don't know and don't want to know."

I hear none of the warmth she has in memories of Benheim neighbors. I ask why. "There's no comparison! In Benheim we grew up together and went to school together. My father fought side by side in war with his neighbors. When someone was sick, my mother always sent me over with soup. It was another time. It can't be recaptured. It just can't be recaptured. . . ."

Right before I leave, Lotte shows me a postcard that she received from Benheim last year. It's an aerial view of the village, green and lush, full of red tile roofs, and it begins, "Liebe Schtumpela." That's what everyone called her, Lotte says, amused, because she was short and squat as a child. She translates the handwritten words:

> We were talking with a heavy heart about former times. Do you remember when we met at Erna's house in Israel? How would it be if you came to Benheim?
>
> Best Regards,
> *Hedwig and Klaus*

"So what did you answer?" I ask, thinking I will look up this Christian couple up when I go to Benheim this summer to see what people there have to say.

"I didn't answer them," Lotte says coldly.

"How come?"

"I don't remember these people." She sounds as if she doesn't want to.

Lotte slips the postcard into the back of the photo album and opens to the front page: a photo of her father's school class in 1887. I see forty-four Jewish children looking safe at a time when Benheim's Jewish population was at its largest: 50 percent of the village. Their parents and grandparents were German citizens, they voted, they prospered, they belonged to the glee club and the fire brigade, one had even been head of the village council. Yet fifty-five years later, many in the photo were murdered by the country they trusted and loved. How does one live with that betrayal and legacy? Some repress and move on. Others let anger rule. Lotte does both—balancing joie de vivre and bitterness in a way that lets her be a smiling Schtumpela, able to light the Hanukkah candles for her progeny of thirty-four near the giant wood stove.

6 | FOUR STORIES OF THE TORAH

> Whether a memory or a . . . scandal, we will return to it an
> hour later and retell the story with additions, and this time
> a few judgments thrown in. In this way history is organized.
>
> From Running in the Family, *Michael Ondaatje*

I

Ever since I saw the rescued Torah in the Memorial Room, I imagine this scene like a movie playing in my head:

KRISTALLNACHT — BENHEIM: *November 9, 1938.*

The Christian villagers (I can't see how many) sneak through the darkening night, up the alley, and through the side door of the synagogue. Minutes later a truck light beams on the two stone pillars outside. Voices are heard: loud and clipped. Feet stomping. "Heil Hitler," many times.

"Hurry up!" whispers a man, blond and handsome. I picture a German version of Brad Pitt. He quickly takes the Torah from the Ark and puts it into a gray sack. Another grabs the silver breastplate and some prayer books stacked nearby. Torches flare outside, the large front doors open just as they escape out the side door.

"What should we do with them?" someone young whispers as the men hug the darkness, running close to the fence of one of the Jewish houses, toward the church. "Our priest will hide them."

"No, keep going," says an older man. "Go to the Jewish cemetery. We'll bury them there." Everyone agrees, except for one dark-haired man who heads back to his farm. He has a new baby and can't take any more risks, especially since his father-in-law was caught listening to the BBC.

The other men, avoiding their neighbors' lit windows, take the dirt path up toward the cemetery. They stop for shovels at the Brenner farm. Brenner, the gravedigger for the Jews for centuries, tells them to dig to the left of the stone gate, where the ground dips. Below them are flames, but here in the woods all is dark. An owl hoots, leaves rustle, and they dig two deep holes like graves. They bury the Torah in one hole, the breastplate and prayer books in another, and stomp on the loose dirt. "Hurry, hurry!" Their brows are wet, faces flushed, even in the chill November air that, fortunately, has not yet frozen the ground. They scatter dead leaves over their cache.

"May Jesus and their Lord protect them," they say, and return to the village, where all the curtains are drawn—not to see the flames, not to hear the shouts. "Heil Hitler! Heil Hitler!" Seven years later, after the war, one man returns with a shovel. He is the only one left from the group who didn't die as cannon fodder. The man finds the hole that holds the Torah and carries the sacred scroll back to his house. Somehow, in the postwar chaos, he manages to mail it to his former Jewish neighbors in Oleh Zion. "It's all I could do!" says his note.

True, the old man in the Memorial Room said only that Christians saved the Torah, buried it beside the Jewish cemetery, dug it up, and sent it to them. The rest came from random facts and bits of memory, plus an imagination that likes turning sketchy lines into a full-color canvas of heroics. I was especially drawn to a story that challenges the usual ones of hate and meanness, like in Theo Richmond's *Konin*, about another Torah in another little village on Kristallnacht:

> Before long there was no synagogue in which to pray. The Nazis wrecked the interior, shattering the magnificent Holy Ark, the pride of Konin Jewry. Jews were forced to carry the Torah scrolls into the Tepper Marik where a great bonfire was prepared. . . . Rabbi Lipschitz and his fellow Jews were made to watch while the scrolls were set on fire. The dignified bearing of the white-bearded rabbi must have irked his tormentors, for they rammed a woman's hat on his head and taunted him while the parchment rolls went up in flame. The rabbi was "made to stand against the wind so that the smoke blew into his face. The Germans pushed him closer and closer to the fire so that his beard got singed." The bonfire blazed for three days. One boy observed the scene with his usual eye for detail: "The colors of the flames from the parchment," recalls Izzy Hahn, "were unbelievable—every color of the rainbow. I stood and watched." (p. 79)

That kind of sadism and humiliation didn't happen in Benheim, everyone assures me. Which is why the story of Benheim's Christians saving the Torah, even if they saved no man, woman, or child, keeps being a comfort against the atrocities of the majority.

II

Gretl Dorfman, with her stern face and strong handshake, tells me that the Christians never sent the rescued Torah to Israel. "It was my Simon who brought it there," she says proudly, as we drink tea in her small, neat apartment. I don't want to believe her and tell myself that her husband Simon is always her hero:

Simon saw what was coming. Simon founded the group that escaped to Israel. Simon brought her to America when she got sick. But her honesty is compelling and her details become more credible than my Hollywood epic:

KRISTALLNACHT, *November 9, 1938.*

We heard someone yell in the street, "The synagogue is burning," and Simon rushed out. He had been an officer in the fire brigade, you know, so when he got there and the firemen were just standing around, he shouted. "We must do something!" But the others pointed to a truck with strangers in brown shirts, who had guns. Only when the neighboring house started to smoke and someone shouted, "The whole village might burn!" did the men bring out hoses and water pails.

The next morning we heard a knock on the door. The policeman had come to arrest Simon. The man was very apologetic, saying he had to follow orders, and led Simon, along with other Jewish men, to the *Rathaus* jail, a tiny room, a closet. Then they were sent to Dachau and I was desperate. I had two young children and didn't know what to do because Simon always made the decisions. But I had to do something. I sold all our furniture for a song, beautiful things, so we'd have money to eat and hopefully leave. Then I took the train to Stuttgart, by myself, to the Gestapo headquarters. I was terrified but planned to beg to have Simon released. Fortunately for me, I was sent to the office of Herr Otz, who reassured me, saying he would see what he could do. Three times I went to see him, and three times he said be patient. The day after my last visit Simon came home, very thin and pale, but alive. Herr Otz had kept his promise. We immediately began packing—we had our visas because we'd been planning to leave—and decided to arrange for visas for Simon's parents and my grandparents once we got to Palestine. We had been trying for months to get theirs, going to every consulate with no luck. "They are too old!" we were informed by the Germans, the British, the Americans, whoever we asked.

The next night, there was another knock on the door. Again it was the policeman, and we were sure Simon would be arrested again. Instead the man took off his hat and said, "Don't worry!" He wanted us to know that he had a Torah from the synagogue in his house. Did we want to take it with us? It had been lying in the gutter, and he thought this is not right, so he took it and hid it in his garden. I was afraid of a trick, but Simon said yes immediately. The policeman was a good man; they'd been in the singing club together. And besides, had he not let the women sneak baskets of food and clothing into the jail before the men were shipped to Dachau? So I agreed.

An hour later, another knock. The policeman was carrying the Torah. It was dirty, damp, there was a slash mark from a knife or axe, but the words were clear. We took it from him, he left, and we said a prayer of thanks. Then Simon rolled the Torah into a carpet we were packing into a crate of our furniture. I worried that the customs inspectors would find it—no small thing, a Torah—but Simon said he would make arrangements, and a few weeks after we arrived in Palestine, our crate came and there it was.

Our parents and grandparents were not as lucky! We tried desperately for two years to get them out, Simon went twice to Jerusalem, a dangerous trip when Arabs were attacking every road. But the British, they were in charge then, kept refusing them visas. Simon could do nothing. . . .

Her strong voice trembles, and my fantasy of heroes fades. For there was only one Christian, not four or five, who was brave and true. Or maybe two, if you believe that Herr Otz of the Stuttgart Gestapo did help Simon come home four weeks earlier than the other Benheim Jews. Or three, if Simon's customs inspector ignored the Torah wrapped in the carpet, a man like the one who told my father, "Herr Loewengart, pack whatever you want. I will not stop you!" and winked as he said, "*Heil Hitler.*" My father had taken no chances, packing nothing forbidden such as money or jewelry—certainly not a Torah. But her Simon had dared.

III

Six months later in Burlington, Vermont, I find out that not one Torah but two were rescued from Benheim. The second Torah, according to Ilse Loew, is in the synagogue a few blocks from her house, brought here by husband Harry, who hid it in his crate of furniture when he sailed to America two months after Kristallnacht. Ilse is a small, pert woman of eighty or so, who reminds me more of a New England matriarch than a girl educated in *Volksschule* in Benheim. She speaks English fluently and with authority, telling me how Harry found a job teaching German here soon after they arrived via England in 1942. They moved into this blue split-level house near the college, and she's still here over fifty years later, a widow of ten years. Harry was called "Heinz" in Germany, she says, and they weren't married until they came here. In fact, they lived hours apart until the day after Kristallnacht, which, as she recalls it, "changed everything":

November 10, 1938.

I was working in Kanden near Stuttgart and staying at a rooming house when the landlord—he was a Jew, you could only live with Jews by then—rushes in. "Did you hear? The synagogues are burning!" He closed all the shades. We began hearing shouts outside, someone yelled "Hang the Jews!" and we huddled together, hearing objects smash, glass shatter, but no one stormed the house, thank God. The next morning Heinz calls from Berlin, saying I should pick him up at the Bahnhof in Stuttgart and we'd go by train to Benheim, to our mothers. I said, "But you don't know what is happening there. If you have black hair and look halfway Jewish, you can't walk down the street. You come here to Kanden, and we'll see what we can do." He made it unmolested, thank God, and then we called the man who ran the bus company in Benheim. He was married to Mayor Kinkele's sister and was no Nazi. "Can you pick us up in Dorn?" we asked. He said he was terribly sorry but he'd already been in trouble for driving Jews. We took the train anyway, hoping for the best. In Dorn, we went to the pharmacy—we knew the people well, they had always been friendly, non-Jews—and asked if we could stay until evening. Hitler youth and SA gangs were roaming around; it was very dangerous. The pharmacist let us in, but after a while, apologizing profusely, he said that we had to go. He could do nothing more for us. Harry was furious, but I could see how deep the man's fear was. So we walked to Benheim, it's only a few kilometers, with no incident, thank God. Our mothers were okay. A few Jewish windows, not theirs, had been smashed and the synagogue had been partly destroyed. They had heard rumors of arrests, but no one had bothered them at home. We decided to stay in Benheim and make immediate plans to leave for America. I had an uncle in Boston who had offered to help me, and Harry had some cousins. We contacted them right away.

A few nights later, the gendarme—there's really no equivalent, okay he was a policeman, the only one in Benheim, known as a *Landjäger*, if you've ever heard that term—knocked on the door and told Harry, "You don't have to fear anything for the time being." Harry, you see, wasn't registered as living in Benheim, so he wasn't on the roundup list. "I don't have a warrant or anything against you, but I have a Torah which I saved from the fire. If you want it, I'll give it to you." And now it's here in the synagogue in Burlington!

I can't believe my luck! A second Torah in the middle of New England (confirmed by my own eyes, the next day), and no one seems to know about it! Neither the Jews in New York nor the old man in Oleh Zion. I, searcher of good stories, have rediscovered it—not buried outside the Jewish cemetery as I had first heard, but in the policeman/*Landjäger*'s garden, the same man who saved both Torahs! My elation fades, however, as the dark side of Ilse's story slips into the room with the late afternoon sun, its shadows lengthening as we sip more and more cups of coffee. . . .

My uncle in Boston sent me the affidavits and wrote that as soon as I arrive, we will help get my mother out. I can still see his handwriting . . . every night. You just have to live with it. . . . Have some more coffee. . . . It took us a whole year before we made it to America—we spent months in detention in northern England—and by then it was 1941. No one could get out. But . . . my mother, at least, was not completely alone. A woman had moved into our house, assigned by the authorities to take over the second floor. This woman, a Frau Holle, was very good to my mother. This woman had lost her husband in the war, didn't know a soul in Benheim, and when my mother became sick, Frau Holle took care of her, right to the end. She is still alive, and I saw her when I went back. She is still in the house and wanted to show me through the whole place, how she fixed it up. She has a garden like we did, and has lovely flowers.

I ask Ilse if she feels resentment. After all, this stranger took over her house. But she says Frau Holle helped her mother, she was a good woman like the *Landjäger*, both risking what was possible in a small village where every move was known.

Look, there were people who were good at heart and did what they could—and some were even not that afraid. I met a woman in Vermont recently who grew up in Holland and had been hiding some Jews. One day someone knocked on her door—it was either the Dutch police or a Nazi—and demanded she hand over the Jews. She offered him a cup of coffee and while he drank, she got a gun and killed him. She had a friend she could trust, an undertaker, and he helped her get rid of the body by sticking it in a coffin with another dead body, an official one. This woman is now a frail, little old lady, about my height, white hair, and is a psychiatrist. Mrs. Pritchard is her name, and they did a movie about her. She had guts. Can you imagine doing that? I cannot!!

Ilse, like Hannah, has seemed such a take-charge woman with life well under control; but now, suddenly, all I see is a face of great sadness in a kitchen of loss. And it is this image, I know, that will impose itself on every story I hear of the saved Torah, one or two—or more. It won't matter. "More coffee? More plum cake? . . ." she offers. "It's good, yes? My mother's recipe . . . I . . . we . . . . we thought we could save my mother once we were in America. A foolish thought, but . . . Look, I have to live with it, my husband did too. His parents also didn't. . . . Here . . . let me put on some light."

IV

In Brooklyn, off Ocean Parkway with its benches of white-bearded Orthodox Jews, next to Sikhs in turbans, next to Hispanic, Asian, and Arab mothers pushing strollers, I hear the fourth story of the Torah's rescue. It is told by two sisters, Hettie and Clara Gilder, who have lived in the same speckled, beige row house with a black wrought-iron fence since they came from Benheim in 1940. Hettie, the older, does most of the talking about Kristallnacht. Clara keeps correcting:

November 10, 1938.

The morning after I still knew nothing. I was getting my fifteen children from the nursery school ready to go to the synagogue as we did every day, when a woman calls through the window, "Go home! It is dangerous. Take the children home. They are making arrests." Then another woman, Brunhilda, comes in. She was the niece of Zundorfer, the pilot, Jewish, of World War I, and she says the synagogue had been burned. She'd seen it on the way home from burying her uncle's sword outside the Jewish cemetery so they wouldn't get it. Can you imagine? She asked a Gentile, one of the farmers, for a shovel. ("It was Brenner, the gravedigger!" corrects her sister). I don't know. . . . I was nuts. I didn't know what to do . . . no one knew from nothing. ("Willie Welder knew," corrects her sister.) *Ja*, Willie did know. He was the head of the synagogue, and he did a good thing. Two weeks before, he took the silver from the synagogue, and also the Torah's breastplate and crown, and he brought them to me. He said he was worried that something might happen, and asked if I could take them with me to America. And I did. I hid them in my trunks and now they are in the Young Israel congregation in Staten Island!

They beam, and so do I. For the old man's Torah story is true once more, even if its facts are scattered into four parts. Something was buried at the Jewish cemetery! Not a Torah, but a sword (even if Jews buried it!). It is listed in a catalog of memorabilia printed for a museum exhibit forty kilometers from Benheim. "Donated by Zundorfer's niece who remarried a Gentile in Mainz," according to Herr Adolph Stolle, who, when I visit Benheim in a few months, will show me its picture, unsheathed.

I love the image of a Jewish sword surviving in Germany, a warrior image of Jews who win. I love it almost as much as the rescued Torah in Israel. And the other Torah in Burlington.

And the breastplate and Torah crown in Staten Island. But even more, I love the people telling me these stories: these old Jews who may have been the ones who pinched my cheek at the *Nachtmittage* reunions. Their refugee faces had scared me then, their smiles too full of a loss I sensed without knowing. Now they nourish, retrieve, and affirm what have become the real stories of rescue for me, the ones I most need to hear.

7 | THE REVOLVING ROOM

I am sitting in the San Francisco Hyatt, high up, surrounded by glass in a revolving restaurant. The Golden Gate Bridge looms a majestic red before me while I tell my colleague Angie about the article in my Dad's folder. "No byline," I say, "but as soon as I read that the whole village was saving goose liver to sell in the city, I knew my Dad wrote it. Something about the voice brought his voice back."

"What's the name of the village?" Angie asks, stopping my segue into my paper tomorrow for this conference on teaching literature.

"Oh, it's just a tiny place near Stuttgart. No place anyone has heard of."

Certainly not a Texan like Angie Watson. Thick curly blond hair I always wanted, intense blue eyes, and a figure that must have ruled the Gulf Coast surfers in younger days. We'd met on a panel here years ago, found out we used the same reading glasses (I'd forgotten mine and borrowed hers for my talk)—and that we both drank only decaf because of scares with breast cancer in the same year. We'd been meeting yearly ever since, drawn by the small surprises within our big difference: I'm Jewish New Jersey; she's a Texan WASP.

"So what's the name?" Angie asks again. "Of the village?"

"Oh, Benheim, near a place called Dorn," I say impatiently, wanting to get back to my talk on the power of voice. Angie always has good ideas.

59

"Ah, in the Schwarzwald!" Her enamel hoop earrings bob with delight, as their lemon yellow centers, matched to her suit, catch the light. "I know Benheim well."

"My God, how?" I've never met anyone not directly or indirectly related to me who ever heard of Benheim.

"My mother's family comes from Ilhausen, practically next door. We visited there every summer when I was little and walked all through the hills. I remember a *Gasthaus* where we'd go to eat *Spätzle*, my favorite!"

"Don't laugh," I laugh nervously, "but my Aunt Hilda's family owned a *Gasthaus*."

"No!"

"And she made great *Spätzle*." She leans forward, and I lean back. "You're from Germany?" After years of dodging strange relatives who hugged too hard, I pride myself on detecting even a trace of German a mile away. "You have no accent."

She laughs. "If you arrive in Dallas in 1946, and are in the second grade, you get rid of your accent as fast as possible, believe me."

I still can't believe she's not the all-American girl, the type I remember as being cheerleader and prom queen and getting the all-American varsity boy. On our first panel five years ago, the room was packed with admirers of her wit and charm. Myself included. That's why when she sent me a postcard before the next conference saying, "How about lunch?" I answered right away. Sure. And it's been a same-time-next-year lunch date ever since.

If she came in 1946, she must be Jewish, even with that blond hair. *Did she survive a concentration camp? Did her family?* I look for numbers on her arm, but Angie is wearing long sleeves.

"My older sister, Ruth, also came as a child," I say, and describe how the neighborhood kids used to call her "Kraut" until she brought all her paper dolls onto the front stoop and gave the leader two of them. "That bought her more time to learn English."

I pause, hoping she'll start her story, but she smiles like a therapist encouraging me on. I tell her how my family left Germany in 1936, and how they had to wait in Switzerland for months until they could go to America, and how they sailed on the Dutch ship *Van Dam* and settled in a row house in Queens for three years surrounded by relatives, the women knitting hats and baby booties for money while the men tried starting a business in a strange land.

The Golden Gate has almost disappeared, and Alcatraz has drifted into view, too slowly to notice. "I am sorry your family had to leave Germany," she says, "but they were the lucky ones, were they not?"

Yes, now I hear something, maybe a rhythm or word inversion not quite right. I do that, too, if I'm not careful, the echoes of my parents' hard-learned English. I nod. "Yes, very lucky."

The waiter asks about coffee and dessert. We say "decaf" at the same time, reject dessert, and gaze out the window for a while. Alcatraz disappears and a giant clock appears, like a stern face. She asks me when I'll be speaking, what sessions I've attended, and where I got my sweater. "I love that blue. It suits you." I tell her my mother knit it, that she's the knitter for the family and my grandmother was the seamstress, so I do neither. I laugh. She does not.

"I wish I had something from my mother . . ." Angie's strong, clipped voice has become a whisper. "I have nothing—no letters, not even a photo of her. The bombs destroyed everything in our house."

"They bombed your house? Where were you?" Now I imagine her hiding in a false closet like my friend's cousin, or escaping across wild mountains to Portugal and then Palestine.

"We were in a small village near Munich, not unlike your father's. My father sent us there to be safe, but the Allies found us. They bombed our house, the only one bombed in the whole village." I hear some anger now. "My brother and I were in school, but my mother was killed." She takes a deep breath. "It was a week before the end of the war."

I mumble I'm sorry, thinking, *My God, she's a real German!* I, who still buy nothing German (except for my Krups coffee maker), am talking about Hitler with someone whose family might be Nazis. . . .

"They bombed us on purpose," Angie's voice has sharpened. "They wanted to punish my father."

"Who did?"

She takes a long sip of coffee. "The Allies. My father was working on the bombs used in the blitzkrieg. The British, especially, wanted him dead."

Now I see Teutonic lines around a tight mouth and imagine her a child in thick, blond braids, waving Nazi flags and singing Nazi songs in Hitler parades. I remind myself that she lost her mother senselessly while I still have mine knitting sweaters for me. But my empathy feels as false as my next words: "You can't know for sure they were after your family." *Her whole story is irrational!* "How could the Allies single you out in a rented house?" I say, trying to soothe.

"I saw the plane. It dropped away from its squadron, swooping down. I was in the schoolyard. The sky was clear blue, only one small cloud . . . I still hear that bomb." She looks smaller, like that child. "A farmer's wife took me to her house and told me that my mother had gone to Munich, and I believed her. Why should I not? Three days later she took me to a gravestone and I read my mother's name, so I knew. We walked back past my house, but there was nothing, only a charred pile by the roadside, and the woman said, 'Don't stop. And don't cry!'"

Angie straightens up, as if she still hears that voice. Behave. Be strong. A good German girl. She shrugs. "But life goes on, does it not?" We look out the window, at the sun that has just come out, making the bay sparkle. An all-glass pyramid shimmers like ice on our right.

The waiter pours more coffee. I sip, but have trouble swallowing. I'm thinking of Helga, whose office is next to mine at school, and how her mother at least hid someone—a Jew or maybe a resister?—and got caught. Helga, the only other German Gentile I've talked to about the Nazis, spent the last year of the war in a Berlin jail with her whole family. Saved from execution by the Russians.

"Did you know any Jews?" I ask Angie, sounding casual, I hope. After all, the past is not her fault. She was only six or seven years old.

"There were no Jews in our village," she says quickly. "My parents never talked about Jewish issues." A strange word, "issues." I worry. Her earrings bob. "I knew nothing until *The Diary of Anne Frank* came out," she says. "A wonderful book. I remember how shocked I was. You read it, of course?"

I nod, struggling to accept the "wonderful book" and the "I didn't know" argument. But how could she know? She was my age, and what I knew about the Holocaust came from watching Hollywood movies and reading Anne Frank's diary when I was twelve. There were no Holocaust museums or movies like *Schindler's List*. And no one in the early 1950s, Jew or German, talked much about what had happened, especially not to children of parents starting again.

I picture us both in Benheim, two little schoolgirls, me on the third floor of the school with Moses, Angie on the second floor with Jesus. That's how my father had described it: Jews had one floor of the *Volksschule*, Christians had the other two, and all shared the dirt playground. I picture us after school, going into the forest together to make doll blankets out of fern leaves and wildflowers, the way Hannah said she used to do.

But then what? What happens after her father begins making bombs for Hitler and my father begins taping his money to toilets of trains heading to Switzerland? And what if I have to wear a yellow armband with a star and she is a poster child for "good Aryan blood"? Would she throw sticks at me? Or watch her friends pull my hair, or sing the popular Horst Wessel song:

When Jewish blood drips from our knives
It solves the problems of our lives. . . .

Or would she just pretend I am no longer there?

The sun keeps ducking behind clouds, its light bouncing off buildings and then going dull. Maybe her father was not really for Hitler, but just someone not wanting to make waves. Maybe as a scientist, Angie's father had no choice: Work for the Führer or be shot. If he had been a Nazi, he'd have been tried as a war criminal. I had seen *Judgment at Nuremberg* with Spencer Tracy dispensing justice enough times to believe that. Unless her father was brilliant, another Wernher von Braun, he wouldn't have been allowed into America.

"It must have been hard getting into America," I say, feeling like Columbo minus the trench coat. "Did you have family here?"

"No, no one." She looks straight at me, and we both know what is unsaid: that the Americans *did* need her father's brain power in case the cold war with Russia became hot.

I tell myself it was long ago, and her father could have been a good man in terrible times. And besides, even if he was a big Nazi and hated Jews, Angie is not like that. Doesn't she ask me to meet for lunch every year?

So what am I to do? Bury the past? Pretend it never happened? Storm out? For the first time in my American life I feel the weight of those verbs—pretend, bury, storm out—and what they meant during Nazi times when it was so easy for Germans to say to Jews, "So what if your mother dies!" I can't imagine Angie like that, but Nazi groupthink changed so many, so fast. Maybe she would have said it! And what would I have said if *I* were the "Aryan" and she, the Jew?

I think again of stories like the one about the Torah being saved. And Christian carpenters fixing the Jewish windows after Kristallnacht. And the story of my father's business friend in Frankfurt who would turn the picture of Hitler to the wall whenever my father visited and say with great joy: "Für meinen guten jüdischer Freund, Artur" (For my good Jewish friend, Arthur). And how the head of the Stuttgart Gestapo saved my Uncle Fritz. They played cards together for twenty years, so when Jewish passports were taken away, he told my uncle, "Tell me when you want to leave and I will give them back for that day." And he did, justifying himself by saying: "You are not *typische Juden* (typical Jews)." Then he rounded up thousands of Jews he didn't know personally for deportation.

"Did *your* father ever talk about Germany?" Angie asks softly, surprising me.

"About growing up in Benheim, all the time," I say, hating my cheerfulness, as if Hitler had never happened. "And about his escaping the Nazis. Those stories I loved because my dad was the hero, leading our family out of danger, like Moses." I smile. She smiles.

"What about *your* father?" I ask, as the Oakland Bay Bridge comes into view, reaching over the whitecaps in the bay to touch the tiny houses, like dots, in the Berkeley hills. It all moves so slowly, like a still life trapped by time, as we are.

"Oh, he'd talk about how wonderful and beautiful my mother was, and how I looked just like her!" Angie tosses her hair behind her ear and says solemnly, "He loved her very much, you know."

"And nothing else?" She shakes her head. "And you didn't ask?" Suddenly I hate the bobbing earrings. *Stop them, for God's sake!* "Nothing else?" I ask again. *She lost her mother, remember. Love is love.*

She shakes her head. "All he'd say was, 'Ach, Schatzie'—that was what he called me—'you can't know what life was like then. Difficult times, difficult times.'" She sits up straighter. "He was too sad for me to ask more—and then, too soon, he died. It was my first husband, you know, who put me through college." She takes my hands in hers. Soft palms, long pink nails. "But I am glad that we are good friends, Mimi." I'm waiting for "Liebe Mimile," what my relatives used to say. "And who knows . . . ?" she says with the smile I've seen light up a room. "Without

Hitler, we might have met and eaten *Spätzle* together in that *Gasthaus!* I would have liked that, wouldn't you?"

I would, I would not, I would, would not. The voices in me collide, as I reach, with both my hands, for my coffee cup. For Hitler is always there, the gas chambers are always there, no matter how much I want us just to be two affable Americans having lunch. Beneath our good intentions, unsaid words linger *It's not my fault. . . . I know, but . . . I wasn't there. . . . I know, but. . . . Sorry. . . .* Words of anger, loss, and guilt that change nothing in the past, resolve nothing now—except the possibility of friendship that needs more open talk than we risk in this revolving room.

In the next few years, I will have such talks, but I don't know that yet. I will go to Benheim many times and will meet my father's former neighbors and other Germans willing to tackle the stories and silences of who we are. I will be armed with a yellow pad of questions, no surprise encounters like today. And after a while I will tell them about Angie and admit that I feel vulnerable in their country until someone *proves* to be nice. And Germans who are nice will tell me about a grandfather who is still a Nazi, and a father who was a train engineer near Auschwitz, and a grandmother who received *Mein Kampf* as a wedding present. And in between we will exchange our mothers' cucumber salad recipes and hike through the woods and talk about jobs and children as we step in and out of dark rooms of legacy with the hope of moving on.

But none of that seems possible in San Francisco, where history has caught us off guard. I am not ready for Angie, the child of possible Nazis—and whatever is behind our smiles. She invites me to the annual conference Talent Night: "Come! I'll be in it. It should be great fun!" and I nod, thinking I'd rather go to Fisherman's Wharf for crabs, if the weather holds. We stand up to hug goodbye as the Golden Gate reappears, now gray against a graying sky. She mentions next year in San Antonio and I mean to keep in touch, I really do. But so far we keep missing each other.

1. The village Torah, rescued by the Christians during Kristallnacht, and now in Memorial Room in Israel. *Photo courtesy of Heinz Högerle.*

2. The author's father, Arthur Loewengart, with his brother Sol, as soldiers in World War I, circa 1916.

3. Jewish families from the village that escaped the Nazis and resettled in New York, circa 1940. *Photo courtesy of Johanna Zurndorfer and Heinz Högerle.*

4. A Jewish girl in the village, standing with her cousin, circa 1920s. *Photo courtesy of Johanna Zurndorfer.*

5. The Jews in the Fire Brigade, circa 1931.
Photo courtesy of Fred Sulmer.

6. The inside of the synagogue before it was destroyed during Kristallnacht, 1938. *Photo courtesy of Heinz Högerle.*

PART TWO | AN OCEAN AWAY

8 | OFF THE RECORD

He stands in front of the Hertz sign at the train station in Stuttgart, as we had arranged, and I recognize him right away from the picture he sent me. A boyish twenty-five, with blond hair and well-scrubbed cheeks, Rolf is what I imagine as the perfect German poster boy of sixty years ago, dressed in uniform for the Fatherland. Today he is in jeans and sneakers, carrying a knapsack and a pink print umbrella.

Rolf, my translator, is a Protestant graduate student at the University of Mannheim doing research about how such a thing as the Holocaust could have happened in his country. Together we are going to Benheim, where, I was warned, no one speaks English. It's too small, too much in the boondocks, so my crash course in conversational German, plus some Berlitz tapes, won't be enough to interview Herr Adolf Stolle—and whomever else he's arranged for me to meet. Herr Stolle has been doing research on the old Jewish cemetery; he's the man who sent the Benheim Jews in New York photographs of their family graves. "A decent man," everyone agrees, "a good Gentile contact."

Rolf and I are expected this afternoon at two *if* my phone call last night from Zurich was understood. I had written out pages of possible dialogue before dialing Herr Stolle and had gotten through the part about my arrival time and that I was bringing a friend (Rolf). I was on a roll, I thought, until Herr Stolle said "Erinnerung" and kept repeating it as I shuffled through my yellow pad of prepared script, clueless. *Erinnerung, Erinnerung.* Again and again.

"Ich verstehen nicht, entschuldigen," I said. I'm sorry, I don't understand.

"Ich *verstehe* nicht," Herr Stolle corrected me in a neutral voice, and then dropped the unknown "Erinnerung," thank God. He said he looked forward to meeting me, his low, even voice soothing my sense of error. *Verstehe.* Singular verb form, not plural. I should know that.

After I'd hung up, I looked up *Erinnerung* in my dictionary: *Memory.* Of all the words not to understand. For memory is why I have come, to find out if what the Jews remember about Benheim is true: that neighbors were decent and that even in the 1930s "it was better than most places." I want to meet whoever is left—and decide for myself. Of course, I have a bias that comes from having grown up in 1940s New York at a time when all Germans were called Nazis, not to be trusted, not one. And old fears linger. But I'm happy to be wrong; in fact, I would love it. Decent people, even in one tiny, overlooked village of 1,200, would be very comforting. It would affirm my own New Jersey town, where I feel quite at home among my neighbors, decent people all.

"How about you drive?" I say to Rolf, holding out the keys to my rental car. I don't feel like tackling the Mercedes-Benzes and BMWs doing 100 miles per hour on the autobahn, and he's used to that, I figure. He takes the car keys with a big grin, locates our red Volkswagen, and opens the door for me. "What?" I hear my father saying from his grave, "A German car you are renting?" I climb inside anyway. "Dad, a French Peugeot would cost $200 more."

Three tries to start the engine. "I must tell you I don't drive so much," Rolf says as we pull out of the parking lot into Stuttgart traffic. "Only when my grandfather lends me his car." I hope he's as cautious as he looks, but I know nothing about him. His name came from someone I met at the Holocaust Museum in Washington, a young man working at the Oral History desk. When I mentioned I needed a translator for my trip to the Schwarzwald, he suggested Rolf, whom he'd met the year before when Rolf had a one-year fellowship at Johns Hopkins University. Three e-mails and a phone call to Germany later, it was settled. I would pay Rolf's expenses, and he, I hoped, would save me from impasses such as *Erinnerung.*

Rolf tells me he only learned about the Holocaust when he was fifteen. "I was shocked!" he says, leaning over the steering wheel like an old man. "No one in my family had mentioned a word!" It's a clear day, and we are in the right lane, driving as if in heavy fog. Even *I* want him to go faster. "I heard of a group in my town (it's near Mannheim) that was doing research about the Jews and I signed up. I was the youngest by ten years!" He beams. "The others were professors, teachers, doctoral students . . . and two from the clergy." He reaches behind him, groping, the car slowing until he pulls a thick red book from his knapsack.

"What happened to *our* Jews is all here," Rolf says proudly. I leaf through chapters on Jewish customs and community life; on what happened during the Boycott in 1933 when Jewish stores and businesses were attacked; and on Kristallnacht, which Rolf calls "the Pogrom of 1938." The term *Kristallnacht* should not be used, he says sternly, "because it means only 'night of broken glass.' What happened in my country was a national pogrom, plain and simple!"

He flips to the *Personenregister* section (as the car swerves), pointing to thirty-five pages of data about the eighty-eight Jews of his town: the names, birth dates, addresses, family members, and fates of those who died in the camps and those who survived. "I compiled this list," Rolf says with satisfaction, "and had contact with Jews all over the world."

Grass-roots projects such as his are not uncommon, Rolf says. In the 1970s and 1980s when the post-Hitler generation, like Rolf, wanted to break the silence they'd grown up with, German regional governments offered small grants to publish material about local Jewry. In Benheim, a church group had produced a slim, hand-stapled booklet, but nothing like this thick red book.

We discuss American culture—Rolf loves jazz, hates Big Macs—and the disorder of American politics. He asks about "Pat Buchanan and this Farrakhan. Are Jews afraid of them?" I say no, of course not, but worry. *Does he know something I've ignored?* I'm alive, after all, because my father spotted the danger signs and knew to leave Germany even when many people he knew were like Rolf, nice.

I tell Rolf that we are going to Herr Stolle's house first and then to interview others that he has, I hope, lined up. "But we must go to the *Rathaus*—to the archives," Rolf says anxiously. "In the archives you get the *real* information."

"What do you mean *real?* People are real."

"People's stories you can't believe so well, even if they are willing to talk honestly to you. And most are not. You mustn't be naïve."

I've heard this caveat before, from the Holocaust scholars at my college who said to trust the records, not anecdotal stories. Were any Jews hidden? they'd ask. What was the voting record? What percentage of the village joined the Nazi Party? I didn't know. All I knew was that the eight Benheim Jews I interviewed so far blamed Germany, but not their Benheim neighbors. And that intrigued me enough to come.

Rolf tells me how in his town people like to *say* they weren't anti-Semitic before Hitler, yet the mayor led the charge on the synagogue during Kristallnacht.

"Benheimers did *not* take part in Kristallnacht!" I say emphatically, trying to sound mild. After all, this is only the first hour of a three-day trip together.

"You must be careful not to be naïve," Rolf repeats softly.

I try to be amused that this young Protestant German is cautioning me, a middle-aged Jew, about being naïve about the Holocaust. And with such paternal certainty! I had expected

Germans to tread softly on the past, sidestepping delicate issues. That's why, when I wrote Herr Stolle for help, I made no mention of Hitler or the deportation, or my main interest, which, as I tell Rolf, is how decent people remember and live with the past.

But Rolf sidesteps nothing. He is ready to lead a direct charge into the Third Reich. He tells me, proudly, that his mother's father was a member of the Confessional Church, the one German religious group to speak out vigorously against Hitler's racial and anti-Christian teachings. His other grandfather, alas, was an ardent Nazi, one who still hangs the Nazi flag in the upstairs hall. "I pass it every day," Rolf says bitterly. As a poor graduate student, he has no choice but to live rent-free on the third floor of his grandfather's house.

"So how do you two get along?" I ask, amazed. A grandfather still mourning Hitler, a grandson getting a doctorate in Holocaust Studies.

"We don't talk politics!" he says with a wry smile, no absurdity lost on him.

Just after the sign reading B E N H E I M , we turn off the highway, as instructed, and climb the *Osterhaldenweg,* a steep switchback road. Below, we can see the red-tiled roofs of the lower village, clustered around an old church, its tower scaffolded. But up here it is suburbia. Number 12, where Herr Stolle said to stop, has a shiny black Mercedes parked in the driveway of a two-story townhouse set into the hillside. Large picture windows, wraparound balconies of white stucco, lush pink flowers climbing over low stone walls are more reminiscent of San Diego or Haifa than of the Schwarzwald village with cow dung and chickens in a rutted dirt street. That's what I remember from 1953 when my father, eight years after the war, decided to show thirteen-year-old me the Europe he grew up in. We spent two weeks seeing the Tower of London, the Eiffel Tower, the canals of Holland, and one day visiting my mother's Stuttgart and his

Benheim. By nightfall we were safely in Switzerland, neither parent wanting to sleep in Germany again. The message I got then was "enemy territory," a feeling I keep trying to shake ever since I crossed the border into Germany again.

Herr Stolle is waiting outside, dressed in a navy plaid sweater and gray slacks. He is a handsome man with a barrel chest and salt-and-pepper hair. He looks to be in his mid-sixties, but he fought in Hitler's army, so he must be in his mid-seventies. All I know about him, aside from his cemetery research project, is that he's the postman's son, was manager of a factory somewhere in the north before retiring to Benheim, and doesn't speak English.

I apologize, in German, for being late and introduce Rolf, who half bows and expresses great delight to be here. "*Your* German is excellent," Herr Stolle says to him.

"Why not? I am German!" Rolf explains that he is a graduate student in Mannheim (leaves out the Holocaust Studies part) and Herr Stolle nods, inviting us inside. We must meet his wife, have some coffee and cake, and then we will go to the cemetery. Tomorrow we will visit the synagogue and Frau Rieber, the former mayor's wife, who had foot surgery. "Frau Rieber was born three houses from your father," Herr Stolle says, "but he lived already in Frankfurt. Sol was in Nagold, only Julius was still at home."

He talks about my father's family as if it were his. He knows that my father enlisted in World War I at seventeen and later moved to Frankfurt to work and marry. He knows my Uncle Sol joined a leather firm in Nagold, my Aunt Kaethe married Max James from Stuttgart, and only the youngest brother, Julius, stayed in Benheim until 1935. Soon after the whole family left Germany and started a leather business in New York.

Yet no one in my house ever mentioned Herr Stolle or his family by name. Nor do the Benheim Jews, except for Ilse Loew in Burlington, who was a childhood friend of Herr Stolle's sister Elisabeth. The others remember the Gentiles as the nice postman, the kind policeman, the decent shoemaker, as if the intimacy of names had been cut like an umbilical cord when the Jews fled the homes that Herr Stolle still passes every day.

"Did you know my father well?" I ask, my German loosening up when we use the familiar vocabulary of house and family, the words my grandparents used when my father wasn't around to say, "Speak English! We are Americans now." Which was fine with me, the first Yankee in the family.

"*Nein*," says Herr Stolle. "Your father was much older. But the family everyone knew. The Loewengarts were well respected."

Rolf interjects. "What about the *Rathaus*, the archives? When can we go there?"

Herr Stolle says he must get permission and people are away. Rolf scowls until our host says he'll see what he can do. I want to take the edge off Rolf's pushiness, explain about the need to supplement interviews with documented records, blah, blah, blah; but my German is not up for that. I settle for garden talk. "Seine Garten ist sehr schön." (Your garden is very lovely.)

"*Ihr* Garten ist sehr schön," Herr Stolle says pleasantly, correcting my pronoun as we walk past blues, purples, and whites, all blooming and nameless to me.

Inside is a spacious living room with a black leather couch, Oriental rugs, and a stereo, TV, and VCR tucked into built-in bookcases. This could be New Jersey. I search the walls for clues as to how "safe" these Germans are. An odd word, I know, except if you are meeting people old enough to be the ones your family had to flee. A large wooden Jesus on the cross hangs above an easy chair. Unnerving. To its right, a wall of photos of wholesome children and grandchildren. Promising. To its left, a large Chagall lithograph of a bride and groom flying above a Polish ghetto. Surprising. And in the window, a stained-glass shield with lions in a garden, dated 1702. Strange. My family's name means "Lion's Garden."

Frau Stolle comes out of the kitchen, wiping her hands on a bright red and yellow apron. She looks like a German Barbara Bush: sturdy, stout, and straight-backed, with white hair framing a face that could be nice or not, depending on the smile. She has baked a linzertorte for us. I worry about betrayal. Should I be eating here at all? Other Benheim Jews and their children have returned to visit the family graves, stop at the synagogue, and drive by their old homes. But none has sat at a dining room table, admiring the panoramic view of their village that now has no Jews, not one!

Frau Stolle pours coffee and Herr Stolle points out the remains of the castle of the Johanniter, the Order of Knights who first invited the Jews to settle here in 1645. He points out what was the synagogue, built in 1837, and became the Protestant church in 1953. The man does love dates. I take out a tape recorder and Frau Stolle looks fearful. Tell her it's because my German is so weak, I instruct Rolf, who goes on with a much longer, convoluted explanation that produces a nod. I click it on.

"Please, a slice of linzertorte for you," says Frau Stolle in German, cutting a hefty piece with raspberry jam oozing over a dark wall of cinnamon, flour, cocoa, and nuts. The real thing. She puts a slice in front of me and watches my first bite anxiously like my Aunt Kaethe in Queens did. I smile, she beams. A worthy Benheim housewife, it seems, is only as good as her cake—wherever she lives.

"That was your father's house over there," Herr Stolle says, pointing to a cluster of old stone houses below us. My eye had been on the white cross on the opposite hill. "I've arranged for you to go inside the house if you like." A pause, waiting for my thank-you, but I'm not sure. I remember long ago, a man with a leather cap inviting us in, and my father backing away. *Nein, nein, danke.* (No, no, thanks.) "A blacksmith, Herr Dinkle, bought it in 1935—for a fair price," Herr Stolle continues. "Your family never asked for more. They were satisfied," he says with satisfaction.

Rolf leans close to tell me, in English, that restitution money to the Jews is still a big sore point in Germany. "If your family had asked for more money after the war, you might not get so much coffee and linzertorte." He laughs, and I look quickly at both the Stolles, who keep eating. I wonder what they really understand.

Two visits from now Herr Stolle will tell me his version of "fair price": how the Jews wanted to sell their belongings quickly and their neighbors agreed to help, paying what they could. And how, after the war, these neighbors were accused of cheating and what a personal insult that was. "To think we were untrustworthy, only after their money!" he will sigh, followed by a *Na ja*, his usual expression when the Holocaust comes close. "But it was a complicated issue. It was the children of the Jews who mostly filed for more restitution. They were angry. Very understandable. They didn't know about the private deals their parents made, because their parents didn't survive." Another *Na ja!* and I believe this sensible man who seems to see all points of view. Only later, in bed, will I worry again about being naïve.

Herr Stolle pauses to sip coffee. "What's that?" I ask, pointing to the white cross in a high meadow surrounded by wildflowers.

"Ah, the *Marienkreuz!*" Frau Stolle says. "We are Catholic here, you know."

"Not so Catholic anymore," corrects Herr Stolle. "We have now 20 percent Protestant. And the Muslims, they are also 20 percent." The man also loves percentages. I want to know more about "the Muslims," but I stay with the white cross on its pedestal.

"Is that where the swastika used to be?" I am sure that it must be, the spot overlooking the village that Lotte described.

"Swastika?" Frau Stolle asks, her fork in midair. She looks confused.

"*Hakenkreuz*," says Rolf. "Was there a *Hakenkreuz* where that white cross is now?"

"*Ja,* right on that spot—but that was much before I came!"
Frau Stolle is quick to tell me she comes from the north (desirable) and not from Swabia (less desirable) and didn't move here until her husband retired in 1976. She points to the rest of the linzertorte. Rolf nods enthusiastically. I decline with difficulty.

"Your mother must also make this, no?" Frau Stolle says to me. "I have this recipe from Adolf's mother."

"Adolf?" I jump.

She points to her husband and cuts me another slice anyway. Her son is in America for two years, she says, in Los Angeles. He is a doctor. Another son teaches history in Aachen, where she is from. A third is a biologist. They have done well, these children of a poor farm boy who has also done well.

"So," Herr Stolle says, standing up abruptly, "come now with me." Rolf doesn't need to translate.

He leads us into a small, neat study with a giant mural of small black rectangles. "You see here the thousand graves in the Jewish cemetery, starting in 1716," he says proudly, "and this is the *exact* map that shows the *exact* size of each tombstone, drawn to scale." He shows us bookshelves full of black ring binders with Jewish tombstones, each with a photograph, family name, first name, father, mother, spouse, where they came from, date of marriage, children, occupation, and date of death. Some have German translations of Hebrew inscriptions. It is very methodical, his ordering of Jews who died, mostly before he was born. And unnerving.

I ask how he became interested in this cemetery project, which he works on without financial support. "It's not a matter of being interested," says Herr Stolle, sharply. "It has to be done. The stones are eroding, so in a few years no one will know who is buried there. We must preserve local history." I bristle at his correction. If eroding stones were the only issue, why does he volunteer to host people like me, offering tours of the cemetery and the synagogue-turned-church for hours, even days? Why field questions that strip away the scab covering old wounds of guilt and blame for the millions his generation murdered? And disposed of without neatly marked graves.

"I hope you are doing more than just photographing gravestones," says Rolf, sounding peeved. "In *our* book, we include Jewish *life* and what happened to it: who died in the concentration camps and where the others went. I myself found out that. . . ."

Herr Stolle turns away and walks to his desk. "I have this for you," he says, handing me an eight-by-eleven-inch packet in a plastic cover, #1401. "Your grandfather and great-grandfather are in it, back to Rubin Veit Loewengart. He was born in 1794." Inside are photos of six tombstones, inventory lists from the family house in 1894, fire insurance bills, all in a fine calligraphy made by a quill dipped into an inkwell. There is nothing personal here. No diaries, letters, or photos that reveal lives lived, but his gift feels weighty in my palm. "It's what I found out about your family," says this former soldier in Hitler's army, softly. He was an aerial photographer over France, he told us—and what else I don't know. But I feel myself drawn to him.

"Thank you," I say, as if to a kindly uncle I have finally met.

We go in his Mercedes, down the hill to the village center, and pass two teenagers in leather jackets, smoking. One in a Grateful Dead T-shirt, another with orange hair and a ring in his ear. Neo-punk in Benheim? It seems like an oxymoron. I can hear my father's outrage—and the battles we had over my wanting to hang out with friends at Penn Drugstore on Friday nights after high school basketball games and smoke. *In Benheim we didn't do such things.* They do now, Dad.

Herr Stolle slows down at an old stone building. "Here is the Gasthaus Kaiser, owned by the Gideons," says Herr Stolle. You have met the daughter, your Tante Hilde, in Israel?" I nod. "She is well?" I say yes, fine, though I haven't seen her in several years. "The Kurds and Yugoslavs live in there now."

I watch two women in chador and long peasant dresses pushing a stroller out the front door of where my Aunt Hilde's family
cooked kosher for generations—and love the irony. Hitler would
turn over in his grave if he knew more "non-Aryans" were here.
Daimler-Benz, it seems, has a factory twenty minutes away and
invited guest workers from Turkey and Yugoslavia in the sixties
when German labor was tight. They stayed. "Our community
is quite mixed," says Herr Stolle, "causing some difficulties but
no big problems."

"What kind of problems?" I listen carefully, thinking that the
way he sees Muslims is how he sees—and saw—Jews.

"Nothing big. *They* like to stay up late, we Benheimers are in
bed by nine. And also some garbage problems. Small things."
He nods at the two women, who smile shyly and look away.
"They are very conservative—from the countryside, not from
the city, like Ankara. Very religious."

"Just like the Jews!" I say, thinking of my country-boy father
being raised much more religiously than my city-girl mother.

"Can't be compared," Herr Stolle says, insulted. "The Jews of
Benheim were old, old neighbors. Can't be compared."

"But the Turks are also neighbors," says Rolf, on the offen-
sive. Herr Stolle's face reddens, but Rolf presses on, as if his
generation's innocence depends on Herr Stolle's guilt. "The
Turks live in the Jewish houses, do they not?"

"From our point of view, it is not the same," Herr Stolle says,
recovering his equanimity. "The Turks are strangers here. The
Jews lived here for four hundred years."

Silence. We are calming ourselves down as Herr Stolle drives
on. We pass the *Volksschule* where he, and my father before him,
went to school. "They had the top floor and did not go to school
on Saturday. We did." When I hear "we" and "they," I think seg-
regation, but both men assure me that this arrangement was
"normal." I ask Herr Stolle if he had had any Jewish friends. "Of
course, this is Benheim! We all got along," he says huffily and

points to an old linden tree where all the boys played marbles. At the crossroad there's a street sign, JÜDISCHESTRASSE, that points right. It goes to the Jewish cemetery, says our guide, and the other street goes to the Catholic cemetery. I'm wondering how much of the harmony of this village "where everyone got along" was based on separate classrooms and street signs of clear difference. We turn right.

Halfway up a hill, we stop at an old farmhouse. "The Brenner family still keeps the key to the cemetery as they have for centuries," Herr Stolle says, taking a rusted key off the dark wooden peg. I remember the peg, the low stone wall beside it, and my father taking the key so long ago. And for a moment the two men morph into one, father and stranger from a shared world, both taking me into a past I have yet to claim.

We follow the road higher, around the bend, and there it is: the same large stone portal in the woods, as if leading to a hidden castle. The old key turns in the old lock, and the iron gate opens effortlessly, as if spirits are waiting. A strange thought for secular me, but this is that kind of spot. The looming trees, the thick bed of leaves, gravestones rising from shadow into shafts of sunlight: all create an eerie calm divorced from the red roofs of the living below us.

"This *is* special," Rolf whispers to me. I nod with the same sense of awe I had at thirteen, feeling mysteriously rooted to these giant dark-green conifers. We follow Herr Stolle through rows of graves and Rolf tells me he's impressed by how well preserved everything is. Even the old limestone gravestones, their names blurred, their edges crumbling, are still standing. "In my town, the Jewish cemetery was badly destroyed by vandals," Rolf calls out. "Did you not have that here in Benheim?"

"A few gravestones," Herr Stolle says, moving forward. "Some young ruffian schoolboys in 1941. A complaint was filed by the Jewish schoolteacher, and the stones were repaired. Nothing else."

"An official complaint in 1941 by a Jew?" Rolf asks, incredulous. "In our town, he would have been shot!" This is definitely unusual, Rolf whispers. "We must look for this document in the archives, definitely."

Herr Stolle drags away a large branch that has fallen on one grave, grumbling that the city of Dorn, now in charge of the cemetery, is not doing its job. He shakes his head and stops to pull weeds hiding an inscription. "Here is your grandmother, Anna," he says, "and next to her is your grandfather, Rubin." I try to conjure up the faces I saw framed in my parents' room: a beautiful woman of thirty or so, with my daughter's face; a debonair man with a handlebar mustache who didn't look as if he traded horses and cows.

"Are you planning to put down some stones?" Rolf asks. Herr Stolle points to broken rocks jutting out under the leaves. They are waiting for the Jewish ritual for honoring the dead, and I feel like a relic on display, like the Navajos must feel doing a rain dance in Arizona for tourists. I choose four stones and lay them on the granite, wishing their souls peace. "It's how you pay tribute to the dead," my father said on this spot, so long ago, looking strangely gaunt despite his bulk. "The weight helps the souls rise upwards more easily." He placed his stones. "If the Jews still lived in Benheim, there would be stones on every grave." I can still see his lips moving, as in prayer. Herr Stolle and Rolf keep waiting, perhaps for the Mourner's Kaddish, but I don't know the prayer well enough on my own. I stay silent.

Herr Stolle removes a dead yellow wildflower from another Loewengart grave, Manfred. I'd never heard of him, but don't say that. He tackles fallen tree limbs and encroaching weeds, full of energy to tidy up these old graves from before the Holocaust. *The souls piled in ditches or sent up in chimney smoke are not in these woods!* "And here is your Tante Rosa." Herr Stolle says, pausing. "She died the day before she had to leave for the East." Rolf points out, in English, that Herr Stolle doesn't use the word "deportation." *So the Holocaust is here too.*

I read the inscription: Rosa Sara Loewengart. Born 1875, Died, March 4, 1942.

"Selbstmord," Herr Stolle says sadly. "Suicide," Rolf translates.

"Why?" I ask, wondering why no one in America mentioned Rosa's suicide. I heard only about her Hanukkah parties and her love of life, and that she refused to leave, saying, "I'm an old woman. Who will bother me?"

"Did Tante Rosa know where she was going—and choose suicide instead?" I ask Herr Stolle.

The vein on his forehead bulges. I'm on turf we've both been avoiding: what people did or didn't know about the Holocaust. "*Na ja,*" he sighs. "That's not so clear. Many old people didn't want to leave their homes, even to go to an old age home, which is what the Nazis told them."

"But of course they knew more," Rolf snaps. "In my town people knew."

"I was not here, and so I am not so *sure* as you." Herr Stolle speaks almost in a whisper to this young German born over thirty years after the deportations. "This is a small village, isolated. People say they didn't know. . . ." Somehow my sympathy is with Herr Stolle, who sounds so reasonable.

More silence. We near the gate and stop in front of a large stone monument erected in 1947: "To those who died during the Nazi persecution—1932–1942," translates Rolf. The words are as cold as the black granite they are carved into. No names on this village memorial or even how many died. I think of Ilse's mother and the others too old to get visas; and the fifteen children in Lotte's class photo who didn't make it out; and Doris Gould who stayed to care for her sick parents; and the Salomons who couldn't afford boat tickets. There is no room for their stories on this stone, but at least their names, and all the others, could cover its smoothness.

"The granite was paid for by our villagers," says Herr Stolle. "They bartered food for the stone since no one had money then." A small gesture, but at least the villagers cared enough to build a memorial despite personal hardships. Or so I think until Rolf whispers, in English, that the villagers might have had no choice. In his town archives he saw an official order to build a memorial. His look says "naïve."

Day 2: Rolf is behind the wheel, stopped at a red light that sits on top of a portable stand next to a large CONSTRUCTION sign. The same light stayed red for fifteen minutes last night on our way to our Bavarian-style inn at the end of a long dirt road. This morning, we are headed back to Herr Stolle's house, talking about how much English he understands. Hard to tell. And about how much more impressive he is than Rolf expected: "One man working so hard alone—and much more open than old-timers in my town, especially about Prague."

"What about Prague?"

"He was captured near Prague by the Americans and then escaped with a friend and made his way back to Benheim."

"I thought he spent the war in France, taking aerial photographs."

"That was earlier. Later in the war he was a foot soldier in the East."

"But when did Stolle say all this?" I asked.

"You were in the bathroom."

"Oh." *Did he wait till I left the room?*

"Today I will find out more!" says Rolf, fired up for battle. He will check the voting records and how many were tried for war crimes. Yet he waits patiently at this interminable red light.

"They don't need a light here," I say. "There's no traffic on this road."

"They are repairing the bridge."

"What bridge? There's ten feet going over a barely moving stream—and not one car has come the other way."

"It is the law."

I tap my fingers. "Come on, let's just go."

Rolf looks shocked. "We must obey the law."

This is Germany's problem! Anyone sensible, any American

surely, would ignore this broken light on an empty dirt road. I put my foot on the imaginary gas pedal just as the light turns green.

Herr Stolle is standing outside again when we pull up twenty minutes late. We are going first to the *Rathaus*, he says proudly. He got permission. "But we should not be optimistic about finding much in the files. What there is . . . is not so much . . . they didn't save anything about the deportations." Now he uses the real word.

"Also in my town," says Rolf, and for a brief moment they are on the same side of history. I ask about the interview with Frau Rieber, and if others also agreed to tell me their stories. "Later," Herr Stolle says as we pile into his car. I will meet them all later.

The *Rathaus* sits on the curve in the road that divides the upper and lower village, an unassuming stone building, boxy and functional. Herr Stolle has the key and leads us into a large high-ceilinged room where the village council met before Dorn swallowed up Benheim and ten other nearby villages. "Another blow to our village identity," says Herr Stolle, "along with the arrival of television and the loss of the Jews. No one knows any-one anymore," he rues, "and no one has a sense of history." Which is why he is working on his project. "Too many don't even know that Jews were here."

I walk over to a wall of photos. "They are the soldiers who never returned," says Herr Stolle. He doesn't say which war. "We lost seventy young men, my brother and two cousins were. . . ."

"You had ss in Benheim!" Rolf says, looking at the photos. He is noticing uniforms; I see only dead German soldiers.

"He was a boy, only seventeen. He knew nothing about what the ss would do," Herr Stolle says, quickly moving us across the room. "These are photos from World War I"—and he points to a framed list of fourteen Jews who died in that war. "Half of our Benheim soldiers in 1914 were Jewish, and many were war heroes," Herr Stolle says with pride. "We even had a Jewish fighter pilot, Frederick Zundorfer. My cousin knew him well."

"I counted *three* ss men," Rolf whispers, in English, as we climb the stairs to the archives. "So you see, Mimi," he says with his most annoying paternalism, "Benheim had its ardent Nazis! I also counted ten officer hats."

"How many were active in the Nazi Party in Benheim?" I ask Herr Stolle.

"Very few, a few louts," he says, continuing upward, as his credibility goes down.

"But there are *three* ss photos on the wall and *ten* in officer hats!" Now I sound like Rolf. "Who were they?"

Silence. I should push harder, I know. I should grill him about the ss and the mysterious boy, only seventeen. Rolf complained last night that I wasn't asking tough-enough questions, but I'm afraid that if I do, Herr Stolle will clam up, introduce me to no one.*

At the top of the stairs, Herr Stolle takes out a large black key. "So," he says, breathless, "my room." Inside are a large wooden table, two metal chairs, and six metal bookcases with four shelves devoted to Jews. Rolf pounces like a lion. Where are the deportation files? Where are denials of passports? Where are the newspapers from 1938 on? Herr Stolle points to a row of fat blue binders and pulls down a dusty brown book for me. "Here are the records about the building of the synagogue and a list of what each family gave: Pressburger, Weinberger, Loewengart. . . ." All in faint black ink.

---

*On future visits Herr Stolle tells me his brother died in Normandy on the same day as his old Jewish school friend who came back to fight as an American. "What a waste! Two Benheim boys, friends, killed on the same afternoon." He also tells me about his uncle, a priest, who was sent in 1933—*Did he have to flee?*—to be schoolmaster on an Indian reservation in Arizona. But I still don't know who that ss boy was to him.

"Your grandfather was a rich man," Herr Stolle says, showing me a tax return for 100,000 marks. "A millionaire by today's standard!"

I think "rich Jew" and tell him (defensively?) that in my father's house a piece of chocolate was like gold.

Herr Stolle smiles. "*Natürlich* (naturally), in Benheim no one threw money away. Chocolate *was* gold then." I do like that smile.

Rolf calls from across the room, "Here's a newspaper article about the boycott in Dorn." He has several books open on the oak table under the windows. "You should record this on tape!" He begins translating:

> The Jewish stores of Dorn shut down today as the citizens obeyed the new decree: it is forbidden to buy from the Jews. A group of schoolchildren, led by their teacher, Herr Shutz, smashed every Jewish store window. . . .

"That's Dorn, not Benheim," I say, just as Herr Stolle begins reading me a tax estimate for my great-grandfather, circa 1846. "He owned two sets of dishes, six chickens, one pearl ring . . ."

Now Rolf has found the voting record of Benheim. Only 16 percent voted for Hitler in March 1933. "That is very low," he says enthusiastically. "In my town 44 percent voted for Hitler. That's more typical of Germany." I'm feeling up again. Benheim is looking more special—and with archival proof.

Rolf asks to see the formal complaint about the broken gravestones, filed by the Jewish schoolteacher in 1941, and Herr Stolle disappears into another room. He returns a minute later. "It must be in the archives in Dorn," he says, and Rolf and I look at each other. *He's stalling.* "This is the only thing I have here," Herr Stolle says, handing me a small, stamped piece of paper. "It is a train receipt." The stamp reads April 21, 1942, and I think, *More stalling?* "It is for the last Jews sent from Benheim to Stuttgart and then to the East." I am stunned. Such an innoc-

uous little paper to record so much inhumanity. I hold it deli-
cately in my palm. Eighty-seven lives erased by an official stamp
indicating bodies paid for, bodies that will end in unmarked
graves in Lublin, Riga, and Theriesenstadt so Herr Stolle will
never be able to document them. I turn the receipt over. The
paper is still so white, I shiver.

Before I can ask for a copy, it has disappeared and Rolf is
reading a letter from Göring's office: "Nov. 14, 1938. In order
to insure the necessary unity in handling the Jewish question,
which is very important in the economic situation. . . ."

I am being tossed between two generations of Germans
searching the past to understand: Herr Stolle, through the
comforts of old Jewish records; Rolf, through Nazi documents
that prove guilt. I keep listening to what's in the air, said and
unsaid, as if what passes between us, off the record, can tell me
how good and bad people were—and are. But, of course, Rolf is
right. I am naïve. All I can know is the three of us in this room,
recasting bits of fact into narrative that each of us will use "not
only for the sake of *what was*," as Michael Heller says in *Living
Roots: A Memoir*, but "in order *to be*." Because history—on or off
the record—is always about the person asking, selecting, and
filtering out ambiguity until we have a story that lets us sleep
easier at night.

Herr Stolle interrupts with a notice of a lawsuit filed by
Sigmund Fröhlich against Abraham Gideon in 1875. "You see,
this is a big surprise to me!" He sounds excited. "The Jews
fought with each other. I didn't know that. We thought *they*
always stuck together."

Rolf cuts in with more of his letter. "'. . . you will have to let
me know everything you do about the Jewish question, so I can
approve it.' . . . Signed by Göring. You see, this proves. . . ."
What exactly?

The two begin speaking at once. My tape recorder will mix
them up, but I do not know which one I should tell to be quiet.

9 | A LITTLE RESPECT, PLEASE

"We have a huge spiritual crater in the center of this village
and people walk around it with no holding of hands."

The school principal of Benheim in the late 1990s

We are walking the three blocks that make up main street, Herr
Stolle again our tour guide to the past. "And this was Kramer's
butcher shop where we all bought meat, the Christians too."
Rolf and I look at a store window full of vacuum cleaners. "And
this house, half of it, was sold by the King of Württemberg to
Ruben Fröhlich, who gave it to his son-in-law, Hirsch. To this
day it is called the Hirsch house." We look at a large stone building leaning on two others, like an old friend. High up are tiny
old windows, like ship portholes, but below are modern casement windows we've seen in many of Benheim's old houses,
part of a village effort to live in historic structures made new.
Whatever is inside, the outside of everything appears as it did
two hundred years ago—and people like it that way.

"The Hirsch family was highly respected," Herr Stolle continues. "One was a children's doctor. He shot himself when he
wasn't allowed to practice. Another escaped to London, a phys-
ics professor, very famous." The level of remembered detail is
astounding, as if these Jews still live here in shadow. "And this
Gasthaus is where I used to pick up my father on Sundays and

sometimes get a little beer." It's one of the few personal facts he has offered without my prodding—and without mentioning the Jews. "But some days he went to the Jewish *Gasthaus*, the Rosa." *No, the Jews always with him!* "And this Christian house was built in 1829 by Jews. You can still see the . . . how do you call it? . . . with the paper . . . ?"

"Mezuzah," Rolf says before I can. Tucked into the right-hand corner, near the door, I see the biblical "sign upon the doorpost" of a Jewish house, its blue glaze chipped into rust. How easy to pass this doorway and miss this lost world, one I sometimes doubt exists except as myths of memory. Yet here it is made tangible at #6 Eilingen Weg—*if*, like Herr Stolle, you know where to look.

Down a narrow alley, also easy to miss, is an oversized house with two stone pillars in front and five arched side windows. I remember it: the synagogue. My father had stopped the car here, long ago, to show me where he prayed every Friday and Saturday as a boy. We had walked around but didn't go inside because, he said, nothing was left. It was just a shell.

Three Muslim men are squatting in a terraced yard below the five windows, drinking Turkish coffee. They live next door, Herr Stolle says, in state-run housing. "It was a Jewish *Gasthaus*." The men don't talk or look up as we pass. At the entrance, above the pillars, Herr Stolle points to a dark, wooden crossbeam with these words carved into it: *Hier ist nichts anderes denn Gotteshaus und hier is die Pforte des Himmels.* Rolf translates for me: "Here is none other than God's house and here is the door to heaven." A few feet above the crossbeam is a Hebrew inscription carved into a stone plaque. "It says the same thing," says Herr Stolle. When the Protestants took over the building after the war, they decided that using the same words "would show respect for the Jews who were here before." I want to say how convenient that the words fit whoever is praying inside, but resist. Joking about tolerance isn't funny in Germany.

A tall young man with a bit of a stoop comes out to greet us.

He is the new vicar of this Protestant church and, pointing to the Hebrew plaque, repeats what Herr Stolle said about respect for the Jews. Then he apologizes for the building's bad condition, saying, "It's a pity because we give so many official tours here—to school groups, church groups." The veins on Herr Stolle's temples bulge. "The weight of the roof is cracking the walls, and the Council won't give us the money to fix it." The vicar invites us to go inside, saying he'd give us a tour himself if he didn't have another meeting. He smiles and nods to Herr Stolle, who does not smile back.

"The synagogue was built *very* solid," Herr Stolle says as soon as the vicar has disappeared. "The only reason it is sinking now is because the Protestants put a bell tower on the roof. It doesn't belong." His annoyance extends beyond building repairs, I learn later. It's about the old rivalry about which "House of God" should be closest to heaven. The Catholics, who came first, built their bell tower. Then the Jews built a taller building, but without a bell tower, so everyone was happy until the Protestants moved in, added a bell tower—and ruined everything, according to Herr Stolle. They had no business putting it on the synagogue—or giving tours about the Jews. That belonged to *his* old world, he made clear, not to be appropriated by newcomers with no village memory and no historic responsibility.

"Do you have something to wear on your head?" Rolf whispers as we climb the stairs to the sanctuary. I shrug, annoyed. Whatever his good intentions to be respectful, I resent being the Jew he expects from German books and movies, especially since I rarely go to synagogue. My father's compulsory attendance here "every Friday night and all day Saturday" did not draw him to the Forest Hills Jewish Center in Queens except for an occasional wedding or funeral. His detachment, now mine, is so unlike Hannah, Gretl, and the other Benheimers I met, for whom the spirit of this synagogue remains so powerful.

The sanctuary of their memory, however, with its thirty- or forty-foot ceiling and graceful candelabras hanging down over the center aisle (I've seen photographs), has been sliced in two horizontally. The top half, still used for praying, has a low ceiling in need of paint and peeling, cracked walls are decorated with posters for a church dance, a raffle, and children's drawings about the Road to Confirmation. The balcony of carved balustrades that was once the women's section is now suspended in midair with no stairs to reach it.* Two large windows on either side of a life-size cross have giant cracks running ceiling to floor on both sides. I try to imagine my grandfather, head bent, shoulders covered with his tallis, and my grandmother looking down from above, and my father waiting for "the three stars in the sky" so he could go home. I don't feel their spirit here.

We walk downstairs, now used for meetings, and there is a wall-size fresco of Jesus in white with a golden halo on his head. He is flanked by two men and all are on a hill of pale pinks and greens lit by a white sun. "This is where the Torah Ark used to be," Herr Stolle says and I, secular or not, am shocked. "How could they put *that* here?" I blurt out. It seems so in-your-face disrespectful to Jews.

Herr Stolle straightens up. "It was meant as a symbol of the unity of religions under God. Isaiah is to the left and Moses is to the right." He sounds hurt. "But the Jews were unimpressed." The rabbi from Stuttgart refused to come here for the ceremony honoring the Jews on the fiftieth anniversary of Kristallnacht! "We tried to convince him by saying, 'It's still God's house, not a factory or gym like in other villages!' But the rabbi said, 'It's *not* God's house; it's a desecration!'" Herr Stolle sighs. *Na ja.*

"Can you not understand that?" Rolf says sharply. "For the Jews . . . Christianity, after two thousand years, has won here. The Christians now occupy their synagogue." *Yes, yes, tell him!* I am totally on Rolf's side for once. Herr Stolle shrugs, turns, and leads us to a glass case with a Torah breastplate, three prayer

---

*In Orthodox synagogues women and men sit separately, and in this part of Germany, women sat in a balcony above the men's pews.

books, a Seder plate, and a yarmulke, all labeled in a childlike handwriting. "This is not so well done," Rolf snaps, still on the warpath for both of us. I seem to be mute. I tell myself it's because my limited German can't say, "What tokenism!" which many Jews standing here would say. Or maybe it's my cowardliness—or reasonableness, I am not sure.

"The Protestants set this up. Nothing here is from our village," Herr Stolle says defensively. "*Our* Jewish things were taken or destroyed, except for one Torah—and that is in Israel." I try to tell him about a second Torah in Vermont, but Herr Stolle has started up the narrow, winding steps. so worn that the edges curve. Easy to fall off, I think, and touch both walls as I follow him back to the main entry hall where we stop to see another display about the Jews, this one not generic.

Herr Stolle points out my grandfather in a photo of stern-looking men surrounding a bus. "It's the board of the bus company started with 41,000 marks donated by Jewish money in 1910." "Bus company" is a generous term for a single vehicle going to Dorn's train station five times a day until the army commandeered it for World War I and people returned to walking and horse carts for another five years.

"And here is the list of those who died in the Holocaust." This is the first time Herr Stolle has used the word with me. "Some were not from Benheim; they moved here the last year or two because they felt safer here."

"Now *this* shows respect," Rolf says, and I nod. A centrally posted list of the eighty-seven who were killed by the Nazis is certainly better than the name-free memorial in the woods. "In my town," Rolf admits, "there is no public list. The names of the murdered are only in our book."

Herr Stolle nods, pleased with Rolf's acknowledgment, and shows us other pluses for Benheim: a framed essay about the Jewish cemetery, written by high school students who won a national prize in 1982. And a hooked rug with the Hebrew word *Chai* (to life), "made by Frau Seilig, who sent it from Israel," says Herr Stolle, happy for good feelings made tangible on this wall.

Finally, he stops in front of two large stone tablets with names and dates carved in black. "These were also saved during Kristallnacht. You see the Jewish stars were knocked off but otherwise they are in excellent condition!" Herr Stolle's usually cautious eyes are bright with pride as we read the list of Jewish World War I soldiers. It's the same list that we saw in the *Rathaus*, but here, in stone, they seem weightier, like the Ten Commandments: *Gideon, Goldstein, Lemberger, Loewengart, Lowenstein, Schwarz, Schwarz, Weil, Weil, Sinn, Schorsch, Wälder, Zürndorfer, Zuerndorfer. . . .*

"How were these tablets saved?" Rolf says, his interest high now.

"One can't be sure!" Herr Stolle's usual qualifier. "Perhaps someone knew that the synagogue would be damaged during Kristallnacht and removed them beforehand."

"I thought no Benheimers took part in Kristallnacht," I say, my antenna up because this core story, agreed upon by everyone, is suddenly under threat. "If they were not involved, how would they know something was going to happen?"

"Benheimers were *not* involved," says Herr Stolle, emphatically. "The people were from Sulz! But someone must have let the mayor know beforehand," he says calmly, "and someone in the office could have overheard . . ." Plausible, I tell myself, relieved.

"I found the tablets in the archive room," Herr Stolle says with great satisfaction, "behind a cabinet, and I placed them here last year."

"*When* did you find them?" asks Rolf, the interrogator.

"When I came in 1976."

"And you waited so long to hang them up?" Rolf says sternly, as if to a child.

Herr Stolle's blotches reappear in full force, the veins on his temple now dark purple. "A little respect, please," he says quietly and turns his back on both of us, angry and hurt that his version of "good" will never be enough for us, the ones who came after, full of suspicion and blame. He heads toward the double door of the entrance. We follow. I take a photo of the two of them under the two inscriptions about God's house. Then Herr Stolle takes one of Rolf and me. Then Rolf takes one of Herr Stolle and me. We nod to the Turks still sipping coffee on the lawn and we pile into the car together, hoping our good intentions count as Respect.

10 | THE GOOD RAINCOAT

In the afternoon we visit Frau Rieber, the former mayor's widow who had foot surgery. She's a small, sweet, well-lotioned grandmother with a pug nose and friendly blue eyes. Tiny wrinkles sometimes gather near them, but only when her lips pout. It happens when she talks about her daughters, Ulla in France and Heidi in Berlin, and how she misses them—"Even though, of course, it's the best thing. They have no future in Benheim, taking care of an old mother!" It happens again when she talks about a former Jewish neighbor who didn't answer her holiday letter, and another who sent her a check for the booklets Frau Rieber sent about Jewish life in Benheim. "They were *gifts!*" she says. Her five-foot frame bridles with insult, reminding me of my aunts when I forgot a birthday or didn't call enough. But then *I* bridle. If the Jews want to pay her—*Thanks, but we'd rather not owe you!*—why shouldn't they?

Yet Frau Rieber—"Anna" to all the Jews in New York—is "the Gentile" remembered most fondly, the one who keeps sending greeting cards, the one they contact when they come back to visit their family graves, and the only one whose house many enter for a cup of coffee, my father included.

"He was sitting right here at my table, having a *Kaffee,*" Anna tells me as I sit, with Rolf and Herr Stolle, around a small, dark table in a small, dark house with low-beamed ceilings that make me want to stoop. It's a much more modest house than Herr Stolle's on the hill, probably because Anna's husband died unexpectedly, leaving her in their old house in the Lower Village. "It was once a Jewish house," she says.

"Bought *after* the war," Herr Stolle adds quickly (meaning bought fairly).

"Your father," Anna continues. "was here in 1970, a year or two before he died . . ." *How can she remember so exactly?* "And he promised to find my daughter a place to stay when she visited Israel. One month later a letter came, all was arranged." Anna's blue eyes are practically electric. "An excellent man!" she says, as if a Jew who would help her family *after* what happened under Hitler is right up there in heaven!

Anna sings the same praises for Erna Gould, who "ran out of her house in Israel to greet us and invite us for *Kaffee* and *Kuchen!*" Herr Stolle nods. He and his wife were on that same government-sponsored trip to Oleh Zion in 1977. "These Jews brought a little Schwarzwald with them!" Anna says, and "even in the desert heat, your Tante Hilde cooked *Kartoffelsalat* and *Spätzle* for us." Her face is smooth with pleasure.

After that trip, Anna kept in touch with her former neighbors, especially my two aunts: "With Hilde and Thea I stayed very friendly. We wrote, but then Thea couldn't see so well to write anymore. When they came here for the spa in Wiensbad, we visited them there. Once they called and said, 'Anna, we're in Freudenstadt!' and we went there."

"It's amazing the contact you have with the Jews!" Rolf says with gusto. Anna's charm has won him over—and me too. "It was the silence in my house that made me interested in Holocaust Studies." Anna nods. "In my town, it is very different with people of your generation. Do you think it is because as children you had such good relations with the Jews?"

"Well, of course! They were our neighbors!" Anna says, arching like a cat under threat. "We fought as children do, but I didn't feel they were different people. They were blond and tall like we were." *She's five feet, hardly tall, and my Aunt Kaethe had dark hair.* "No," Anna insists, "one didn't know a difference . . ."

"And did they speak exactly like you?" asks Rolf. "The same dialect?"

"*Ja, ja,*" she says impatiently, her lips starting to pout until she offers the traditional Schwarzwald balm: food. We decline, having just had a big lunch at Die Sonne, Benheim's only restaurant. "It was very good food, yes?" Anna says in broken English.

"Sehr gute Maultaschen," I answer. Which was true. The liver dumplings were delicious, even if the place was filled with locals who nodded at Herr Stolle, but stared at Rolf and me—especially when "Juden" and "Hitler" kept rising up from our conversation. I was glad to leave.

"Next time, you must try their bratwurst," Anna says. "Also excellent." She has switched back to German.

Food triggers nostalgia, as it did in the Jewish living rooms in New York. Anna talks of *Berches,* the bread her neighbor brought her family on Fridays as a gift. "What a good, thick taste it had, nothing like the light bread that we Christians baked!" And that leads to "Every Friday night, the whole village would be lit up and quiet, except for the sound of Israelite prayer." And to weddings in the synagogue—and fancy dresses: "I still remember Tony Weil, who was a born Loewengart. God, that was a beautiful bride! For us, it was . . . well, our brides were more plain. Tony had a white veil, a white dress with embroidered leaves." Anna laughs. "I'll never forget that in all my life. And then we went up the stairs to where the women sat."

Rolf looks surprised. "You Christian children also went up there?"

"Why yes."

"Did it happen often that Christian children went to Jewish weddings? Also to their baptizing?" *He must mean "bar mitzvah."*

"We all went." Herr Stolle says, jumping in. "But only with our mothers."

"*Ja, ja,*" Anna says, nodding. "Only with our mothers.

4 cups flour

3 tsp. salt

1 tbs. salad oil

1 package yeast

½ cup grated potatoes—
    boiled and refrigerated for 2 days

1¼ cups water

Poppy seeds

1. Finely grate the potatoes.
2. Dissolve yeast in 1 cup of warm water (at room temperature).
3. Add ½ tbs. salad oil.
4. Put flour in large bowl. Add salt. Add grated potato.
5. Add another ¼ cup of water as needed. Knead for 5 minutes. Dough should be firm.
6. Place towel over bowl and let rise for 3–4 hours.
7. Preheat oven to 500 degrees.
8. Make a loaf out of 4/5 of dough. Divide the rest into three strands (hand-rolled so they are ½-inch thick by 10 to 12 inches long) and make a braid for the top of the loaf.
9. Sprinkle with poppy seeds.
10. Put bread on middle shelf on foil that covers a cookie sheet.
11. After 10 minutes, reduce heat to 375 degrees and continue to bake until golden, about 50 minutes.
12. Five minutes before done, peek in, and if not dark enough, raise temperature to 400 degrees for last few minutes. Don't bake more than one hour!!

Anna's mother and father, both from large farm families in Benheim, were married in 1920, the year Anna was born. Her father became a barber, and many of his customers were Jews. He kept cutting their hair, Anna declares proudly, long after the Nazi mayor ordered a sign posted: JEWS ARE NOT WELCOME HERE.

"To lose the Jewish customers was a big hardship, no?" Rolf says, implying more than altruism, but gently. He's not on the attack as he was with Herr Stolle, and when Anna says she doesn't really know because she was in Switzerland with a cousin, learning to cook, Rolf nods. We both do. I've decided Anna's charm is more convincing than her pout, and besides, she is well respected in New York. And didn't my father help her daughter out?

Anna gets up, her left foot in a plaster cast, and limps to a small bookcase. Her face in pain, she takes a paperback book from the shelf. "I couldn't believe what I read here, such terrible things." The book is by a Jewish woman, Rolf whispers, who was hidden in Berlin for three years before being caught and sent to Auschwitz. He'd read it, too. "I had no idea that Germans could hide Jews!" Anna says, her face pale and suddenly older. "Germans took this woman in, but how could we know that? If we had taken in Frau Pressburger . . ." She looks at Herr Stolle, practically in tears. "Where would we have hidden her? They could have turned our houses upside down, looking for her. Or what if she became sick? What would we have done? Or worse, if she had died? Or . . . or . . ."

"You couldn't hide anyone. Not in such a small village!" Herr Stolle says, standing up to help Anna back into her chair. He is very protective of her, the widow of his childhood friend, the one he was supposed to do the Jewish history project with if he hadn't died so suddenly, soon after they'd begun. "If extra wood was burned in the chimney," says Herr Stolle, "if you had more garbage, everyone would know it. In a big city maybe, like Berlin, you could risk it. Not here."

"This woman who writes in this book . . . ," Anna is turning pages now, "says she received letters from Poland and sent them packages—and apparently they arrived." She hands me the open book as proof. "I sent packages, too, to Bette Fried, and she wrote me back under another name. . . ." *That's absurd. I never heard of Jews getting packages or sending letters from the concentration camps.**

"We always assume," Herr Stolle says, again in Anna's defense, "that one knew what was happening. But if the Jews knew, they would have defended themselves with all their might. There were men among them. No, they didn't know—they knew as little as we knew."

Rolf leans over the small table. "The word 'concentration camp.' Was *that* not known to you?" he asks softly.

"No!" Herr Stolle says, straightening, as Anna shakes her head. "No!"

"But 'labor camp' you knew, correct?" Rolf continues, pushing harder now. For him, this is the conversation he never had with his grandfather.

"It was called a work camp in the East," says Herr Stolle.

"But Dachau was nearby."

"One knew about that," says Herr Stolle, grim-faced.

"But what Dachau *was* we didn't know," says Anna quietly. "It wasn't only for Jews, you know. Christians were sent there too—even someone from the village."

"And no one talked about it?" I ask, finding that hard to believe. The ten Jewish men who were arrested after Kristallnacht and released a few months later came back to Benheim with their

---

*Later, when I ask one of the survivors of a camp if this is possible, he says, "Anything was possible. The woman may have been in a special work camp, not a death camp." And then I read about a packet of three hundred letters from Sala Garncarz, a survivor of work camps, sent to America, where it stayed in a trunk for almost fifty years. The letters are now being published (*Princeton Alumni Weekly*, November 17, 2004).

heads shaved, their bodies thin from near-starvation. Did no neighbor ask what had happened?

"No, it was forbidden," Herr Stolle says, and Rolf nods in agreement. "According to my knowledge," says my young Holocaust scholar solemnly, "if someone spoke of what happened, particularly to people not from his family, he could be sent back again."

"*Ja*," says Anna, "they were not allowed to speak about it. It was true."

How quickly the mood can shift from light to dark! It takes only one image of a Nazi sign in the barbershop to make the memories of Benheim as Paradise fade. I expect the same explanations I heard in the Jewish living rooms: *People were afraid. What could they do? They were helpless, too.* After two days in Benheim, I can understand that better. Being brave *was* dangerous and a risk to your family, especially in a village of six streets.

"So fear stopped people from resisting or helping," I say. Anna and Herr Stolle look at each other.

"You had to be careful . . . ," Herr Stolle says cautiously, "you had to watch what you said to your children, but . . . ," he sits up, "you couldn't say we lived in fear."

Anna nods vigorously, to my surprise. They both shy away from using fear as the culprit and resist the excuse that otherwise people would have done more. Later, Rolf tells me why: that the "fear alibi" is what many Nazis, postwar, used to escape blame during the Nuremberg trials: *We were following orders. We were helpless. It is not our fault.* So people like Herr Stolle and Anna, who weren't hiding great atrocities, avoided these words and the guilt by association that they brought. We're not like *those* people. Besides, *those* people (who may still live down the street) would not like any unfavorable comparisons. So what? I keep thinking. I don't grasp the dilemma until I imagine Americans whose family once owned a slave plantation saying, "We treated our slaves humanely." Sneers would overwhelm them: You bought and sold *people* like everyone else did. Nothing special about you.

Anna tells me that she didn't vote for Hitler, but that she was attracted to Hitler's promise for more law and order, more jobs, less inflation.

"Not that things were as bad in Benheim as elsewhere," Herr Stolle interjects. "Here there were no factories, no unions, no street fights with the Bolsheviks—and there was always food. In Berlin, people needed a wheelbarrow of money to eat!"

"And what violet eyes that man had!" Anna continues. "It was terrible how the women were drawn to him, like to . . . to the Beatles!" She shakes her head. "Terrible." I believe that she didn't want to be one of those adoring women, but her blue-eyed peppiness makes me picture her anyway, watching from the edge of a Nazi parade, waving?

"Were there any Nazi parades in Benheim?" I ask. "Or other Nazi events?"

Yes, she says after some silence, she remembers a parade through Benheim after the '33 election. I ask about the other danger signs I know. Yes, she remembers *Der Stürmer*, the rabid Nazi newspaper that was posted on a billboard. But her family never read it. And, yes, there was the swastika on the Denkmal. But it was not important; no one knew what it would mean. And, yes, some did sing that Nazi song ("When Jewish blood drips from our knives . . ."). But she never thought much about it. I want to say, *You can't sing those words and not know what's ahead!* But what Anna is saying is what Lotte and Ilse said about the black swastika on the hill. *It was there, but we never thought much about it.* And didn't I sing "Rock-a-Bye Baby" to my children for years without paying attention to the words?

When the bough breaks the cradle will fall
And down will come baby, cradle and all.

Go to sleep little one, I'd whisper . . .

I'm still assessing how much of "How could we know?" to believe, when Anna says that she wants to tell a story she has never told before—"not even to you, Adolf!" She laughs uneasily, Herr Stolle shifts in his chair, and Rolf and I lean forward for some kind of confession.

> It is about Lily. She didn't go with her family to America and was living alone. Her children were still trying to get her a visa, but the war had started. It was impossible. . . . She had little money left and too few ration cards, so she would come to eat at our house, for lunch, and when she didn't have anything, she also came in the evenings. Then one day she arrived very upset, with a list. It was an official order to get ready to leave in a few days and to bring these things with her: sheets, underwear, things one needed in a household, and also a hat. And I gave her my hat; at that time one wore hats. And a raincoat, which I also gave her. Such a beautiful raincoat I never got again. At that time things were of very good quality, not like now. How grateful she was! A brand-new raincoat. How could we know?

Anna looks so dejected, for Lily and for the raincoat—and suddenly, for a very dumb reason, I know she's telling the truth about not knowing what was in the East. *In Benheim, neighbors helped each other! In Benheim, we never wasted a thing!* This was the double refrain I always heard in Queens: the first, to make me generous; the second, to make me thrifty. For Benheimers like Anna and my dad, the inherent contradiction didn't matter; they were paired values, second nature to Christians and Jews alike. And both were at work in this raincoat story! If Anna had known what lay ahead, that Lily was being sent to die, Anna would still have wanted to give her a raincoat—I'm sure of that—but not her brand-new one. It's absurd, tragic! Yet it's irrefutably Benheim!

The "good raincoat" story changes how I understand German collective guilt. True, millions of Germans were involved in some aspect of the concentration camps—and knew what was going on there or chose not to know. But there must have been Annas, too. Out of geographic isolation and failure of imagination, they lent raincoats instead of saving lives—and now live with deep regret each time they say, "How could I know?"

It's a refrain still used today. I just read about a factory with slave workers from Thailand being held as prisoners in a California neighborhood for two years. People living nearby told reporters they knew nothing, even though they passed the factory daily, saw the barbed wire and faces pressed against windows. "How could I know?" was the defense offered. True, they were talking about half-seen strangers, not lifelong neighbors who "disappeared" one morning; but the mix of inattention and denial feel the same.

Anna's cast is to come off next week, she says, and she will start her daily exercise routine again: walking up the hill to the Jewish cemetery. She goes with Frau Brenner, the gravedigger's wife, whose husband's family used to bury the Jews when they lived in Benheim. I wonder why these two seek out what others avoid—or don't even know exists. These women find rest, or something else, up there in those woods.

"Have you seen the heart carved in the big tree?" Anna asks me. "It was made by Alfred Weinberger who married Erna Kahn before they left for Palestine. They didn't really love each other," she confides, "but got married anyway so they could both leave. The day before he carved their initials and the date, 1939, in the tree."

"I told the forester to take good care of this tree," says Herr Stolle with pride. "It's the straightest in the forest."

"Ja," says Anna, "the lumberjacks are always looking at it with an 'Oooh, we'd like that one!' look. But we have saved it, right, Adolf?"

They smile at each other without irony. Anna tells me that in the cemetery I should also look for another tree, a small one near the memorial to the Jews. "I planted it myself, a little seedling that I dug when I visited Israel for the second time. It was in Hans Gideon's garden and I wanted it here. For years now, it has survived our terrible Schwarzwald winters, a little evergreen, very special in our German woods!" Her smooth face shines like the girl she once was, as she talks about spring, her favorite season. She hopes her foot heals enough to be walking in time to see the wild anemones. "They blanket everything in the woods in white and pink, just for a few days. It's amazing. Like a miracle!" Anna speaks with such conviction, her delight so contagious, that, for the moment, she remakes the woods, the old Jewish graves, my ancestors, all in a glimpse of rich color.

11 | HEDWIG, FRITZ, AND "SCHTUMPELA"

I remember Hedwig as a Nazi bitch. She was Magda's
older sister and she told us we weren't allowed to play
together anymore.

Fritz Helm, age 72, in New York

Hedwig Luger, who lives five houses from Herr Stolle, pulls out
her "Jew file" (her term). It is a fat brown envelope filled with articles, photos, and correspondence with the Benheim Jews. She
shows me a photograph of a thin, sharp-eyed teenager next to a
chubby little girl with wild curls. "That's me with Schtumpela!"
she says, and I realize that the little girl in the photo is Lotte Pressman—when she had joie de vivre in Benheim, before Hitler and
Kristallnacht and her father not coming home from Dachau in
time for Hanukkah.

"I interviewed her in New York!" I say, delighted that, thanks
to Herr Stolle, the dots I came to the village to connect are connecting. This woman must be the German who sent Lotte the
postcard she didn't answer. "Why should I?" Lotte had said,
making it clear that her nostalgia for Benheim did not include
Hedwig Luger.

"We called her Schtumpela because she was so short—and I
remember how she loved animals." Hedwig talks with anima-
tion. She is a stocky, assertive woman, confident in manner and

happy to speak English without fluency, and without apology. Rolf does not have to translate. "Schtumpela was always in the fields, helping with the cows and chickens. Whoever would let her. And what a beautiful older sister she had, Tanya. I hear she married to a rich grocer on Long Island. Right, Adolf?" She looks to Herr Stolle, as if for affirmation that Lotte and Tanya were her closest friends.

The Luger living room has the same built-in bookcases and state-of-the-art stereo as the Stolles'; but instead of a wall of family photos, there's a "This Is Your Life" poster made for Hedwig's seventieth birthday by her nephew. "We have no children," she says matter-of-factly as husband Klaus opens the blinds, revealing the same hill with the white cross that you see from the Stolle dining room.

Hedwig passes around photos from a trip to Florida where they visited an enclave of Benheim Jews who spend winters there. "We saw them all in Fort Lauderdale," says Klaus proudly, also in English. I don't recognize anyone, but Herr Stolle recognizes everyone, nodding at each reconnection to someone he'd grown up with. Klaus says that he also brought the Jews some photographs. "I took pictures of all the Jew houses in Benheim, that was their wish." Herr Stolle nods. "And they knew everything from every house. They said, 'Let's start at the bottom of the street. Who lives here and who lives here?' And about every house they knew everything exactly."

He is a large, boisterous man with a big belly and double chin, not unlike my cousin Roger in looks. And he speaks with the same tendency to turn quiet description into loud declarations. He brags about visiting Israel twice (the Lugers were on the same trip as Anna and the Stolles)—and how thrilled he was with his reception: "I was walking by foot and suddenly a Jewess comes toward me. In the first moment I didn't recognize her, and she threw herself around my neck and said, 'You are Klaus! I am Hilde!' Or maybe it was Thea, her sister, I forget. I asked her, 'How do you know me?' and the woman said, 'You look exactly like your mother.'"

"More like your father, I think," says his wife.

"Well, she thought more like my mother."

Klaus tells us how "Hilde, or maybe Thea" invited them in for "real *schwäbischer Apfelkuchen*," and how this village "is a Swabian oasis." It's the same story of reunion that Anna told, but Klaus makes everyone too chummy, as if Hitler were just a blip on a small radar screen. I pull away, especially when my aunts seem so interchangeable. Hilde or Thea? Anna and Herr Stolle would never confuse them.

I ask Hedwig if she remembers Fritz Helm. When I met him in New York, he was the only Jew from Benheim with no fond memories of childhood. Any nostalgia was overpowered by anger and fear.

"Of course I remember him!" Hedwig says. "Little Fritz was always in our garage, playing with our father's car tools and the gears."

She acts as if Fritz couldn't possibly remember her as a Nazi bitch (true, he was six and she was thirteen) and that there could be no reason for Fritz's night terrors that years of therapy haven't eased ("I remember being curled in my bed on Kristallnacht, sure I was going to die as I heard windows being smashed"). And that she never bullied her little sister into believing that Hedwig would report any contact with Fritz to the Nazi mayor, and that would be the end of Magda and Fritz.

"Hedwig loved to strut around in her BDM* uniform," Fritz recalled bitterly, as we sat in a New York bagel place, next to an overly loud jukebox playing heavy metal. He did add that if he hadn't been Jewish, he probably would have done the same. "All the Jewish boys secretly wished we could join the Hitler Youth. They had great flags and songs, and parades that made you part of the great 'We.' Unfortunately, we were 'They' not 'We.'"

*BDM was the Hitler Youth group for girls. There was strong pressure for Hedwig and others her age to join it. "Aryan" boys were all to join the Hitler Youth.

Hedwig remembers herself as a victim, not as a bully, and that's why she outwardly supported Hitler:

I was in high school in Dorn at that time. You know Dorn? It's a few kilometers from here and those who went to high school went there. Benheim had no high school. Even today. On the day after Kristallnacht, a teacher came to us in the morning and announced, "Let's go and break all the Jewish windows in Dorn!" I wouldn't go and stayed in the schoolyard for hours. I didn't think to go home because I knew my father would say, "What are you doing here? Go right back to school!" In those days one didn't dare leave school without permission. When my classmates came back, all but two jumped on me and wanted to beat me up. I didn't know why. Someone said they had seen my father driving his taxi to the train station with a Jewish woman inside, and her baby. My classmates ran after the car with stones. My father told me later that on this day he realized something was really foul, because in Benheim there hadn't been much against the Jews. So what was going on, the hatred, wasn't known yet. My father decided not to stop at the train station and drove in the direction of Switzerland, two hours away. The police followed, but he knew tricks to elude them and the woman got away. At least that's what I heard. After that things really went sour for me. I got in big trouble with the principal, who wrote my father a letter. I don't have it anymore, it got burned; but it said that my father should remove his daughter from the school because she undermines the morals of the other children. My father wrote back that he wouldn't. Then in the spring-time, before I could finish the year, I was expelled for having a bad report card. It was 1939. I had no diploma so my father sent me to a boarding school three towns away. Nothing worked the way it was supposed to.

Hedwig still sounds upset with her father for the dangers he brought into her family. "They took him away in the middle of the night, and he disappeared for three days. When he came back, he was pale and frightened, and I begged him not to help the Jews anymore!" Her outward enthusiasm for the Nazis began that day, she says (although Fritz remembers it starting much earlier). The basic story must be true, Rolf assures me later, because the same story appeared in the local newspaper—Hedwig showed him the clipping—and she wouldn't have told a reporter a made-up story. Too many old-timers like Anna and Herr Stolle would challenge her on a lie told in order to look good.

Klaus's stories are easier *not* to believe. He is certain he went skiing with his Jewish friends after Kristallnacht. (Never! says everyone I've asked.) He is certain that on Kristallnacht, "In Benheim nothing much was going on."

"A fire of some kind was lit," Hedwig says, "and some things like curtains and smaller pieces of furniture were burning. There wasn't a lot."

"I did not notice anything," says Klaus. "The Gasthaus Kaiser was between my window and the synagogue."

"It can't have been a lot," Hedwig says, closing her "Jew file."

I ask if they heard about the Torah being saved. Yes, they knew it was the policeman who did it. A good man. They hadn't heard about the Burlington Torah, and, like everyone I tell, they grin with pleasure at another rescue story. Rolf asks how people reacted to the deportation. Were they sad? Klaus says he knew nothing, even though, unlike Herr Stolle and Anna, he was living at home. (Why he wasn't at war, he doesn't say. He seems old enough.) He offers me a glass of sherry, which I decline—it's ten in the morning—and says that "only by coincidence" did he know about the last *Abtransport* (transporting someone away). "Had I not lived on the main street, I wouldn't have seen people coming with their little carts. I asked someone, 'What is going on here?' and they said the Jews were going away. They were mostly old men and women." *Did he not see the children? Were they also interchangeable to him?*

"You have to remember that people were struggling with their own lives," says Hedwig, passing out glasses of apple juice. "The war was going on and reports of dying husbands and brothers were coming back daily. I wasn't here except on weekends, but one day I came home to a different village. My mother said, 'They took the Jews away.' I asked, 'Who did?' Strangers came in uniform, she said, she didn't know from where—and they packed the Jews into trucks. We heard they were being taken to labor camps to work and believed that was true because one man wrote to my father, saying he was in Theresienstadt and was allowed to get packages. So we sent, but never heard from him anymore. He didn't die there. She heard he went to Switzerland."

There's a matter-of-factness in their talk about the past that is both unnerving and honest. The Lugers have none of Herr Stolle's *Na ja*'s or Anna's looks of helpless grief. The Lugers remember the Jews without sighing. And they remember the Nazi takeover and her uncle Kinkele's removal with neutral acceptance. "Sure, he was a Jew friend, so he couldn't continue here as mayor. A different wind was blowing here. The next mayor was in uniform. An SA uniform." No eulogies for the loss of a good man. No laments about the growing isolation of the Jews, ending in deportation. After the Jews had to wear the Jewish stars, "one didn't have much to do with them anymore," says Hedwig. "One didn't really see them walking around any-more—maybe to the store and back. One wasn't allowed to give them anything anymore."

That's how it was, the facts of history. And now the Lugers have moved on to visiting Florida and Israel and filling their "Jew file" with whatever information comes their way. "We have the list of everyone who got away and also who was killed." All the names are in her file, tucked between a greeting card and a postcard from the Big Apple.

The Nazis took over, I decide, because people like the Lugers "blow with the wind." They are not the kind who hurt people for fun, but they don't help either. And they don't seem to suffer for that. The scale of justice that sits on Herr Stolle's window sill, balancing, would not find a place here.

Yet their unabashed pragmatism has its upside. When Herr Stolle complains, yet again, about the Jews' ungratefulness that the synagogue is still "God's house," it is Hedwig who says, "But if they made our Catholic church into a mosque, would you be grateful?" And when Rolf asks if schoolchildren visit the Jewish cemetery, it is Hedwig who gives the politically incorrect, yet honest, answer: "They come often, in fact too much. The cemetery is becoming a tourist attraction, the classes tramping around on graves. I feel sorry for the few who are really interested."

Herr Stolle stands up to leave. "So! We must go!" He points to his watch, but I have one more question to ask. It's bothered me since I saw the thick woods surrounding the village. Why didn't more Jews try to escape? Why were they so passive? After all, Benheim is an hour from France, two hours from Switzerland. There are thick forests to hide in. Herr Stolle, Hedwig, and Klaus shake their heads. No, it wasn't done.

Why not?

The Jews were all registered. Everyone had a number.

But why didn't they just *not* register?

Herr Stolle shakes his head again, and I hear the wheels of propriety clicking. *In Benheim you didn't do such things.* That meant everyone, the Jews, too—even when the law abandoned them. The idea makes me mad.

"I hid someone, or rather my father did," announces Klaus. We all look up. Herr Stolle, too. "It was in Dorn, in the Digmans' apartment, in the basement. My father brought food. It wasn't in the town itself. Maybe half a mile outside. I don't know the name anymore. The woman left after the war and never even said thank you. I don't remember her name, but it annoyed my father and Digman."

Another unlikely story by Klaus! Rolf and I say, as we head down the hill on our way back to Stuttgart, our trip together over. "Except for his complaint about the woman's lack of gratefulness," I say. "*That* sounded authentic."*

"He's the only one I met who I did *not* believe," says Rolf. "I wish I could say the same of my town." Rolf is happy he came here, saying he liked these people very much. They are less anti-Semitic than in his town—"and they donated more to the archives in Stuttgart than any other village in Württemberg."

"What archive in Stuttgart?"

"Oh, I checked the village listing there before I came. Nothing of interest for you." His clipped certainty makes me picture him in military uniform again.

"Do you ever wonder if Hitler would have appealed to you?"

He slows down. "Sometimes," he says gravely. "I am a conscientious objector, you know. But that is now. And I am a lover of what is great in German culture—Goethe, Heinrich Heine, Beethoven, Brahms. But we Germans have, under our thick crust of culture, a deep, dark lake with cracks we must see in time. That is why I study history. To find where those cracks may be hidden."

"And did you?"

"I think more than before."

We are quiet. I am thinking about cracks so small they are almost invisible; yet when the Lugers and others add their weight, we all fall through. The clouds have thickened; it looks like rain but the sun is still out, shining on the white cross above us. It makes me think of Herr Stolle's last story before we left,

*A year later, in Dorn, I will in fact hear the same story about one hidden Jew on the edge of town. But no one will mention Klaus or his father, and when I asked, no one knew of them.

about the big swastika that was once there "before it was blown up in 1945, three hours before the French troops marched in. Some of our old people were smart. They knew it would get everyone in more trouble." And he laughed. I wish he hadn't. It rings in my ears, even as half a rainbow appears, one end reaching above the village before fading.

12 | THE SECOND GENERATION

As soon as Otto Stolle opens the door, I think, *So this is what his father looked like.* Handsome, dark-eyed, and in his mid-forties, Herr Stolle's son is holding a baby who is sucking on a yellow pacifier. Otto lives in a two-story townhouse in Aachen, five hundred miles north of Benheim, with a new wife, her three children, his eldest son, and the baby. His other two children live with his former wife, he says, as we settle into a small, bright living/dining room to talk about Benheim, his postwar childhood, and what his father told him.

"So how did your father react to your new marriage?" I ask, imagining Herr Stolle in *my* father's voice shouting *In Benheim we didn't do such things.* That happened when my cousin got divorced and when my sister was contemplating it. (She decided to wait until after Dad died.)

"Not well," Otto says, with his father's quiet smile. "In his Benheim, people didn't do such things." *Is my echo his as well?* But even in Benheim, he says, the old social codes no longer hold. Divorces, single mothers, higher crime, and, recently, even drugs are commonplace. "It may look like a quaint old village, but today's problems are all there."

I like that he does not weigh his every word. I like that I'm not judging his every word. Maybe it's because we are both "the second generation," as historians call those of us born during or soon after the Third Reich. We grew up with our parents' secrets and silences, we live with them, but we don't own them except in the collective sense: as in *our* country, *our* family, and so *our* legacy.

Otto teaches German history in a multicultural high school. His students are "a mix of Germans, Turks, Italians, Nigerians, and Kurds, all getting ready for jobs, not the university." Otto teaches about the Third Reich, but there's great resistance from colleagues who would rather limit the subject "to a few paragraphs of facts in a more glorious German history." And many students say, "This is not our problem. Let's focus on issues that directly concern us, like the merging of East and West Germany." But they *must* study the past to learn from it, Otto says firmly, putting the baby on his other shoulder. He can understand their frustration, being handed a history they can't feel proud of. "Even our national anthem is politically incorrect, thanks to the Nazis who appropriated the words *Deutschland, Deutschland, über alles* (Germany over all things). To avoid any echo of racism and warmongering, we are Greens, our cause to protect the environment. Except that we still have Skinheads who hate foreigners, outsiders, and Jews."

I like his honesty. He is much less guarded about prejudice than his father and the other old-timers of Benheim. Or even Rolf, who prefers to judge the past rather than the present. Otto seems comfortable connecting the two, as if we were anywhere, even New Jersey. It's easy to forget he's German, a nice feeling.

I tell him about Monika, a friend in Frankfurt who is also a history teacher, and that before coming here I visited her class, also very multicultural. Her students had been assigned to give talks about their backgrounds, and those whose families came from India, Iran, Nigeria, and Turkey stood up proudly to describe "their great heritages." But four students (out of twenty) said nothing—except to whisper to each other in the back of the class. I expected Monika to quiet them, but she didn't, explaining later that "the Germans were too embarrassed to talk. They feel a great loss of national pride and so they don't participate."

Otto nods. That is a big problem. Another problem is teachers not using discipline, he says, starting to feed the baby. "We are afraid of too much obedience, another Nazi legacy we try to erase, but . . . we also must be careful that the pendulum does not swing back the other way."

Now I hear his father talking. The need for balanced thought is pure Herr Stolle—even if the cluttered dining-room table with its stack of diapers, a black teddy bear, and half-eaten banana is not. His father's love of order may be another Nazi legacy the next generation feels the need to avoid. Order, obeying orders. No thank you. Or maybe it's just the chaos of a new baby.

We start talking about Benheim, where he spent every summer as a child. His family lived near Hanover in the north but spent holidays on the family farm run by his aunt and uncle. "I loved it!" Otto says. "The animals, the fields, were wonderful. When I think about it now, it still seems perfect." *He sounds just like Lotte reminiscing.* "Many of Benheim's Jews," I say, "remember the same childhood landscape that you do," I say, "as if, for children, Benheim never changes. . . ."

"Now it has changed," he says, evenly. "The old mountain road where our farm is, for example, now has many houses owned by people of Turkish personality. They came initially to work, but want to stay, and have bought the older German houses in Benheim."

The way he says "German houses" makes me think of the issue of who is or isn't German. In the States, if you are born American, you're called American. It's a matter of geography. But here, it's possible not to be called German, even if your family has lived here for generations. The Iranian and Nigerian students in Monika's history classroom were born in Frankfurt; yet she didn't mean them when she talked about "the Germans being embarrassed." And Otto described his class as "a mix of Germans, Turks, Italians, and Kurds." The Jews were also considered "other." Their families lived here for centuries, and by 1900 many saw themselves as 100 percent German. Quite a few were even baptized, not realizing until Hitler's racial laws, thirty years later, how many of their countrymen saw them only as Jews.

"How well have the Turks integrated into Benheim?" I ask, figuring Otto doesn't have a village to protect, the way his father does.

"The children in the schoolyard don't seem to play together," he says. "But the next generation will be different. These Turkish people are very industrious. They have fixed up old homes, added new roofs, made them new, their home. Their children have learned the language. It will be better."

On a future visit, I will meet one of these "industrious Turks" in the upper village of Benheim. He will invite me into a house that he has gutted and is remodeling for three families: his and his two sons'. In broken German he will point out every window he has redone—and the wiring, plumbing, and plastering, plus three kitchens installed, all by working every Sunday for two years. This has caused some problems "among the German neighbors," Herr Stolle will tell me. "Too much hammering on the Sabbath! Too much noise!" (And that's before fifteen people move in!)

Otto and I compare fathers. I tell him how whenever I wanted to chew gum or wear lipstick, my father would say (and now I say it out loud): "In Benheim we didn't do such things!" Otto laughs. He heard that plenty, too. We talk about the irony of those words, given the Holocaust. And how little our parents spoke about what happened. "Did your father mention anything at all?" It's the question I was afraid to ask my colleague Angie over lunch in San Francisco. But Otto and I both knew this conversation was coming. It is why I came, and why he said yes when I called.

He talks about the white cross high in the meadow and how his father never wanted him to go there. "He kept saying it was a bad place and we should stay away. 'But why? What's wrong with it?' I'd ask, and once he answered that a Nazi cross once stood there. I was a child and didn't know what he meant, but I could tell it was a bad thing."

Otto also knew there was something in the forest with a locked gate, and that the farmer down the road had the key. Sometimes strange people would come into the village and stop at the post office where he worked for his aunt. And she would tell Otto to take them to the Brenner farm. But his father kept being vague, only telling him "the people buried there were former inhabitants of Benheim." So what Otto knew came from what he saw from outside the stone gate: "Very old graves, many were tipped, some falling over, with plants growing over them. And that it was something . . . strange."

It's hard to imagine Herr Stolle, so dedicated to the cemetery's history now, being so silent then. I ask, "Your father never mentioned the Jews?"

"Once when I was sixteen, I insisted on knowing more. I'd become interested in history, the old history but also the new history. We had teachers who lived during the Nazi times, and they were of two groups. The younger teachers, who tried to give us new insights into these terrible times, and the older ones . . . [great pauses] who feared we would get the wrong impression. They talked about the Weimar Republic, inflation, and the Treaty of Versailles being the beginning of a bad development, and that was it. The younger tried to explain that they had . . . , the good Germans, . . . that in the good Germany . . . there had been a certain immunity against the developments of official political . . . a pervasive abdication."

For the first time in our two hours together, Otto's lucid English is replaced by fragments of jargon about Germany's ignoble past. I interrupt him. "Do you have a Facing History program here?" I ask. Monika had joined one in Frankfurt that was devoted to countering such jargon with personal stories. Each year they invite Jewish survivors and German resistors to come to classrooms and talk about their experiences. According to Monika, the Hitler past becomes instantly real and relevant to students. She showed me letters her students wrote afterward to the speakers, full of admiration, regret, and empathy. New immigrants, in particular, identified the most, "for they know what it is to be an outsider." As does Monika. She and the other teacher from her school who participates are not appreciated. The rest of the faculty "would like us to disappear into the walls with this past."

Aachen has no such program, as far as Otto knows. He speculates that it's because the Jews living here have no roots in Germany. They come from Belgium and most recently from Eastern Europe—Poland, Galicia, and the Western Soviet Union. "One of Hitler's aims, unfortunately," Otto says sadly, "was successful. There is no continuity of Jewish life in German life today, and that is a crime and loss that will be felt one hundred years from now."

But in Benheim, he says, "Jewish history is still everywhere, which is why I kept telling my father, 'If you won't preserve it, no one will.' I eventually convinced him, but it was a calling, not something he liked doing, like fishing. And he had no academic training—he was a retired textile engineer, after all." Otto believes this work helped his father confront his own history, something he had avoided. "You can't spend six hours a day in the archives or the Jewish cemetery without asking yourself: What did *I* do in this time? What did my neighbor do, and the friend on the other side of the road, what did he do?" The answers, Otto says, ran the spectrum. "Some thought what was happening to the Jews was okay, including the new Nazi mayor, not from Benheim. Many were indifferent and looked the other way. And some felt it wasn't right, one even spoke up in church. But mostly they were the quiet people, not organizers. They didn't know how to form a resistance, or didn't want to, or couldn't perhaps. . . ."

"They did save the Torahs!" I say, and tell him about the one in Israel and the other in Burlington Vermont.

"I never heard that before!" He sounds delighted.

"I wonder why not," I say. "Why these stories get lost, especially in a small village where everyone seems to know everything anyway."

"Because such acts are something normal, something self-understood." (Yes, he uses that very phrase.) "People who do such things are not helping Jews or non-Jews, but their neighbors, people they know. To brag about such gestures would make them, and everyone else, uncomfortable."

I ask who, in the church, had spoken up for the Jews, but Otto doesn't know. What he overheard as a child was that there was a sermon, some heated discussion, the SA showed up, and someone was taken away for questioning. Nothing discussed openly. Even today. What he does know is that his father ran into opposition when he began doing his research. People were afraid he would put what he found out in the newspaper, and he had to keep reassuring everyone that he wouldn't. Otherwise he could not have kept living in Benheim. "The archives told a lot about who took advantage of the Jews and who didn't. Some people bought fairly; others got a big bargain. It was all perfectly legal, but people didn't want that information out. They didn't want their parents' reputations ruined."

It surprises me that people still worry that their reputations could be hurt for cheating a Jewish neighbor fifty years ago—and with Nazi permission. I think of Gretl in New York saying (reluctantly) how almost every villager paid his debt on her store accounts, even after Nazi law absolved "Aryans" from all obligations to Jews.

Otto's baby, a husky boy with fat cheeks and his father's brown eyes, who's been happy in a baby seat beside us, begins to cry. And Otto's wife magically appears. Her name is Anya, and she's a lovely, slim blond, looking in her thirties. We try chatting, but the wails get louder, and she and the baby retreat. Climbing the stairs, she tells Otto, over her shoulder, to offer me a cold drink or coffee. I like their marital balance of power, more like my house than our parents', where mothers managed babies *and* served iced tea, while fathers held forth in large easy chairs.

He asks when my parents left Germany and I tell him in 1936. "Yes, your father was smart," Otto says, while rummaging in the refrigerator. He finds iced tea, two glasses, and makes room for them on the dining table. "Too many Jews kept waiting to see if . . . ," he hands me one glass, "Hitler was going to stay in power. There was opposition at first, in 1933, and they thought they had a chance. But by 1935–36, the Nazis were firmly established and there was an exodus, over 400,000 Jews. You know only 1 percent of the German population was Jewish and 75 percent got out in time." He has his father's love of statistics.

"Only 1 percent? I thought there were more."

"In Poland, yes. They were 10 percent, over three and one half million. And 90 percent were killed." He shakes his head and I half expect his father's *Na ja*. "They had so little warning to leave once our armies invaded. The same in Czechoslovakia and Hungary."

"Was your father in those places?" I am still trying to solve the mystery of where, exactly, Herr Stolle was in the war.

But Otto, too, could never pin his father down. He knew that he'd taken aerial photos over France and that he'd been captured in Hungary and escaped to the American zone. *I thought Czechoslovakia.* And when Otto had pressed him, they'd had terrible fights, especially when he was a teenager. "I was furious. 'How could they let such a thing happen? Why didn't they go into the streets and stop the deportations?' I'd yell. '*Everyone* knew when the Jews were being deported!' My father would become equally angry at my accusations against his parents and brothers and sisters—he was already in school in Rotenberg. (*Wasn't he a soldier in France by then?*) Dishes would fly, things were smashed in our fights, as I demanded to know why Germans didn't do more, and all he would say is 'You can't imagine the times.'"

You can't imagine the times. It's the same phrase that Angie's father told Angie. And the old man in Israel told me. And what all who were there tell those who weren't. Otto says that nowadays he is more open to understanding than he was. After studying history, he realizes how little could be done by 1939, and by 1940–41 when the Jews were deported, there was no way to stop that locally. The time to stop the Nazis was in 1933, we both agree. I say my book project has made me reassess my own unearned virtue. "At first I assumed as a good person I would have been good. But now I wonder how much I would have dared. It's a humbling experience."

"I have come to this, too," Otto says, just as Anya's son comes in to ask him a question on his math homework. Otto opens the textbook and pulls the boy close, and I can picture this man, sixty years ago, a good man, a decent man. Someone who might have brought soup at night. Someone who even might have saved a Torah if he could do it safely. But I don't imagine him protesting publicly in church about what isn't right! He and his father (and me, too) are "the quiet people" who disapprove from at home. We don't willingly, like Monika, join a group that makes work life difficult, and we don't instinctively, like Monika's friend Sonya, confront an angry man who yells, "Forget the Jews. Go home. It's over!"

That's what happened last week on a plaza near Frankfurt when Sonya was showing me a memorial to the Jews. It was one of four that she'd helped set up so her town would *not* forget. The man kept circling as we looked at the exhibit of life-sized photos of men, women, and children crowded on the train station, bags in hand, waiting, fearful. *I could have been on that platform being deported.* The man, staggering and drunk, kept closing the circle. I wanted to leave, but Sonya stood her ground—and mine. She had told me that her father had been a train engineer during the war (*Had he been to Auschwitz?*) and yet she defied any such legacy, hands on hips. She stepped toward the man. "How dare you?" she shouted, glaring until he backed away, disappeared, while onlookers stared or pretended not to notice. To her, there was no alternative action. "It was self-understood"—and not even a story worth retelling.

7. The black swastika erected by the Nazis in 1934.
Photo courtesy of Heinz Högerle.

8. The white cross that replaced the swastika after the war. *Photo courtesy of Heinz Högerle.*

9. The entrance to the synagogue that became the Protestant Church in the early 1950s. Inscriptions in Hebrew are still over the doorway. *Photo courtesy of Heinz Högerle.*

10. *Berches*, the potato bread that everyone remembers. *Photo courtesy of Heinz Högerle.*

11. The Jewish cemetery in the woods above the village. *Photo courtesy of Heinz Högerle.*

12. The tree Anna planted in the Jewish cemetery with seeds from the garden of her former neighbor whom she visited in Israel. *Photo courtesy of Heinz Högerle.*

PART THREE | BACK AND FORTH

13 | WILLY FROM BALTIMORE

I went back to Benheim in 1945 . . . It was unbelievable.
I mean every house—one after another as you go up
the main street—had been a Jewish house. Gone. I mean
really unbelievable. You are lost.

From Willy Weinberger's memoir, unpublished

If it weren't for Hitler, Willy Weinberger would have been a cattle dealer in Benheim like his father and grandfather and great-
grandfather. Instead, he ended up as half owner of a kosher
butcher shop in Baltimore, Maryland—and credits God. Willy,
one of the two Benheim Jews to survive the concentration
camps, was deported on his eighteenth birthday and released
four years later, in 1945. Yet his smile is real. "I thank *Hashem*
(God) every day for His kindness and mercy—*Baruch Hashem*
(blessed be He)—because I have nineteen wonderful grandchildren and nine great-grandchildren," says this small, good-
natured man of seventy-eight. Many who survived the Holocaust
declared that "God is dead," but not Willy or his sons. Both
became rabbis, Willy says proudly (though maybe with a hint of
regret that they didn't take over his business).

He's now retired, but the butcher shop still has "Weinberger"
in fat black letters above the doorway. "You see? The new owner
didn't change the sign!" Willy says happily as we drive by on our

way to lunch at "the kosher Chinese restaurant." He eats here often since his wife died two years ago, and the Chinese owner greets us like old friends. "Just remember, it's my treat!" Willy says, delighted that I've taken the train two hours south from New Jersey to meet him. Despite apprehensions about talking to a survivor about the Holocaust, I want to know what Hannah, Lotte, and the others who escaped Nazi Germany cannot know firsthand: What happened in Benheim and Dorn after they left?

"If you buy a cow and make a profit on it, you don't want to leave!" Willy says about why his father and uncles ignored the early signs to emigrate. By 1934, signs of JUDEN SIND HIER UNERWÜNSSCHT! (No Jews Wanted Here!) were posted, literally, at every marketplace they visited in southwest Germany. But the Weinbergers and their non-Jewish trading partners continued to buy and sell cattle as before. I always imagined Jews who defied Nazi orders getting beaten, hauled away, or shot on the spot—especially after 1935 when new Nazi laws left Jews unprotected, at the mercy of anyone's hatred.

"So how did you get away with it?"

"We managed," Willy says, and sips his egg drop soup. "People were loyal. My father's business lasted until 1938 when the last of the inns he stayed at became unavailable." *How gradual it all was!* No wonder the Weinbergers got lulled into a false sense of safety, if it took four years for one lodging to become a Nazi headquarters; another to be placed off-limits because a Christian woman lived there (Jewish men weren't allowed to live under the same roof with unmarried Christian women); and a third, owned by "two lovely old people," to be closed to them because of fear of reprisal. Finally, even the farmer who came to the house at night to trade disappeared.

"People became too afraid," Willy says without rancor. I'm thinking, *Same old, same old.* It's just what the other Benheim Jews said: *People were afraid. What could they do?* But then I realize their empathy was rooted in the safety of America, while

Willy was living the nightmare of Germany. So where does *his* empathy come from? Does surviving with a smile depend on it? And where is his rage?

"Most of the older Benheimers didn't change their behavior towards us—except for one ne'er-do-well who strutted around like a real Nazi," says Willy. "But the children were a different story." Every day in school they learned that the Jews were vermin destroying German purity. And the belief took hold quickly because, unlike their parents, they had no sense of village history to counter it. Kids would pick fights with Willy and his brother Sigfried, and once, on his way to the baker for hot water after Shabbat, a boy his age was waiting in the alley. "He wanted to beat me up, but I cracked him on the head with my water pail. His mother came to mine all upset, but my mother calmed her down, saying, 'You know my son didn't start this. And what was yours doing in the alley?'"

The woman didn't file a complaint, because she didn't approve of her son's behavior. "Most didn't, but they were afraid to say much, afraid they could get into trouble." After that incident Willy stayed away from places where he could be jumped. "It was my brother Sigfried who was the fighter. He had his share of wins, but got beat up too."

He and his brother sound so normal, their boyish punches countering my image of cringing Jews, afraid that one gesture of opposition could leave them dead. Which happened elsewhere, but evidently not in Benheim. Even Willy's mother felt safe enough to defend her son with "My son didn't start this." I wouldn't have thought she'd risk the honesty.

Willy compares what happened nearly seventy years ago to the Middle East today, his calm voice becoming agitated for the first time, as if putting the past in present tense is too much to bear: "You know, it was like the Palestinian children today. They also are so indoctrinated to hate the Jews, hate the Jews. That is all they learn, so what else should they do?" His words are loud enough to reach a Chinese couple two tables away that look up, surprised. But the two old men with yarmulkes, next to us, keep leaning over their rice bowls, not missing a beat. They have heard these words before, probably said them even louder to themselves.

Willy saw the flames from the synagogue on Kristallnacht from his bedroom window. He and his brothers woke his father, who jumped out of bed, saying, "My God, maybe the *shames* didn't extinguish the candles!!" Willy tells this dark moment lightly to show "how little my family knew!" Only the next day, when Benheim's Jewish men were arrested, did his family realize they *must* leave, and quickly. But time was against them, for the Weinbergers had no visas in hand. They managed to ship their furniture to Palestine in a huge lift, "the size of the kitchen," but they never followed. The war started, the visas didn't arrive, and the Weinbergers were trapped in Benheim while their furniture sailed away. It sat on the dock in Haifa, an uncle there paying storage for eight months, hoping—until he finally had to face that they weren't coming and sold many things to pay the storage fees.

The family still had one sliver of hope for Willy: *Hachshara.* In 1939 these farms, run by Jewish organizations (with Nazi approval), were still preparing German-Jewish youth to emigrate as farmers to *Eretz Israel* (the land of Israel). The Weinbergers sent seventeen-year-old Willy to one near Hamburg. "It was the best year of my life," Willy says wistfully. "We were all young people, studying, dancing, working in the fields with the hope of a new life still looming large." But by 1940 the Nazis closed all these farms down. The plan to eliminate the Jews by emigration was over; the plan for genocide—the "Final Solution"—was soon to begin. Those unfit for slave labor, and that meant children, old people, sick people, were to be systematically murdered by the state.

Willy, like all Jewish males over sixteen, was to report immediately to the Labor Board in nearby Dorn. He wanted to work with his father and uncles, digging local ditches and repairing roads, but was assigned to a farmer from Sulz-am-Neckar, fifteen kilometers away. "Luckily, the farmer was a decent man," says Willy, again opting for a good spin on what others might tell darkly. This farmer honored Willy's constraints against eating nonkosher meat and "gave me plenty of cheese, bread, milk and eggs, all I wanted." He even honored the Jewish Sabbath, letting Willy go home by bicycle to Benheim every Friday despite Nazi laws forbidding that. When deportations started, the man volunteered to hide Willy, and said, "If you want, I will try to keep you here." But Willy declined. "I told him that wherever my family went, I had to go too."

This "non-Jew" was not the only one to help Willy and his family. The mayor's assistant, the day after Kristallnacht, saved his father from being sent to Dachau with the other Jewish men. "Why did you pick Weinberger? He has four little children!" the assistant told the mayor, and Willy's father was let go. And there was "the kind policeman" who saved the Torah (everyone mentions him) and the policeman's wife, "a very decent person" who, when the Jews only got half the allotted rations, brought his mother extra food at night. And the man who bought his father's house for a fair price, Herr Damon, "a fine man." And the family's servant girl, Mary, who used to say the Jewish prayers with Willy nightly in Hebrew. *Ha Malach Ha Goel Osi Mikol Ra* (May the Angel redeem me from all Evil). "She didn't know what they meant, of course!" but she was a wonderful person. Willy and his father visited her after she was married, "maybe it was '35 or '36, and she was so thrilled to see us, she offered us an orange! Do you know what an orange meant in those days? Like gold!"

There's a tough kind of twinkle in his eye, the same kind my father had, one not easily dimmed by hardship. Whether because of strong faith or pragmatism like my dad's, I don't know, but Willy refuses to raise a fist to the sky to ask: "Why me?" Such an impulse may appease rage but demands the role of victim; and Willy prefers to be the boy who receives oranges of love, despite Hitler.

I get a new slant on the tradition of kindness from Willy: how for Benheim's Jews, it was more than personal impulse; it was a survival technique. "It kept our Gentile neighbors kindly" in a country where before the mid-nineteenth century Jews could be thrown out at a moment's notice. "I remember my father cleaning the manure off the streets on Saturday night after Shabbat, so they would be clean for Sunday church. We didn't want our horses' droppings to upset them. And the women in my family were always making a thick potato soup for non-Jewish neighbors. My grandmother brought it to the old woman next door, and my mother brought it to someone every time she had another child. Eight of them! But that soup didn't help us!" Willy says, as if telling a funny story. "After Kristallnacht, one of her sons came and threw stones at our house, and my father said, 'You see, you didn't make them enough soup!'" Levity, in the midst of hate, seems to run in the Weinberger family. Another survival technique.

The waiter removes our soup bowls and puts down chicken in broccoli and vegetables in garlic. Willy fills our plates with gusto. "Everything here is extra fresh," he says, and behind him a red Buddha sits smiling, his hands in prayer, resting on a round belly of fullness that Willy also celebrates.

The boy who threw stones is a blip of meanness in stories mostly about "the nice." *Is this denial or truth?* "You didn't have to fear physically in Benheim except if you met some boys in an alley," Willy tells me. There were "a few brownshirts with leather straps across their chests, but they never did much." The others were like the old man next door who raised his arm *Heil* Hitler! for parades, "but he could hardly keep it up!" Again the twinkle. "He didn't know better. He was doing whatever everyone else did." I ask him about Joseph Bodenheimer, who I heard had been shot over a land dispute. Willy shrugs off this darker image. "Well, I was young. I didn't know so much. I thought he just died." *Denial or truth? How can I know?*

Even on the morning of deportation, Willy remembers one comfort: "a neighbor crying in the shadows." The others were not to be seen, he says ruefully, because they were ashamed, or asleep, or afraid. "The policeman's wife, well-meaning as she was, was not about to see the Jews off." He still sounds hurt by the silence of goodbyes that day, his birthday. "At six in the morning a farmer came with his wagon for our heavy suitcases and heavy clothes.* But we had to walk to Dorn, to the train, the little children too. The streets were empty, silent. We carried food baskets of whatever we had in the house, which wasn't much. My mother baked cakes with some apples maybe. Potatoes, maybe. Who remembers? People were numb, leaving a place where they had lived for hundreds of years—and trying to get little children to walk so far. . . ."

Willy and the others rode in a railroad car to Stuttgart and then to Latvia; but it was not a cattle car. In fact, Willy remembers no real guards, only two policemen. "We knew we were going to the East to work for the war, but not much more," says Willy, echoing Anna's "How could we know?" They were still optimistic when they arrived in Riga, three days later, "to more snow than even we from the Schwarzwald had ever seen. We had warm clothes; so even as we stepped onto the platform of a small railway station called Kirotova, we knew nothing. When men in uniform came towards us with canes, we thought they were invalids from the war, greeting us. Within minutes, we knew better. They were ss who used the canes with all their

---

*The facts here contradict Klaus and Hedwig's stories of strangers and a truck, but there were three different deportations between 1940 and 1942, so both versions might be true—or not.

strength to beat whoever got in their way. We had to march through miles of deep snow. I was with my parents, and my three brothers, who were fifteen, nine, and six, and when we saw our destination point—a large barren farm with huge empty barns—my father said, 'From here we won't leave alive.' The place was called Jungfernhof, and it was to be my home for nearly three years."

The waiter brings the check with some sliced oranges, no fortune cookies. The stories stop as Willy sucks the juice from the wedges, and I join him, thinking of the Neumeyers who used to come to our house in Queens. They had survived Auschwitz but lost two children there. I still see the numbers on Mrs. Neumeyer's arm as she hugged me hard, and I look at Willy's long sleeves, picturing the indelible ink, as we take a break from memory. He asks how my family is, if I have children, and I tell him their ages and names, as if his world, like mine, didn't collapse at age eighteen.

Willy is the only one in his family to survive the camps. His mother and two younger brothers died first, his mother of typhus in a freezing cow barn four months after they came. In his unpublished memoir, which I read later, at home, he describes it:

> I saw her the night before. I had snuck in to see her when I learned she was sick, as my little brother stood watch . . . A week later, in the evening, everyone was handed a shovel to clear the road of deep snow, and if no shovel, you had to use your hands. The next morning 3000 to 4000 people were loaded on trucks including my two youngest brothers. My brother Sigfried, who was helping people into the trucks, was bold. He asked the guard if his brothers couldn't stay and was told: "Oh, they will be much better off where they are going to a town three to four hours away. They'll have more food and heat." But the trucks came back an hour

later, and so we feared the worst. A week later we found out they'd been shot in the nearby woods and buried in a mass grave.

For a while, Willy had his father and brother, but then they were sent to the Jewish ghetto in Riga, and the Commandant wouldn't let Willy join them. He did visit them once—"we even went to *schul* together and prayed"—but then they were transferred. "It was the last time I saw them." I want to offer comfort, an apology for not having suffered, a hand on his, but it is he who gives me his arm as he stands up to head for the car.

"If you have *sechel* (smarts) without *mazel* (luck), it won't help you!" says Willy. We are back in his apartment, the sun angling through the slatted blinds. He has poured us seltzer as he begins the story of Leah Kahn, "who proves what luck can do." Without a bit of *sechel*, this old woman lived through everything. "Here was someone who was always sick. I'd visit her with my mother when I was a boy, an invalid as long as I can remember. She was someone you'd think wouldn't last a day in bad conditions. And what happens? She falls off the truck on her way to Theresienstadt, right through the wooden cracks, and spends the whole war in the hospital. Afterwards, she lives until ninety-six, blind and being cared for by nuns in an old age home in Stuttgart. Can you believe that? And her son and daughter, they were with me in Riga, were killed."

Life and death, sad and funny, all mixed up. I never thought it possible, which is why I never dared talk to a Holocaust survivor before, afraid of a breakdown from the horror, taking me along. Yet here is Willy signaling that even in that nightmare, you must find something to laugh at. And believe in. This man, the most religious person I know, one who prays three times a day and studies the Talmud daily, says that "even in the concentration camps, living in freezing barracks where the bunk beds were five bunks high, we got down in the dark to say prayers." The more he talks about surviving in the camps, the more the word "luck" is replaced by "miracle." For Willy, "luck" is godsent.

The first miracle was that he was young, strong, and sent to a work farm instead of a death camp. The Commandant was "a big, handsome German who had killed thousands of Latvian Jews without pause but saw the German Jews as more civilized." He convinced his superiors to let him make a model farm, "a showplace of our blood and sweat—and if we worked hard, he left us alone." Willy's voice is suddenly hard-edged. "The Commandant let us wear regular clothes without a yellow star. That wasn't official, but he didn't want to be bothered. Which was good for us."

Food was key to staying alive, to keep strong enough to work so you wouldn't be shot. Willy and his father used their old cattle-trading skills to exchange goods for food grown by a local Latvian farmer, "nicer than the rest." Once during a sleeting storm, Willy and a friend risked driving a wagon to the farmer to trade extra clothes for some bread and butter. They thought they were safe in such weather, but in the middle of the deal, the farmer suddenly yelled, "The Commandant is coming!" And ran out the door. "Who would have believed that the Commandant would go out in weather like that? And for what? To count the manure piles we had out there? He stormed into the house and caught us. He hit my friend over the head and hit my back with his stick, saying, 'This time you'll be hanged!'"

The second miracle, Willy says, is that the Commandant didn't hang him. He gives three reasons for that. "First, God didn't want me to get hanged. Second, if the Commandant hanged me, he would make himself a bad name. He always bragged, 'My Jews behave.' Third, he had a mistress who, believe it or not, liked Jews. That she got together with such a man I could never figure out. But . . . she was a poor girl and with him, she lived like a queen." Even here, Willy has empathy for the girlfriend, and I wonder if that response is what made people kind to him. If you had one grain of generosity, you gave it to Willy, because you knew he wouldn't waste it on resentment. You'd get appreciation and a smile from the inside out.

Willy was put in a hole with only an airshaft—"At least it was warm!"—and again, he got help. His friends dropped his ration of bread through the hole: one-fifth of a square dark loaf per day, plus a tin of "soup" consisting of a watery broth with a few potatoes, sometimes barley, "and if there was a bit of meat, horsemeat, you wouldn't know it anyway. It was so little." The next day he got twenty-five lashes instead of death, thanks to someone else who liked him: "The Jewish policeman who was ordered to hit me was a friend who used a rubber hose, not too strong."

The third great miracle was meeting his future wife, Leesa, in a DP camp after the war. She came from a nearby village, and their parents had known each other. He shows me her photo, a dark-haired smiling woman in the middle of grandchildren and great-grandchildren. Images of a thriving family fill the apartment. "And they are my biggest miracle," says Willy, affirming the prayer I used to say with my nursemaid, Mary.

Ha Malach Ha Goel Osi Mikol Ra.
(May the Angel redeem me from all Evil.)

Not the first part, which seems like a bad joke, but the second part—which did come true:

Bless the children so my name and the names of my fathers, Abraham and Issac, be carried on in them and that they may grow into multitudes like the fish of the earth.

Willy moves into the kitchen to stir a big pot of soup. Kitchen jobs, he tells me, saved his life twice in the camps. First, he worked in one "where it was warm and there was an extra turnip or raw potato to eat." He made friends with a boy whose father became the cook and needed workers. "Pick him!" the friend told his dad, and so Willy "stirred pots of thin broth with a wooden stick the size of a boat paddle." Later when he was sent to Buchenwald, he managed again to work over a kitchen stove: "Once again I had luck. A friend who was in charge of the kitchen told me that the next day he could select fifty people to work with him and if I sat in the front row, he would pick me. And he did."

Since his wife died, Willy says, he cooks for himself. He goes to his former butcher shop and they still give him their choicest chicken or beef. "Whenever I come in, they say, 'Take your pick!'" So his soup always has big chunks of meat mixed with broth, vegetables, and potatoes, and he divides it into portions that he can eat all week. Which he does, except when members of his synagogue invite him for dinner, as they often do. "I am lucky," Willy says, "*and* I make a beautiful soup!" His smile, kind and triumphant, is full of the alchemy that turns this man's luck into God's miracle.

14 | FIVE KILOMETERS AWAY

I see an old wooden sign reading TO DORN near Herr Stolle's house and want to follow the dirt trail that my father took daily to high school. Herr Stolle discourages me. Go by car, he says, "not that anything bad is in there . . ." I picture my dad, rucksack on one shoulder, kicking stones without a glance into the dark woods. Worry was not his style. He was optimistic and nervy, which saved him later; but in 1913, at age fourteen, this narrow dirt trail was salvation enough. Dorn was his gateway to the world beyond Benheim with its little ideas. He was a boy with big ideas, and being where *not* everyone knew *everything* about him—and being accepted, Jewish or not—made him feel very German, and quite free. Herr Stolle offers to drive me, but I decline. So far, he has set up all my interviews. But on this visit, my third, I want to see what I can see on my own. Do a kind of compare-and-contrast exercise based on what those beyond the village see from the outside looking in.

What took my dad half an hour on foot takes me five minutes by car. Two lefts and a right over the bridge, and there is Dorn set against a steep hill overlooking the Neckar River. A fortress and a church dominate the high ridge above tiers of red roofs that suggest sturdiness on the edge of picturesque. Dorn's population, which was 5,000 in my father's day, is now 50,000, because since 1996 all surrounding villages including Benheim are under its administration. What remains of official

Benheim, five kilometers away, is the highway road sign and part of a postal address: Benheim-Dorn.

The mayor, Herr Himmel, greets me at the *Rathaus* as if I were royalty, not a random woman who telephoned his office two weeks ago for permission to see the archives. "Of course!" he had boomed so amicably that I pictured a graying, beer-bellied politician, not a slim young man with a round face, reddish hair, and laughing blue eyes. He is the youngest politician in Germany, a liberal who won this conservative district with 60 percent of the vote, according to Herr Stolle, because people like his energy and optimism. With him is a Herr Buchman, "who will take you around and speaks perfect English," says the mayor, also in perfect English. Unlike Herr Stolle, these two seem to enjoy being bilingual and cosmopolitan. I shake hands with a tall man in a button-down shirt and khakis, American style.

"A pleasure to meet you," Herr Buchman says in a clipped British accent that demands cooperation. With a straight back and determined jaw, he leads me to a wall-size aerial view of the region. The mayor disappears. "What you see," says my new guide, "is actually a large, flat plain called the Gau cut up by the river Neckar."

"But I see mountains and forests!"

"That's because the river sawed through the plains, like your Grand Canyon, and we are below the surface—on the wall of a giant crack."

I have always thought of my father's village as a mysterious mountain world, which this annoying man now says is flat as Kansas, only I can't tell because I'm inside looking out. He continues about the Ice Age and soil richness and I start glazing over until I hear, "My father was an ardent Nazi, you know. My grandfather was one of the first supporters of Hitler."

"What?" I say.

"When he and my grandmother married, they not only received the Bible, but *Mein Kampf.* It was their second Bible."

I have no idea how we got from geologic plates to Nazis and *Mein Kampf*, and it must show. He straightens even more. "I was told that you are writing a book about the Jews here," he says. "Is that not correct?"

"Yes, yes, I am." I grope for my tape recorder. "Do you mind?" I ask, thinking he's the first person I ever met who talks openly about a Nazi family history.

"As you wish." He smiles. "In my grandfather's circle, *Mein Kampf* was an automatic wedding present. I still have their copy and dip into it sometimes. It's six hundred pages, a fat book." I'm thinking, *Whoa! Is he a Nazi?* but then he says, "What a lot of crap! How people could believe such rubbish!" I relax. "Hitler was more educated than people think. His quotes came from all over"—I tense—"but he was also uneducated because he lacked a sound moral center." I un-tense.

Herr Buchman is an English teacher at the *Gymnasium*, a latter-day version of my father's high school. Unlike American teachers, he has no duties, he says, like lunch or homeroom, so aside from his three courses, he has time to help the mayor and also do research on his favorite author: Kafka, "the greatest German writer in the twentieth century. He was Jewish, you know." His second favorite is Berthold Auerbach, "one of our best Swabian writers. You heard of him?" I shake my head. He looks surprised. "He was also a Jew." I shrug. "I am curator of the Auerbach Museum in Nordstetten, his birthplace, not far from here. I will take you there if you are interested." Obscure Jewish writers are not why I came here, but I am fascinated with Herr Buchman, his Nazi legacy, and his favorite Jewish authors. "Yes, I'd be delighted to go," I say.

He smiles. "So, now we go to the archives."

I can't help it. I await the click of heels.

We climb up the dusty, cobblestone street, and Herr Buchman points to the water tower across the river. "It was built by my father, who became city architect of Dorn in 1933 when the other man, a Catholic, refused to join the Nazi party." He waves to a boy on an old black bicycle. "My former student, a real *Lausbub*, a stinker," says Herr Buchman, walking with long strides. I struggle to keep up. His classes are full of *Lausbubs*, he says, too many. "German schools are afraid of teaching authoritarian values, so the kids run wild." I nod, having heard this from Otto Stolle, too, but he said it with more tact.

Herr Buchman's father was captured in Russia during the war and was held as a POW until Herr Buchman was ten. "Conveniently, he came home in 1949 *after* the war trials that convicted my uncle." For a second, a tinge of sarcasm replaces his careful neutrality. "We quickly moved away because people resented us, but kept our house. In 1963 I moved back with my new wife, a woman I met as an exchange student in New Orleans. She converted before we returned because it would be impossible to live in Dorn otherwise."

"Otherwise?"

"Being half-Catholic—and with Jewish roots." His "Jewish roots" catches me off guard, which he notices. "You see," he says, "everyone in Germany has a complicated history. My father, an invalid after two strokes, would have a third stroke if he knew his daughter-in-law, who takes care of him every day, is part Jewish! And his grandsons have a Jewish grandfather in São Paolo!"

He grins at this joke against the Master Race, but then turns solemn. "You know, my grandmother, my mother's mother, was also murdered by the Nazis. She became depressed after her husband died, leaving her with five children"—*Who wouldn't be?*—"and the Nazis labeled her as mentally incompetent. They took her away, part of the euthanasia program, and no one in my house was allowed to mention her. I only found this out last year when I discovered the certificate of her so-called death in the bottom of a desk drawer." Now there's a flash of real anger—and then it's gone. The man, who has revealed more family skeletons in thirty minutes than anyone else in hours of interviews, lengthens his strides even more as we climb upward, leaning into the hill.

The archives of Dorn are in underground chambers, and the archivist, I now learn, is on leave to have her fifth child. So all I have are Herr Buchman and the files of Frau Kopf, guarded by a white crib beside her desk. I like the human touch in the middle of bureaucratic efficiency and the innocence of a child's crayon drawing of a train with a fat black smokestack, hanging beneath the harsh fluorescent lights.

We move down aisles of metal stacks, and Herr Buchman hands me File #373 for Modern Jewish Affairs. It's full of news clippings about memorials, Jewish cemeteries, and ceremonies with Israelis. This file was started in 1968, my guide says, when German ties with Israel were just beginning.

Next comes the file for old Jewish history, slimmer than Benheim's, with yellow, crinkled documents that he translates:

1777—a proclamation against usurious Jews.
1811— a building permit that allows a "protected" Jew to add a store to his house.
1815— an announcement that Jewish homeowners had to quarter Napoleon's soldiers.
1875—a complaint by a Jew about ad hoc property taxes.

What strikes Herr Buchman—who wants me to call him Kurt (though he seems more like a Herr Buchman)—is that the Jews became integrated in the 1840s after the Napoleonic laws gave them civil rights. What strikes me is that the archives have special files about the Jews. At home, I am used to disappearing into the majority. Civil rights and affirmative action are essential for blacks and Hispanics, not for Jews like me. These records tell an older story. . . .

There is almost nothing from 1941 to 1945. Newspapers

and documents were burned before the Allies came, says Herr Buchman. He does find a file of memos from 1938. One says:

> Due to the freeing up of Jewish property, it is possible to knock down houses with bad corners so streets can be widened.

The callousness shocks me. At last we can widen the streets! I imagine people walking by as the houses collapsed and thinking: Good riddance. This is the Germany I grew up fearing, the one I expected and haven't yet found in Benheim.

Herr Buchman moves away and returns. "The Nazis didn't find this to destroy!" he says, holding up a small black book that looks like a diary. "Our young mayor found it in the old mayor's office." He opens to the front page, handwritten with a quill pen in an odd calligraphy, and translates: "My name is Paul Knoll, formerly of Alsace, and I am writing this at the request of the authorities of Dorn . . . I am eighty years old and feel unfit for such a task, but I will do my best as a scribe. . . .'" My guide stumbles over the words. Very unlike him. The old German handwriting, he explains, "is long before my time."

Towns such as Dorn commissioned scribes to document the war, but there aren't many records left intact. "This is special!" says my guide, as we thumb through the entries from 1939 to 1944. They read like a ship's log, full of dates, events, and numbers, until we come to one with a heading, "Girl Is Stoned." It describes a Dorn teenager from a good Catholic family being shaved for sleeping with a Polish slave worker. Later, she was publicly stoned for defiling the Master Race.

"Stoned to death?" I ask, thinking of Shirley Jackson's "The Lottery," a short story I like to teach. *This town was certainly mean!* I can't imagine that scene in Benheim. I can't imagine Herr Stolle, Anna, or the Lugers throwing stones.

"The Nazis had control of the youth, remember. Others shut their curtains. If you did more, you would have trouble," says

Herr Buchman. I ask how many Nazis there were in Dorn. "Enough," he says. "The party was powerful here."

Most of the entries are disappointing, full of trivia about rationing laws and new security measures, until we come to the heading "The Last Jews of Benheim," August 19, 1942:

> The last Jews of Benheim were sent to Stuttgart today and from there they would go somewhere to the East.

Two lines, that's it? The previous entry spends three paragraphs on the five bombs that were dropped between 7:15 and 7:25 a.m. The next entry devotes a whole page to the new proclamation that men must stop wearing buttons on their sleeves to save for the war effort. And yet the Jews—they don't say how many—are sent "somewhere to the East" in two lines. Like the collapsed houses, their demise was barely noticed.

We are having lunch, Mayor Himmel and I, and he wants to know why I am writing a book about Benheim. I tell him that the story of the Christians saving the Torah intrigued me. He did know that story, but didn't think anything similar happened in Dorn. Most people, he says sadly, didn't get involved. "Bravery and goodness are not easy," he says, pouring the last of a bottle of Riesling. I tell him about my aunt and uncle being saved by the head of the Gestapo in Stuttgart because he and my uncle played cards together for years. "*Ja*, here is the German split personality," says the young mayor. "To be good and bad at the same time, in the same family, even in the same person." He tells me how his grandfather was good friends with the Jews, but also had an ardent Nazi living on his second floor. "You see, my grandfather owned a pharmacy, and the Jews were both customers and friends. But renting a room was renting a room."

The word *pharmacy* clicks. *His* grandfather must be the man who turned Ilse Loew away on the day after Kristallnacht. I remember her describing how, when she and Harry came home by train, gangs of schoolchildren were roaming the streets with rocks in hand, and the pharmacist took them in. But when the street became silent, he said they must go. He was sorry.

"I heard your grandfather helped Ilse Loew after Kristallnacht," I say, leaving out the betrayal. His eyes are steady and do not look away from the whole story. "Split personality," he says again, and we finish our *Spargel*, the white asparagus that appears every spring and makes every German crazy for it. This *Gasthaus* has a whole *Spargel* menu to choose from—appetizers to desserts.

I'm back with Kurt Buchman, driving to the Berthold Auerbach Museum. As curator, he has his own key, and assures me we can take as long as we like to learn about "Swabia's most famous writer, a true teacher of democracy." He talks as if he and "Berthold" were intimate about everything from politics to love life: "With Augusta it was a very good marriage, not like with Nina, his second wife, who was difficult, a bit demanding but maybe he was also to blame."

The village of Nordstetten, where we are headed, is one of the twelve *Judendörfer* (Jewish villages) in the region, says Kurt, as we wind our way through forest that opens onto fields of pink and white flowers. Now and then, a village not unlike Benheim appears. His father and grandfather must have sneered at that word *Judendörf*, but this Herr Buchman says it benignly. "The local prince invited the Jews to come in the sixteenth century, and they stayed. Three hundred years later, by Auerbach's day, the population of these villages was often half-Jewish. But then many young Jews started leaving for the big cities and only the Germans stayed."

Again, the distinction between Jew and German. "Don't you consider Jews as Germans?" I ask.

"*I*, of course, do," he says evenly, "but *they* did not in those days. Racial anti-Semitism, you know, began not with Hitler, but much earlier. It was the idea of Jews being an alien race, with different blood, bad blood."

"But my father as a boy considered himself 100 percent German. He always said before World War I he felt no anti-Semitism!"

"It is ironic, is it not, how that was both true and not true?"

I think of how 100 percent American I like to feel and wonder how much of that is true. As a child I'd hide behind the front door with a fire poker and Ritz crackers, waiting to crack Danger over the head when it walked in. And I still keep the bathroom door slightly ajar, just in case. *90 percent American? 80 percent?*

The house where Auerbach was born in 1812 is a sturdy gray house with a gated front garden. The Nazis used it as a local headquarters, says Herr Buchman, but now its owner is a Christian woman studying to be a Jew. Again, the split personality. A few blocks farther is a red stone mansion that once belonged to the local count. Windows are cracked and the trim badly needs painting. "No one wants to pay for public spaces like this," my host says and puts the key in the front door of the Auerbach Museum as if he lived there.

"Auerbach, you know, was trying to educate the masses to the need for German democracy." We are climbing what was once a grand staircase that squeaks with every step. "And he did it by telling small stories—not unlike what you are trying to do." That catches my attention. "His most famous book, *Tales of Schwarzwald*, was wildly popular, especially in the big cities. People were nostalgic for the life they left behind, and he told it as it was, the *real* village life of the peasants." I imagine a kindred spirit, 150 years before me. Only his characters live in a richly static world of continuity; mine live in a world of empty spaces they keep trying to fill in.

In the first room, Buchman expounds on memorabilia from Auerbach's baby spoon to a watercolor of local peasantry. I focus on dust floating in sunlight until I hear, "He is one of the few German heroes still considered politically correct." He is pointing to a biography of Frederick the Great that Auerbach wrote "because, like Frederick, he believed in German nationalism, but one ruled by justice like in the American system." My guide sounds so proud, I am liking him better—and his hero Berthold, too.

In the second room, we study photos of Auerbach "in the drawing rooms of the rich and famous of Berlin—publishing people, aristocracy, media people, he knew them all." In one group picture of maybe thirty people, two arrows are pointing to two heads. One is Auerbach, smiling; the other is a scowling face in a French beret. "That is Fontane, an anti-Semitic author, a peer of Auerbach." What amazes Buchman is that the two men were attending the same literary party in 1866. What amazes me are the arrows, and how Jew and anti-Semite are both marked for public display. Where else but in today's Germany would you find the conflict clearly labeled in a glass case? Other countries would keep this photo, without arrows, in a locked closet.

"Berthold Auerbach died a broken man, his life a tragedy," my host says to my surprise. Things seemed to be going well for him, but Buchman says no. "By 1882, Berthold knew his vision of a united Germany of Jews, Catholics, and Protestants living together and honoring the Fatherland was dead. A new kind of anti-Judaism, defined by race, had taken hold, and the ideas of *Mein Kampf* were already waiting for Hitler, who was born seventeen years later." I do the math as we move along and realize Hitler was born within months of my father.

Post museum, we sit in a café on a cliff jutting out over the Neckar River. The waitress is looking stern because in Dorn at 6:00 p.m., one doesn't linger over *Apfelkuchen* and *Kaffee*. But Kurt (the name is feeling more comfortable) seems in no hurry. He takes a leisurely bite of flaky crust wrapped around warmed apples and talks about life right after the war.

"My father didn't starve as a POW, because he was small and wiry. 'It was the big men who starved!' he kept telling me when he came back, very, very thin. I hadn't seen him in seven years." For once, Kurt sounds sad. This, after all, is *his* story, not Frederick's or Auerbach's. He takes another bite of *kuchen* to soothe old memories, and I think of how my father, also a big man, escaped Kurt's grandfather and father—and lived to eat big plates of meat and potatoes in Queens. "It's also a wonder," Kurt continues, "that my mother and I didn't starve. The French commandeered our house and we had only an hour to get out. I don't know how my mother survived with no husband, no livelihood, no house." I think of all the Jews who told me the same thing: that they didn't know how they survived. "Luckily, there was farmland all around. My mother grew onions and traded them for milk from the farmers. And then she took the seeds from the green ears of corn that we gleaned all summer and made a sack of flour, four hands high. It lasted us the winter, every winter for ten years."

Now the waitress is wiping tables around us, glaring, but he continues, "Do you know Millet's painting *The Gleaners?*" I nod. "Two peasant women are stooped over, another is half-standing. Well that was I, gleaning and bowing!" He leans closer, to help me enter that field of gathering. "We spent our summers following the peasants as they harvested the corn. My mother had made a special apron, kangaroo style, for carrying. It was red, probably from a Nazi flag. We were not allowed to use scissors to harvest, for cutting the stalks would be stealing. We could only use our hands, like birds picking up crumbs."

That story triggers others about his mother's friend being burned in a train station bombing, and his diving into the woods when shot at. And one about a little wagon. "My mother bought it with all our savings to drag coal seven kilometers so we'd have heat that winter. All was fine until a rain shower surprised us, turning wheels we thought sturdy into cardboard."

I feel for this man who was a starving boy and for his mother who lost her sister, and even for the tired, scowling waitress who closes the blinds, comes over—all smiles—and says sharply that we must go. The young mayor was right about indifference and empathy. I feel both; they can coexist in one person at one time.

I find Auerbach's *Tales of Schwarzwald* in my local library. His stories of love and thwarted love are set in rich Schwarzwald splendor. Men "in fur caps with gold tassels and blue jackets, scarlet vests" woo girls who become brides in "a crown of glittering silver foil with hair . . . tied in red silk ribbons. . . ." I always pictured my father's world in the blacks, browns, and grays of obligation, but here is this countryside of "yellow rapeseed blossoming among green rye fields, while the skylark trills his gladness, and the thistle finch sits on a twig of a cherry tree." This beauty is what my father and the other Benheim Jews seemed to miss most in exile—and one that, until reading Auerbach, I never imagined in full color.

I did expect more of a window into Jewish life, but Auerbach mentions it only in passing: "A knot of boys had collected there, including George and his old friend, a Jew, commonly called 'Long Hartz.'" His focus is on a larger definition of German: how *all* Germans must stick together for justice. In "The Axe Story," my favorite, the hero, Buchmaier, opposes a new law that undermines civil rights and gets others to follow him. If only, knowing the future, more Germans would have taken Auerbach's tale of long-ago resistance to heart.

From this day on, the story begins, men can no longer carry axes, according to an ordinance, that rescinds a right people had "for time immemorial." A crowd gathered, muttered, and shook their heads—"these are our privileges"—but they would have acquiesced if it wasn't for Buchmaier, who "marched up to the ordinance and took his axe in his right hand and with a Whew, he struck it into the board in the middle of the ordinance." He said to everyone: "We are citizens and without our consent no such ordinances can be passed and everyone who agrees should strike their axe into the board as well. . . . By degrees, all the village assembled and everyone contributed his stroke amid shouts and laughter." The judge stormed and wanted to lock everyone up, but Buchmaier said there can be no locking up without a trial for everyone. And how could you lock up everyone anyway? After many threats and posturing, "the men carried their axes on their left arms as they had done before."

Unfortunately, there were few Buchmaiers to strike their axes at Nazi injustice. Instead, people turned away, and if someone did speak out, like the man in Benheim's church, no one joined him publicly. So Buchmaier's warning to the judge came true for everyone. "If judges like you continue making so many unjust laws," Buchmaier prophesied long before death camps, crematoriums, euthanasia, and Catholic girls stoned by a crowd, "you'll end by putting a policeman under every tree to keep it from quarreling with the wind and drinking too much when it rains."

15 | KATHERINE OF DORN

And while the great and wise decay,

And all their trophies pass away,

Some sudden thought, some careless rhyme

Still floats above the wrecks of Time.

William Lecky

"Come in, come in!" say a handsome, silver-haired couple in their late sixties, in German. "Welcome to our sanctuary!" And it is—literally. This four-story mansion that sits on the curve of Dorn's busiest street was built in 1301 as a convent for aging nuns, according to a stone plaque in the courtyard of fading chrysanthemums. Two days ago I asked Kurt Buchman who else in Dorn, besides him, might be willing to talk about the Hitler years, and today we are ringing the doorbell of Paul and Katherine Schutz. "Katherine will be full of stories," he said, "especially about her grandfather, a big anti-Nazi." Given that background, I have high hopes to learn much more about Nazi times in the Schwarzwald.

Antique chests and clocks line the walls of the entry hall. Oriental rugs add warmth on days like this when no sunlight streams down from the high windows above the stairwell. A lovely, hand-carved chest, a graceful grandfather clock, and wonderful etchings and watercolors, all impeccably placed, bring to mind sophisticated New Yorkers more than Germans in a provincial town down the road from Benheim.

Katherine has lived in this house since 1936, she says, as Kurt translates what, so far, I already understand. Her father owned the jewelry shop next door and bought this twenty-nine-room edifice. She leads us up a wide staircase to a huge room with Gothic windows and a high domed ceiling covered with a mural. "We restored it!" Katherine says proudly. "It was painted right after the Thirty Years' War." I look up at the reds, blues, and golds of Europe's bloodiest war, fought between Protestants and Catholics four hundred years ago, and see everything rich in detail. Nothing seems faded.

More wondrous antiques, including a massive breakfront that reminds me of the one we had in Queens. I remember how it loomed over our small dining room, like the foreigner it was, shipped across the Atlantic with other furniture, equally dark and huge, into my American world. I wanted them gone, replaced by sleek blond modern like my friend Maddie had; but my parents shook their heads, absolutely not. Too many memories to sell, just like that.

Katherine seats us on beautifully carved oak chairs placed around a matching oak table and offers us wine and cheese. "Later is better," Kurt says, much to my delight. I realize that he, the son and grandson of Nazis, is planning a long visit with his friend, the granddaughter of an anti-Nazi. And I'm here with them, amazed that by my saying "I'm writing a book!" they have let me enter their world.

Paul brings in two bottles of red wine—French—and some finely fluted wine glasses. We must drink, he insists. He is a tall, slim man, but sturdy—with sea blue eyes, both shrewd and kind. "So what do you want to know?" he asks, pouring the wine. There's an honesty in the air that makes me skip the euphemisms and get to the point. "I want to find out what happened after 1939. Whatever stories you have, especially about the Jews, would be great!"

Katherine nods, her black eyes full of promise. She is tall, regal, and unadorned except for a touch of lipstick that she doesn't even need. Her silver hair, pulled into a tight bun, has just a hint of disorder—a few loose strands hang down—that I trust more than perfection. I expect her to jump into the past, but instead she launches into a lively account of how people scolded her for not playing the organ at church today, just so she could be here with me. "'It is over! Done with! It's time to forget the whole thing!' they said to me. And on and on and on."

"These people are still in denial," says Paul, already flushed from a half glass of wine. He seems to light up after three sips, like me.

"Absolutely," says Kurt.

"I told them we have to remember everything, *very* carefully." Katherine now turns to me. "We must go back to the stories of the Old Testament, the first Bible, the Jewish stories." She looks solemn. "They are important, they are history, and should be in our minds at all times, like myths. Like the Jews telling the story of leaving Egypt and being delivered from slavery, so we have to tell this story of Germany and never forget."

She's become more animated with each word, as if responding to her own pep talk. She then tells what must be a favorite family story: "Whenever my father said, '*Heil* Hitler!' my grandfather said, '*Grüss Gott*' [Greetings]!" Her black eyes dance. "And he did it to everyone—well, not quite. But whenever the doorbell rang I remember being terrified they were coming to take him away."

Her words echo Hedwig in Benheim, who feared for her father's safety after he drove a Jew to Switzerland. But Hedwig made herself a martyr, emphasizing how she became an outcast in school. I hear none of that in Katherine's story—only kudos for bravery and honesty at a time when they were in short supply.

"Did you notice the Holy Trinity painted outside the house?" she asks, still beaming. Her grandfather painted it in 1938 and the Nazis immediately destroyed it because *Yaweh* in Hebrew letters was painted into one corner. "They came in a truck, climbed high on a ladder, and sprayed the whole wall with a black tar. People came into my father's shop for days, crying over the desecration. The church even had an expiation service."

Paul is pouring wine again and Katherine smiles broadly, lifting her glass, her cheeks also flushed: "After the war, he quickly restored it, even asked the priest for the correct Hebrew spellings. That's how my grandfather was." And Paul says, "Hear, Hear!" clicking her glass. We all sip. I make a note to look at the mural carefully on my way out.

More stories follow about Katherine's grandfather holding secret meetings in the basement every Friday night to listen to the BBC. All the priests from nearby villages came to listen. They knew him because he painted their churches and repaired their altars. They trusted each other. I ask how he avoided being sent to a concentration camp, knowing that Germans were arrested for listening to foreign news. "They were, absolutely!" Katherine laughs. "But *he* was not. They interrogated him several times—at party headquarters or town hall, I'm not sure where—but he still had the BBC going!" I swallow more wine, thinking what great people these are, much bolder than in Benheim.

Paul, who had left again, reappears with a large leather book. It is the collected art works of Katherine's grandfather. He flips quickly through wonderful Schwarzwald landscapes to a page with a scowling devil with a mustache. Kurt leans over and translates the caption: "The Devil as Hitler: Hitler as the Devil—carved in wood, 1938."

Katherine is all smiles. "When he painted the Devil with Hitler's face, the priest said, 'You can't get away with that.' But my grandfather said, 'Don't worry! It will be high up. No one will notice him.' And they didn't! So now it is in this book!"

She speaks the way I do when telling my father's escape stories. Small victories, small heroes, but much better than Kurt's legacy of a father and grandfather who are perennial villains. This art book is Katherine's proof that her family really was anti-Nazi. No one can whisper, "Oh, she just says that *now!*" for her grandfather's bust of Hitler as Devil is on the page (and in that church!). I scribble down the title quickly. It will be my proof, too, for those who say I'm naïve.

Fascinating stuff, but no one has yet mentioned the Jews. "Did your grandfather's need to resist Hitler extend to the Jews?" I ask, feeling warm, finally, in these old rooms that deny the June day outside.

"Oh, my father had many Jewish friends!" Katherine says. "They all came into his shop to talk and listen to records on his gramophone. Especially the women. He was a fine craftsman, charming, and they loved the music. The store was called Sigmund Rheinhundt."

"A typical Gypsy name," says Paul, opening bottle three, a Merlot. He has also brought in a feast of cheeses, also French, and cherry tomatoes. "From the garden, sweet as candy."

Cherry tomato in hand, Katherine tells how a Gypsy woman came into a village called Signoiner Talle (Gypsy Vale) and had a child, Katherine's great-great-grandfather. He became an itinerant blacksmith who did kettle and tool mending for the farmers, and his son, her great-grandfather, married "very well into Dorn society." But Katherine still inherited those Gypsy eyes, "and they stopped me from playing Mary Magdalene in a church play as a child. Too black for the part!" She sounds amused. Her family was evidently wealthy enough and Catholic enough to escape the fate of tens of thousands of "too black" Gypsies who were murdered by the Nazis.*

It's been two hours, and my eyelids are getting heavy. "Anything else you remember about the Jews?" I ask, thinking we should go soon. *That chair across the room, those soft brown pillows, look good for curling into. This oak chair is too hard.*

---

*Between 20 and 50 percent of all Gypsies—220,000 to 550,000—were killed in concentration camps, according to the *Holocaust Chronicle.*

Katherine sits up. She remembers a Jewish day laborer from Benheim who was assigned to them by the authorities. It made her parents uncomfortable, but the Jews needed work in order to eat. Their money was gone. "What else could we do for them?" she asks as if imitating her mother, long ago. This man Willy, she says, "wore a Jewish star and ate at the round table. Sometimes I would sit with the grownups when they ate, but we children were told, 'Never, never say that he ate with us!' If someone rang the bell, we put the plates away very quickly because you weren't allowed to feed the Jews like that." Now I sit up. Could she mean *my* Willy? From Baltimore? He never mentioned Katherine's family, but how many Jewish Willys lived in Benheim? I will call him when I get back. He'll be amazed. I want to tell Katherine that, but she has started talking about the deportation and "the Jews coming down the road carrying their suitcases, their heads down. And the Hitler Youth marching around them singing a song, something like 'Die Juden sind daher, daher . . .' (The Jews are here, here)." Her voice fades off. "I have never told anyone this story," she says quietly, "the way I lay in bed, the moonlight, hearing that song, afraid to move. . . ." We are silent. I think of Willy and his brothers and parents passing under her window. "I was only a child," Katherine says. "It was night." Kurt has stopped translating, and I can't help myself: I wonder if he'd been one of the boys singing. Or Paul, who is standing again.

Katherine brightens and, as if to erase the grimness, says coquettishly, "Maybe I shouldn't tell you this . . ." She looks at Paul. "About the matzo?" He nods consent and she tells how a Jewish neighbor gave her a piece of matzo and her father made her take it right back, saying, "*My* daughter isn't going to eat matzo!" She imitates his sharp authority. "But I did it anyway! It was delicious!" She loves being like her defiant grandfather, just as I love being like my fearless father. We wrap their stories of bravery around us like a cloak and hope for the best.

Paul says this rejection of matzo "was purely on religious

grounds, not racial." Kurt nods vigorously, and all agree that her father "was not against the Jewish people like the Nazis. Only against their religion."

Religious anti-Semitism! Racial anti-Semitism! They end up the same, I want to say—and know the perfect quote to make my case, something Martin Luther wrote five hundred years ago that paved the way for Hitler. But it's beyond remembering now. Later, at home, I will find it again in "On the Jews and Their Lies," written in 1543:

> What should we Christians do with this contemptible, damned people the Jews? . . . I will give my true advice. [They] should throw brimstone and pitch upon them; if one could hurl hell fire at them, so much the better. . . . Let their synagogues and schools be set afire. . . . Let their houses be similarly razed and burned."

I think about sending it to all of them, but get stuck on what note I could write: "FYI, Mimi"?

Talk drifts from matzo to furniture and silverware, and I run my fingers along the carved grooves of the table, smooth, worn, no splinters here. I hear Katherine say, "The Strassburgers asked us to ship them their china dishes. They were very valuable, you know, and such a beautiful rich blue, with white trim. I remember helping my mother wrap it up in brown paper." Now I am awake. Who are the Strassburgers? The name sounds Jewish.

The family owned a shoe store down the street, Katherine says, and Frau Strassburger and her mother were good friends. When the family needed cash to leave Germany, she begged Katherine's parents to buy their property and also to ship their dishes to a relative in America. That was the last her mother heard—until a postcard arrived from America ten years later. Frau Strassburger wrote how much the family still enjoyed their dishes, and that she hoped everyone had survived the war and the house was still standing. Katherine's mother wrote back that they had not been bombed, and she and her six children were okay.

I love how the two kept in touch, these friends. "We began to receive packages of clothing from the Strassburgers, much needed. You know we had no wood those early years. And we thought how well the Strassburgers have done in America! They are rich people, and so fast. Only years later, when they came back for a visit, did we find out how little money they'd had. He was an elevator operator and she sold Avon products. Who would have thought such a thing? It goes to my heart every time I think of it."

I love the ripple effect of kindness, the Golden Rule alive and well with these two families, despite Hitler. It even spread beyond them: "Because of their generosity," Katherine says solemnly, "I now send packages to East Germany to help the poor there." Her open face confirms every word.

"What a great story!" I say.

"Nothing like that happened in my family," says Kurt, glumly. "Or in most German families."

Paul is silent and Katherine takes another cherry tomato. "I remember Frau Strassburger sitting here at our table, in that chair, worried to death if she would get out of Germany alive." Katherine leans toward me. "In fact—and I've never told anyone this—our dining room set belonged to the Wolfsheimers, another Jewish family who also begged us to buy from them so they'd have money to leave."

I lift both arms off the table as if electrocuted. I want to leap across the room into that brown chair. *Wait! The Strassburgers'?* Or onto the gray couch. *The Wolfsheimers'?* Suddenly, this lovely, tasteful room feels like a museum of the dead, even when I learn that those who owned these antiques aren't dead. The Strassburgers live in New York and the Wolfsheimers in Chicago, says Katherine, not realizing my revulsion to her trophies of history. I picture homes all over the Schwarzwald like this, full of Jewish rugs and chests and dining room tables that beautify without context or story.

Except that this oak table has its story, and so does the Wolfsheimers' silver. "They wanted to give us a gift," Katherine says cheerfully, "but my parents insisted to pay them." There's pride, not apology, in possession. I try to make peace with her antiques, but my arms stay off the old table.

Paul heads out the door again and returns with two fur jackets on hangers. "Here's what the Strassburgers sent us. Can you imagine?" He twirls them in the air. "Katherine wore this one to our engagement party and she looked New York chic in it. Still does." Katherine puts it on, a black hairy fur, maybe dyed fox, and walks regally around the chair. They want me to try it on, but I say no. They insist. Their faces are urging, as if the whole visit depends on this. I give in, slipping my arms into the torn silk lining, the smell of mothballs mixing with death.

Soft edges of fur brush my neck, and I take the thing off quickly, feeling the lining silently tear away more of their proof of expiation. They keep smiling broadly, full of the warmth these furs of forgiveness gave them through harsh postwar winters. I want to hold onto their version of truth, but suspicions whisper: Would poor immigrants really send furs, heavy bulky furs, from America?

Nothing about Katherine signals deception. So maybe, I tell myself, *she* was deceived. After all, she was a child, and if her parents invented the fur story, how would she know? Or maybe, like the four stories of the Torah, the real facts got shifted in the retelling? Her mother might have bought the furs elsewhere. The Strassburgers might have sent a wool coat that became a fur, because fur makes a better story. And people like Katherine and me eagerly scoop the good stories up, especially when their proof hangs in the closet.

We are leaving when Paul points to two side chairs and an end table that his family got from Jews. He says he doesn't often admit this because people say: "*Ach*, you bought them for a song!"

"But that is not so!" says Katherine indignant. "The Jews begged us to take these things, so they would have money to go!" she repeats more urgently this time, as she leads us to the front door. It is night now, we've been here that long.

In Benheim, I was told, people did not go to the state auctions of Jewish things left behind. They thought it would dishonor the Jews to buy anything, according to Herr Stolle. And no home I was in had rooms of antiques like these, only one piece here or there. A silver spoon Frau Loewenstein left Frau Gekler. A small gray cabinet Frau Pressman left the grocer's wife; it's in her daughter's hallway. Maybe they were gifts of gratitude, maybe they were pieces of abandoned or stolen lives. Or good bargains, like my Waterford glasses that I bought years ago at a New Jersey auction. Fifty years later, who is to know? They must be as old as this oak table and we use them without a historic thought.

Come back soon, Paul and Katherine tell me, shaking my hand vigorously. Next time I am in Dorn, I must stay with them. "We have twenty-nine rooms to choose from." I think of the nuns once living here in austerity, without the lush Oriental rug we are standing on as we say goodbye. And then, suddenly . . . *If Katherine's grandfather didn't have enough money to be a full-time artist, how did he buy these expensive things?* I worry, but smile, as Paul and Katherine shut the heavy oak door studded with its black nails.

Outside, over a large clock, I see the Holy Trinity. I must have passed by many times, as I drove to and from Benheim, absorbing its rich colors and golden halo of charm on a busy main street. No evidence of black tar. That's long gone, Kurt says. "This mural—indeed, all the public murals—have been recently restored in this town that is prospering."

Back in the States, I ask Hannah if I could meet the Strassburgers, but find they died a few years earlier. I tell her the story of the furs and my skepticism that poor Jews would send heavy furs to German neighbors in 1946. "Yes, that was unusual," she says, and Lotte and Gretl agree. We are having another kaffeeklatsch. "But not impossible! We were so grateful to be alive—and some spoke of wanting to pay back those who helped." None of these women had sent such packages.

"Katherine says those fur jackets were a thank-you," I say, "for packing and sending Mrs. Strassburger's good dishes to America."

"*Ach*, yes, I remember those dishes!" says Hannah with delight. "I once visited the Strassburger house for a Hanukkah party, or maybe it was a wedding—and how grand and worldly everything was!" Her eyes light up and I imagine a lively red-headed child in her best dress with matching velvet ribbons. She is standing before a dozen fancy cakes and tortes filled with fruits and cream, arranged in splendor at a giant table, maybe oak, maybe not, but it is well shined. "I remember eating on those dishes here too, in their little apartment on 176th Street," says Hannah. "They were sooo beautiful those plates, a cobalt blue!" her voice riding on one small pleasure of continuity that survived from one life to another.

16 | TRUTH TRANSPOSED

I call Willy in Baltimore to see if he remembers Katherine's grandfather. He says vaguely. When I tell the mural story with the Hebrew writing, he remembers more. "Ah yes, the man was religious—and a big anti-Nazi. I think he made gravestones."

"Actually, he made church altars."

"Gravestones, church altars, what's the difference?" Willy says, the irony resonating, maybe on purpose, maybe not. I'm not sure.

I tell him how Katherine remembers him eating lunch with the family and how she stood guard to warn if anyone came while he was sitting at their round table. "But I never worked for them," Willy says, amused. "The Jews did forced labor on farms, roads, and railroads. We weren't assigned to jewelry shops in Dorn."

"But she remembers you," I say, trying to save my story. "There wasn't another Willy Weinberger, was there?" I know I'm grabbing for straws. Katherine is just wrong.

"Actually, there was. My uncle, but he left for Palestine in 1938. He's long dead."

Willy starts talking again about his farm family in Sulz, how they fed him so well and let him go home on Shabbat—and I realize that, oddly enough, his story confirms Katherine's. True, it was a farm family, not her family, that was humane to him, and another Willy, not him, who was fed in Katherine's kitchen at the family table. But despite the inconsistencies of fact, the emotional memories hold. Non-Jews were nice to one or two Jewish Willys. And Katherine's grandfather was a big anti-Nazi, even if church altars were transposed into gravestones.

I write Kurt Buchman, asking him to ask Katherine more about Willy. Months go by, and just when I'm sure there is no Willy connection, I receive a letter from Kurt (along with an article he wrote on Kafka) and this bit of research:

A Jew called Weinberger worked for the local contractor Marquant and in this capacity worked at Katherine's house. Her mother invited him to share their meals, which was forbidden under the Nazis, so she warned Weinberger to hide in the coal cellar in case the doorbell rang. It never happened.

Was this Willy's uncle before he left for Palestine? Or another Weinberger from Dorn? *Or a Weingarten, or a Weintraub, or a Rindberger . . . ?*

17 | WHAT WILLY'S NEIGHBOR SAYS . . .

We've been talking for an hour before she mentions, as a young girl, keeping the kitchen fires going on the Jewish Sabbath for the Weinbergers next door. "You knew Willy?" I ask, delighted with another intersection of stories. "I met him in America! He's doing very well for almost eighty!" Frau Bidner of Benheim nods, as if his survival after deportation is no surprise. She continues with the past. "Willy was the same age as my brother, a fine type, gentle and kind, not like Sigfried. He was more aggressive, always teasing the girls. Many were afraid of him." Her favorite, and everyone else's it seems, was the youngest, Eric. "*Ach*, what a sweet little charmer he was! He would come into our shop, always wanting something—a notebook, an eraser. His mother would shush him. 'Be quiet! There is a war on!' And one time, I'll never forget, he answered, 'Then I'll go and ask my grandfather for money and buy it myself!' Such a *Lausbub*, a sweet *Lausbub*. Who could say no to him?" She says *Lausbub* with a little laugh, her hand over her mouth as she recalls the imp with pleasure. I look for sadness in the laugh, that little Eric died in Riga, but it is not part of this story.

Frau Bidner still lives in the family house of her childhood. I take her picture in the doorway, a white-haired, robust woman with an unburdened face. Her family was "the only Christian family on this street of Jews," she says, with no attempt to sweeten up that fact the way Anna, Herr Stolle, and the Lugers might do. Her mother ran a small grocery store and her father, a tailor, died suddenly in 1925, leaving no income to care for six children. The Jews, she says with equal matter-of-factness, helped them through that terrible time, buying goods in their shop, making meals for them, even lending some money. I think of Willy's mother making potato soup "to keep the Gentiles kindly." Was the big pot for Frau Bidner's family? And was her kindness returned years later when the Weinbergers were trapped in Benheim?

Evidently, yes. Frau Bidner remembers her mother helping as much as she could during Nazi times. There were special days when Jews were to come into the shop for food, but she gave to the Weinbergers on other days, too—or, rather, at night in the back of the house. Once, someone saw her and she got in trouble, but she said to the Nazi mayor: "You have already taken my two sons to the Front, and if you take me, then take my two small children and then you'll be done with all of us!" She continued giving food at night and had no more trouble, her daughter says. There are no heroics or pride. That is what her mother did. End of story.

She was eleven when Kristallnacht occurred, and she remembers a big noise that she thought was Otto the baker tearing down his oven. Smoke was outside her window and she wanted to look, but a man in civilian clothes was outside shouting, "Close the windows and don't look out!" She kept peeking anyway but couldn't see much. "I do remember hearing Frau Loewenstein calling out the window, 'Our synagogue is burning! How terrible!' And no one answering her." Her words evoke a terrible loneliness in me, how suddenly neighbors abandoned neighbors as shutters closed, the spirit of community disappearing in the silence.

But Frau Bidner does not linger in that moment; she moves on to the next day when "the synagogue was still smoking and her mother said, 'Don't go there!'" The children went anyway. And then to school where their teacher, "the one who wasn't a

Nazi," ordered them to go to the synagogue and help clean up. "We were to save what we could. We were to take the money that was in a cigar box and other things in the building to where the Jewish baths were." His orders were *not* to take any of the money, and they obeyed. But later that day, an SA man came to school with a different message. "He told us to go and break all the windows of the Jews. I was happy because I had the day off from school, but my mother kept me home and put me to work."

Here are the forces that Willy blamed for turning children into Nazis: the indoctrination that encouraged violence, even ordered it. The teacher who tried to preserve decency had no chance against the SA man's demands to hate and act on it—no matter what parents who disapproved thought.

One thing Frau Bidner's story doesn't confirm: Willy's belief that people were too ashamed to say goodbye. Frau Bidner's reason, probably passed down from her mother, is decorum. Goodbyes would be too emotional. "I was sleeping at the time but remember someone wanting to have a flour sack for packing. And there were no big goodbyes—the Jews didn't want that . . . but I think my mother said some sort of goodbye anyway."

Maybe her mother was the woman Willy remembers crying in the shadows, but I doubt it. If the families had been close, they'd want to know about each other now: they'd have questions about family, job, health, children. Nothing. Not from Frau Bidner when I mentioned Willy in Baltimore. Not from Willy when I call to say I met the daughter of the grocer next door. All he says is, "We liked the Jewish grocer down the street better. The one next to us wasn't kosher." Maybe that's religion speaking, but I suspect anger, the same one that made Lotte *not* answer the Lugers' postcard. It's how I'd feel about good neighbors who convince themselves so easily that the families next door, who are forced to leave their homes forever, don't *really* want a goodbye.

18 | THE RED ALBUM

I am sitting in Inge Wolfmann's farmhouse in Benheim, flipping through her red album. I see photos of a girl with blond braids standing beside a hay wagon, lovely and laughing. I see six little girls in white Communion dresses, surrounded by nuns with long, white, stiff collars curving upward. I see a family dressed for church, sitting on a stone fence in a meadow of wildflowers. I see a group of teenagers dressed in satin costumes and outrageous hats holding a sign: December 1938. Except for one young man in uniform, there is no hint of Hitler or the black swastika on the hill, or the synagogue torched a month before the costume party photo. No sign of any Jews either, I think, annoyed at the festive smiles, so full of celebration.

"*Ach*, I remember the Jews like yesterday!" says Inge, returning from the kitchen, tray of water glasses in hand. I shut the album. "Especially on their Sabbath, those beautiful melodies they sang." She has the same girlish smile of the photos, now in a woman, angular and spare, with no round curves except for the upward sweep of thinning hair into a neat bun. What was blond has turned gray, but she is full of youthful energy—ever since she greeted us at the door, shepherded us down the narrow hall past the kitchen ("Oh, it's not fit for such guests as you!"), and seated us on this well-worn brown sofa, plumping its pillows.

I am here because Herr Stolle was not to be outdone. When I told him I met Katherine of Dorn, whose grandfather was a big anti-Nazi, he said, "The Wolfmanns of Benheim were bigger anti-Nazis, and Inge has even better stories. She worked for the Jews!" Until now he has only introduced me to the middle-class tradesmen who once ran the post office, the barbershop, and the bus service. But I've never met the farmers who owned the land they worked, but were cash poor in the village economy. I'd see them in the upper village in front of old wells and splintery barns—they'd stare, I'd stare—and I'd wonder what they thought of the Jews, especially during Nazi times.

With me is Carole, a close friend of Sonya in Frankfurt. When she heard about my project and the rescued Torah story, she volunteered to come with me to Benheim and translate. Within two minutes, I realize how much more than bilingual fluency she offers. "Ooh, it's your birthday next week! Happy birthday!" she says to Inge, who had a phone call of congratulation that we couldn't help but overhear. "And are you sixty-five yet?" she says with enthusiasm that matches Inge's, as if no one else in the world counts.

"I'll be seventy-eight!" Inge beams, gratefully, and pulls up a straight-back chair opposite us. Her smooth cheeks show no signs of the hard farm work that, she says, became her life once World War II started. With no father or brother to tame the horses and plow the fields, she and her two older sisters had to do everything, and after they married, Inge and her mother did it all. "I am a farmer's daughter, still to this day," she says proudly, "even if my farming is now just my garden."

The family farm was sold in the 1980s because their neighbors—who no longer farm—complained of noisy tractors and the smell of manure. Inge now lives on one side of the family house; her son, a plumber, on the other; and tenants live in the middle. Their old barn has become someone's house with a swimming pool full of children jumping in and out as we speak, their delight noisier than any tractor.

"You have seen Herr Stolle's wonderful book, yes?" Inge points to a fat gray book that lies next to the red album. I nod.

Herr Stolle just sent me a copy—a four-hundred-page tome, published with the help of a couple from Stuttgart who bought an old farmhouse near the Jewish cemetery. They wondered who was buried there, met Herr Stolle with his eight years of research, joined forces, and today Benheim has a glossy hard-cover book worthy of New York City in size and number of high-quality illustrations. Two-thirds of his book consists of photographs of Jewish gravestones; the rest is devoted to speeches, articles, and memorabilia related to Benheim's Jews: 1645–1942. The villagers, once hostile to his research, are delighted with the result: a story of shared history made tangible. There is more talk since it is out, I'm told—old-timers remembering, young people asking questions. It must please Herr Stolle, though he hasn't said that to me.

Beneath his book is Inge's "Juden" file. *Does everyone have one?* She shows us a wedding announcement from a Gideon in London, an article about a memoir published by someone's daughter in Berlin, and one about someone's grandson in Brooklyn starring in a German movie about a Nazi general. *Could that be true?* I see a photo of a savvy young boy, dark-haired, dark-eyed, not one bit "Aryan."

"A Jew playing a Nazi? You couldn't make that story up," I whisper to Carole, who is chatting in German, nonstop, with Inge. You'd never know that Carole's father, a rising Jewish socialist, had to escape through the kitchen window in 1933, an hour before the Nazis were at his front door. You'd never know that Carole, born in England, had to follow her father back to Frankfurt in 1953—she was ten—so he could take part in "building the new democratic Germany." With her enormous smile, she enchants older Germans such as Inge; and there's no hint of blame emanating from her, as from me. She doesn't assume that all Germans over sixty are guilty until proven innocent, preferring historian Sebastian Haffner's view that "the first country to be occupied by the Nazis was not Austria or Czechoslovakia. It was Germany." So she nods at the Nazi/Jewish movie star story. Perfectly possible. Why should I doubt it? I see that she will be my new barometer to measure truth against my skepticism, waiting below the surface of my smile.

Inge tells us that as a child she worked "down the hill" where the wealthier Jews lived. She thought of them all as "aristocracy because they had things like balconies and doorbells." She remembers with a childlike awe. "And they had table linen, and silver, and cheese with red rind. And wondrous strange holidays where they built huts in their gardens covered with beech branches and ate sponge cakes and cream cakes, fancy stuff, and lived there for days. And they made wondrous bread called *Berches* with poppy seeds on top. All three of us, it turns out, had childhoods full of this good bread. Inge says she loved the recipe with milk, but "the Jews preferred the other. A matter of taste!" she assumes, until Carole explains that Jews who are kosher don't mix milk and meat, hence, the *Berches* without milk. "I never knew that!" Inge exclaims. "All those years!" The way she claps her hands with this revelation makes me smile. She is so guileless, easy to relax with.

Inge knows what Jews liked to eat and what rituals they observed, but the *why* of religion stays behind a wall of difference, respected without curiosity. "A peaceful boundary," is how Hannah put it, making me think of Robert Frost's "Good fences make good neighbors." His line seems to fit the religious/social life of Benheim, even though it runs counter to my own New Jersey experience—our block parties spill across everyone's lawns—and also counter to Carole's life. She grew up in a Germany with almost no Jews, so no tall fences. She still tries to live that way, which explains her close friendship with Sonya, a Protestant whose father was a train official in Poland during the war. No, seeing Germans as individuals is not a problem for Carole.

Working for the Jews keeps coming up in Inge's stories. Her family did not socialize with them, so she never exchanged holiday cards after the war "like some of the higher-ups of the village." I hear no conscious resentment, but some of her memories, though often couched in humor, make me squirm. She tells about having to find Frau Esslinger's lost false teeth in the sewage pit: "The good woman had a bad stomach and when she vomited, her teeth fell out." And about having to go to the blind Levy to bring manure for his garden. And about how she went to old Frau Baum's at three in the morning—"there was no choice because, by then, working for Jews wasn't allowed"—and she had to be brave, a young girl walking home alone, in the night.

Hitler seduced many Germans with his "What's theirs (the Jews') should be ours!" propaganda, but not Inge's family. Maybe because God fills her house, literally. Jesus hangs, almost life-size, from a wooden cross on one wall of this tiny living room, and on another wall is a framed picture of baby Jesus in the manger. The side table has a giant white candle with WER BETET IST NIE ALLEIN (He who prays is never alone). Being a good Christian seems central to Inge's actions, peppering conversation with "the right thing to do." Her family didn't like Hitler because he competed with the Church—and that's also why she and her sisters refused to join the BDM, the Hitler Youth group for girls. "The Catholic youth group was enough for us," she says, revealing how strongly her family resistance was grounded in her Catholic faith.

The local Catholic church seemed to support this anti-Nazi ethos. In 1933 the Catholic bishop of nearby Rotenberg spoke out publicly against Hitler. His house was attacked by Nazis, his bed defecated on, and he was whisked off to Rome at Göring's request. But his moral example lingered. In 1934 the Benheim nuns, who doubled as nurses, were reassigned to another village because they continued to care for sick Jews against the Nazi mayor's orders. And in 1941 it was the Benheim priest, I found out, who spoke out in church and said, "It's not right what is happening to the Jews." The Pope may have signed the Concordat with Hitler to stay out of politics, but Catholics like

Inge's family—and Katherine's too—continued to try to follow their conscience.

None of this compares to Le Chambon, a Hugenot village in France where the pastor exhorted his parish to hide scores of Jews, but it might have come from the same impulse as a minority religion. The French Hugenots were surrounded by Catholics, the Benheim Catholics were surrounded by Protestants, and as Carol Rittner, an authority on righteous Christians during the Holocaust, told me, "When you are used to being persecuted, you are more likely to help others in the same position."

Only six girls in Benheim did not join the BDM, but they got away with it. Inge thinks that being fatherless gave her family more leeway. "I had a cover. I told the authorities I had to help on the farm, so when, one afternoon a week, all the children left school to do Nazi activities, I went to the nuns. Everyone thought this was a punishment, but I liked to do needlepoint with the sister, Sister Timea. We had fun."

Her sister Margo's lack of Nazi enthusiasm got her in trouble with the young Nazi mayor. "She was the typical blond German girl of his dreams—until he saw her come out of Frau Esslinger's house. Then he told everyone that he could not court a girl who worked for the Jews." But, Inge says proudly, her family did not yield to Nazi pressure, not even "when the Nazi mayor came to our farm in uniform, wearing a whip. He said *Heil* Hitler to my sister, who said nothing. The next day she was ordered to the *Rathaus* for questioning. 'Why didn't you answer my *Heil* Hitler?' he asked. 'Because,' she said, 'In Benheim a German gentleman greets a young German lady with *Grüss Gott!*' He let her go, but the harassment continued and we were called to headquarters often."

Her Aunt Thea, who was a seamstress, also continued to go to Jewish houses after it was forbidden. But, Inge says, her aunt was terrified. She kept saying to everyone, "One day I'll disappear and you'll get my ashes back in the mail!" People had heard about such things happening. A hunchback child of a local family was taken away one night and the ashes were mailed back weeks later. But still she went.

I wonder why Inge's family dared more than others. They did need money, but that doesn't explain Margo defying the Nazi mayor. Or Inge's mother standing up at a farmer's meeting in 1940 to say, loud and clear: "God forbid a Benheim Jew should be forced to work on their Sabbath on my farm! Never!" Inge's mother, I realize today, was the hero of Willy's story, the woman who silenced all the farmers with her boldness. Others then decided to follow her example—despite Nazi orders that Jews must work seven days a week.

Such stories, Carole tells me later, reveal a lot about this village, not just about this family. The Wolfmann family needed tacit approval from the community, or else they would have been reported and punished by the Nazis as Jewish sympathizers. Some variation of my father's *In Benheim we didn't do such things* kept them safe, even from disapproving people such as their next-door neighbor. He knew they went into Jewish houses at night but said nothing—until after the war. Then the man, while tiling his roof one day, threw Inge down some tiles and said: "Here! If you could help the Jews, you can help me!"

The family's safety suggests that more people, like the Wolfmanns, did not replace the faces of their Jewish neighbors with Nazi stereotypes. They kept remembering that Frau Esslinger, long before her false teeth fell into the toilet, came to Inge's farm to make cakes for a family wedding. That the blind Levy, whose garden Inge fed with manure, made the matzo that still makes Inge beam in reverie. "I can still taste it! Oh it was wonderful, freshly baked. Oh wonderful! I would deliver the wash around the time of Lent and get a piece, and it was sooo delicious."

"Did you eat it with butter?" Carole asks, telling Inge how she likes it best.

"No, dry, without butter. It needed no butter. It was like poetry—brown and white bumps. *Ach,* so good. I haven't had it since."

"Not since?" says Carole, an idea forming. "Well, I shall send you a box this Passover!" (And she does.)

How easily these two women get along! This is how it must have been before Hitler's world made such gestures all but vanish, leaving barely a scratch of generosity on the history of those years.

Inge brings out coffee and small round cakes, the kind her mother used to make. "Nothing fancy!" she says. "Delicious!" we say. And then she opens the red album I skimmed through before.

> And here is a picture of my sister. You can see why the Nazi mayor fell in love with her.

> And here are the oxen we bought after we sold the wild horse. He was such a nightmare we wrote my brother on the Front about what to do. He said to sell the horse and keep the foal so we'd have a horse after the war. But it was also too wild—so we sold it, too, and bought the oxen.

So the Third Reich is beneath the bucolic normalcy of a blond farm girl and two oxen after all. I'm reminded of Leo Spitzer in his memoir *Hotel Bolivia*, describing how he kept looking for signs of grief in a family album of the ocean voyage after fleeing Germany. He knew there was trauma, he knew his grandfather had died on the ship; yet there was his young mother against the guardrail, smiling, and his uncle looking debonair in a T-shirt. Only years later, when the photos became unglued, did he find the handwriting on their backs: "Our bad luck ship Virgillo" on one. "Flying Dutchman aboard a ship of sadness," on another.

Inge's photos also have hidden captions, known only if you happen to be sitting beside her on this brown couch:

> And here is my brother before he resigned from the Hitler Youth, saying he had to work the farm. But someone

remembered. When he was sent from the Front to the hospital in Sulz, his feet frozen, the doctor, a Nazi, wouldn't treat him. He died.

It's the first sadness that she has allowed herself, and the first bitterness:

And here we are sitting on the stone fence near the Denkmal. The whole family would walk up there on Sundays after church and a big lunch.

So the black swastika is also in the album, just beyond the peaceful family photo taken on the stone fence. And the pain of the wild horse story. And the story of a young farmboy next to a haystack who died as retribution. For the initiated—the ones who lived during those times—all is there.

And here are my mother and me cutting the hay without any help.

"I thought you had help," I say. "Didn't you say that Rudy Schwartz took care of the wild horse? Or had he already been deported?"

Inge takes a deep breath. "He was gone, I don't know when —1940 or 1941. All I remember was how the little Weinberger boy, a little thing, not more than six years old, would come over. When he saw my mother and me working alone in the fields, he would offer his help. 'I can rake, I can hoe,' he would say solemnly, then shaking his head, 'but I can't mow.' It breaks my heart still today to think of him walking down the hill with his little rucksack and I too afraid to run out or even wave from the window." Her shoulders slump. "To this day it haunts me." She sighs, looks out the window. "We should have done more," she whispers.

And here is my mother in the Aga garden. It made a wonderful salad that we'd sell for ten pfennigs, but the Jews always liked to bargain. It was like a religion with them. Whatever we had, they'd try to trade down.

"But that is part of a Mediterranean culture," Carole says, patiently. "The Jews were traders, you know. They could not own farms in Germany until after the Napoleonic Laws." She sounds like a kindly teacher—with no "Now I gotcha" edge to her voice, the kind Rolf used to prove his lack of naïveté.

Inge says her family never overpriced anything, "never dreamed of it." This Jewish bargaining is the one blackened memory among those filled with delicious matzo, sweet cakes—and the butter her mother would make every Friday for the Jews. "*That* they never bargained for. It was too delicious!" And she beams again, all is "forgiven" by what's delicious.

And here I am with my friends dressed for carnival. We'd go around to all the houses and sing *Burim, Burim, Burim* and ask for little coins for our boxes. And sometimes we'd also get yellow cheese with red rind and sit in the field next to the houses eating cheese and bread. Delicious.

She sits up, and starts to sing:

> Burim, burim, burim is heut
> Weist Du was Burim bedeut
> Burim bedeutet ein langes Leben,
> Sollst was in mein Bindslein geben.

Her face makes me see the child, box in hand. Carole translates:

> Burim, Burim, Burim is today
> Do you know what Burim means?

It means a long life
And you should give me something
For my box.

Suddenly Carole lights up. "Of course! Burim means Purim!"
Carole says in English. "She is singing about Purim and doesn't
know it!" Carole asks her in German, "Did you know the holiday
Purim . . . with Queen Esther and *hammantaschen*?" Inge looks
puzzled. She repeats the refrain in a lovely, lofty voice, more confident than before: "Burim, burim, burim is heut. . . ." The irony
of the lyrics fills the air. The promise for long life in exchange for
the "gifts" that Jews paid rulers, for generations, to live in the village was not enough to save little Eric or the others who, despite
"Burim, Burim, Burim," walked down the hill to their death.

Inge, still cheerful with the song's memory, jumps up, disappears, and returns with another folder. Shyly, she hands it to me,
saying, "I never studied beyond *Volksschule* so excuse my bad
writing." Inside are two letters, handwritten in old-fashioned
German script with a fine-tipped fountain pen. "I sent the letter
instead of myself," She had been too sick to go with the other
Benheimers to visit their former neighbors in Oleh Zion, and
so wrote this four-page letter to a Jewish man she remembered,
whose rich voice of ceremony still sings in her head:

Dear Hans,

. . . I still like to think of that Friday evening when I was
supposed to deliver the starched collars to your house. As
soon as I reached the door, I realized that the Sabbath had
probably begun because I heard your fine clear tenor voice
sound out on the road. I very timidly knocked on the door
and your mother received me in a very friendly way and
asked me into the living room. And I stood there as though
I had been nailed down. There was this wondrously laid
out table with such a festive atmosphere. . . . In spite of
my presence, you, Hans, continued to sing your *Ado, Ado,*

Adonai from deep in your throat. Your father with the typical thing for his head had the book in his hand and this picture I always have before my eyes. . . . The memory doesn't let me go. . . . Is it this very special moment that is soothing to think of? Or is it reassuring to remember how one and the other respected each other?

In this sense I stay connected to you, dear Benheimers and send you my greetings of my family from all my heart.

Inge Wolfman

And my sister Margo sends her special greetings also.
P.S. Forgive me writing with "Du" because that is how I talk to you in my memory.

I hold her letter like some treasured proof, an affirmation of an illusory good embedded in so many conversations that, until now, never quite added up to certainty. Yet here is the ethereal made concrete: a German woman writing to a Jewish man she barely knew, not out of friendship—that would be easy to explain—but because one moment of memory binds the girl of ten and the boy of thirteen in a shared community now lost in guilt and grief.

And he writes back, one page to her four, but with genuine—albeit more formal—thanks:

Dear Inge,

. . . I really do want to thank you for your lovely letter from all my heart. . . . Right away I felt I was reliving the past even though forty-seven years lie in between since we had to leave Benheim. . . .

He offers no forgiveness to the country that destroyed his life:

. . . My parents did also perish during this terrible time. . . .
. . . I have been to Benheim several times to visit the

cemetery . . . and believe me it cost a great deal to tread on
German soil again. . . .

But that doesn't stop his appreciation of Inge's letter, its generosity and regret, one neighbor to another. For the first time
in this project I don't feel the residual doubt that mixes, especially at night, with fears of my betrayal and naiveté. "May I bor-
row the letters," I ask, "to make copies?" I want them, the pair,
with me beyond this moment in this farmhouse with Inge and
Carole beside me. "Yes, certainly," Inge says simply, as I knew
she would.

As we leave, I see a heavyset, middle-aged woman in a black
dress and headscarf watching from across the street. Her
crossed arms and set jaw put me on guard. I imagine her father
as the one who, while fixing his roof, threw down those roof tiles
to Inge, saying: "If you could help the Jews, you can help me."
Herr Stolle will not arrange an interview with her, or with those
who were big Nazis. But so what? It's the Inges I need to meet,
people who are not warriors, but who, amid difficulty, want to
do the right thing. Inge somehow managed to do that—nothing big like Schindler and Wallenberg, or even noticeable like
Katherine's grandfather's mural. But something.

Yet how do we learn about the Inges—and does it matter?
Does it matter that if I saw a gray-haired and gray-skirted woman
in the red album, I would think: Nice-looking Old German
Woman, the Right Age to Be Guilty? And that I would not see
the girl who saved Frau Esslinger's false teeth and cleaned Frau
Baum's house at 3:00 a.m., walking home bravely in the black
night with no moon, scared.

19 | WHERE LEGEND ENDS

The story began in the Schwarzwald soon after the war ended in 1945 and went something like this:

> I remember those Jews of Benheim. They all went to the Holy Land together and built a new village there by the sea, a real Swabian village.*

I first heard it in 1996 from a German reporter whose beat included Benheim. She called it "a legend with a happy ending" because the Jews got away. "No guilt needed. There's even local pride," she said, "that *their* Jews were smarter and tougher than most." A German television special nationalized the legend in the 1960s, and Herr Stolle had a video copy of the program. So he and I watched it together—and there was my Tante Hilde on his TV screen, speaking Schwäbisch in her new home of Oleh Zion and then on a visit to her old one in Benheim. What began with a voiceover of Hitler blaring over the red roofs of peaceful Benheim ended with interviews, thirty years later, about *Heimat,* that uniquely German word for one's sense of home: how it is lost and gained. My Tante Hilde said she no longer feels Heimat in Benheim. A German man with a leather cap, watching a parade outside the Café Sonne, said that he does.

---

*People from the Schwarzwald are often called Swabians, and they call their local dialect Schwäbisch.

The legend has some truth. Benheim Jews did emigrate to the Holy Land together and resettled beside the Mediterranean Sea, a few miles north of the Crusader town of Acre. They did build little houses with red tile roofs reminiscent of Swabia. They did speak schwäbisch in the fields and mounted Swabian cuckoo clocks on their walls. More amazing—and the stuff of legends—is that on the first day of digging foundations, they found an omen, as if God led them to this spot. It was an ancient Roman column with the escutcheon of the Order of the Knights of St. John, the same order that invited Jews to settle in Benheim in 1645! More shards with the Order's cross were uncovered—the knights evidently came with the Crusaders and stayed—and so the Jewish Benheimers voted to make a flag that honored the lore that connected their old and new worlds.

But here truth and legend part company. An entire village of Jews never escaped Hitler together, only fourteen or so Benheim families that had invited a few more from neighboring villages to help finance the *aliyah* (the return to Zion). The arrangement was that two rich families should pay for one poor one, the old with money supporting the young with strong arms. There was not enough money for everyone so, legend or not, many were left behind. Only their names, carved in stone in the Memorial Room, made it to the new village.

"We became Zionists by necessity," says Gretl, whose husband Simon was a founder of Oleh Zion. We are sitting on her blue couch, eating linzertorte, and she tells me, bright with memory, how in 1933 their *Jugendbund* (Jewish youth group) began meeting every Friday night in the *Volksschule*, planning what to do. The Hitler Youth group met in the upstairs classrooms, says Gretl, and because it was against Jewish law to turn lights on or off on Shabbat, their leader would come downstairs to do that for them. "This kind of cooperation was so typical in our village! It was why our parents did not see the dark shadows slowly coming up, but we, the young people, did see them, and after endless discussions, we decided that if we wanted to survive, the only way was to go as a group and the only place to go was our ancient homeland of Eretz Israel."

The idea of group emigration was novel enough to attract the support of German Zionist organizations deluged by individual applicants. So was the Benheim idea of setting up a cooperative settlement, a *moshav shitufi*, where work and income are shared but family life (unlike in a kibbutz) remained private. Their biggest asset, however, was their experience as farmers, which they played to advantage. When "the men of Berlin" came to Benheim to decide why these people should be chosen over the more dedicated city lawyers, doctors, teachers, and businessmen (all trying desperately to flee), the Benheimers showed up as if they had just plowed the fields. "Their clothes and high boots [were] splashed with mud, their fingernails dirty, and the smell of the stable strong enough to show that they were men of the soil who had no time to waste in dressing up, not even for visitors from Berlin," according to journalist Leopold Marx in *Experiment and Promise*, about the founding of Oleh Zion. The gamble paid off. Within a year, half of these would-be pioneers (who all owned suits and ties) were on their way to settle six hundred dunams of land in the Western Galilee, bought from a Turkish prince who needed money to pay gambling debts.

"There was nothing here. Not a tree, not a shrub. I remember only sand—and danger," says Gretl. "This was ten years before Israel became a state, and the Arabs were not happy to see us. Nor were the British. They told us that, *on that same day*, we must build a watchtower with bunkers and a water tower, all surrounded by barbed wire and sandbags. Or else, we couldn't stay—even with our bill of sale for the land. We had only sixteen grown men out of maybe fifty people, but we did it, how I don't know." Gretl's black eyes are full of victory, even if the hard life eventually defeated her. "Working in the hot sun, twelve hours a day for ten years. Never knowing if you'd be shot—it was too much for me. I became very ill." And so in 1947 Gretl, Simon, and their two children left for America, resettling near Hannah and Lotte in New York, which is where we are talking now.

But most of the first settlers stayed, keeping their spirits high with a feeling of possibility. "Everyone knew we had escaped hell, and so a great hope lay ahead," says Jacob Frank, who still lives in one of the original cement houses of Oleh Zion. "Even in this barren spot, people felt a measure of control over life. In Germany, everything was taken away: our swords and guns and civil rights. Here we at least could defend ourselves." Jacob had his bar mitzvah in Benheim, the last one ever held there. Six months later he was on a *Kindertransporte* through Italy to Palestine to the new village.

He and the other children stayed in Haifa fifteen miles away until housing was built, a room made for daily prayer, a vegetable garden started, and the first cow arrived—the gift of a Salvation Army missionary, born in Benheim and living in Galilee, who had heard the Jews had come. But dangers increased daily. Arab gangs of youth began attacking anyone working in the fields or traveling on the road to Acre or Haifa. Every adult carried a gun, stood watch on the tower, and braced for death, even as they reclaimed the land. There was no telephone. When the War of Independence started in 1947, the only communication to the outside world was a light flashing Morse code from the watch-tower to the *Haganah* (Jewish Defense Forces) in Acre. That and their *shomer* (guard), who rode the hills nightly, were their only warnings of an attack.

My cousin Mordechai was a *shomer*. And what a figure he cut, I remember, as he galloped into the village on a white stallion, my dream. It was 1957, and my family was visiting Tante Hilde, her son Mordechai, and the other Benheimers resettled in Israel. My father had been there before, several times, and wanted me to see the Zionist dream he believed in ever since, as a young soldier in World War I, he saw the oppression of Jews in Eastern Europe. Returning to the Jewish homeland, he decided then, in 1917, was key to Jewish survival.

Oleh Zion, by 1957, was lush with almond and carob trees lining walkways to thirty small, but well-kept, whitewashed houses. Green fields and large barns surrounded everything; the barbed wire was gone. I remember Mordechai's horse rearing up and him laughing fearlessly. Better than Gary Cooper or John Wayne, I thought, pleased with a land that has Jewish cowboys.

Mordechai had started guarding the hills at age fifteen. By the time I met him, he was spending his time racing horses with Arab friends from neighboring villages. There was relative peace in those days. The British were gone (1947). The State of Israel had been declared (1948). The local Arabs who fought the new state had left and those who stayed had developed a good rapport with the German newcomers. They traded goods, exchanged services, and formed loyalties, not unlike in Benheim. The Six Day War (1967), for example, did not stop Salech, the Arab man who milked the cows, from crossing the road from his Arab village to do his job. "The cows don't know a war is on!" he told the Jews, who had heard Arab radio's call to loot Jewish villages and expected the worst.

Salech, since then, has become the manager of the cow barns. He lives in a stately white villa set into the hillside of his village, one wing for each branch of the family. "My sons and I built everything with our own hands!" he tells me proudly in 2002, as I sit in his courtyard eating dates and drinking tea. One of Salech's sons is a doctor; another, a judge; and another, together with his daughter, runs the machinery repair shop of Oleh Zion. Salech, though officially retired, continues to come to the cow barns despite the *Intifadas* and suicide bombings. And he has continued his friendship with Yaron, the Jewish boy who for years worked with him in the cow barns. Yaron, now living in New York, says his daughters write Salech's daughter, and he has urged her "to come to New York and stay with us." The day after 9/11, Salech called to see if the family was all right.

Why is it that these two men have been able to do what their leaders cannot? And how long can their goodwill continue to trump the politics of hate? Or will the shared history of milking cows collapse, as in Benheim, under the force of extremism?

2002: Lev Mayer is giving me a tour. We have walked through the cow barns that supply milk to the whole of western Galilee. We have passed the fields of roses, now exported all over the world, and are in the lobby of a hotel run by Oleh Zion. On the wall is a giant quilt, with insets designed and sewn by every family of the community to commemorate fifty years as a village. Lev gives me a running commentary of who's who. "Here you see Itzhak and Clara Stern. Her husband was always going with the donkeys to Nahariya for the milk. She is ninety-two now. And here you see Schmuel Kahn. His daughter was always sending Morse code with the lights. And here you see the mayor, Hurtzl, who was also the baker." Lev reminds me of Inge Wolfmann going through her red album, only instead of private images of Benheim, these colorful hand-sewn squares are what rose from the ashes of that old life, hanging for all to see.

Lev calls himself a *Mensch für alles* (man of all talents) and, indeed, he has been: schoolteacher, commander in the *Haganah* fighters, pioneer rabbi/cantor, Zionist, Jewish lecturer in postwar Germany, author, backyard archeologist, school superintendent of the sciences, botanist, kosher meat inspector, co-keeper of the archives, Orthodox Jew, secularist, German citizen, Israeli.

This small, soft-spoken man was the Benheim schoolteacher who introduced Gretl and Simon and others in the *Jugendbund* to the idea "that Jewish freedom depended on returning to the Jewish homeland." But somehow he stayed in Germany until after Kristallnacht, despite several run-ins with the Nazis: first, in 1934, for teaching self-defense. "The children and I would go into the forests, like Scouts, and make all kinds of games—and somebody told the Gestapo that we were making preparation for war. They accused me of producing secret weapons, which wasn't true, of course." He smiles. "I talked my way out of it!"

A year later this quiet man—hardly a firebrand in looks—was in trouble for a speech the Nazis found subversive: "It was Lemberger's funeral but the non-Jewish neighbors also came. In those days, they still dared. I, in my youthful enthusiasm, quoted the Torah: 'You will go above and they will fall, and they will pay for what they have done to you.' The next day I get an invitation to the Gestapo, and they say, 'What are you saying?' Again I escape, by telling them, 'I was not speaking politically. I was speaking religiously, this was a religious service.' You see?" he smiles again, "I always had a way with the Gestapo!"

Lev casts himself as a crafty Odysseus outwitting the Cyclops, or little David beating Goliath. But when, in 1939, the Gestapo called again, this time for slaughtering kosher meat despite Nazi law, he says, "I talked my way out—but left two weeks later, just in time."

We walk to the sea where an early Byzantine church—one of the oldest in the Holy Land—once rose into this blue Mediterranean sky. Six new concrete columns are meant to evoke past glory, but hold up nothing but sky. Below them is a mosaic floor from the second century and below that are other floors of other civilizations, "their stories still untold," says Lev. All I see are inverted swastikas in mosaic tile, scores of them. Lev says they are an ancient sun symbol, but they seem ominous, just the same. "Not at all," says Lev. "Hitler tried to destroy us under that symbol, and all he accomplished was to make us blossom in a new place above a floor of swastikas, all going in the opposite direction!" Lev is the spirit of this place, its feeling of regeneration, of refusal to be defeated, of every story having a good spin, a good omen.

There is also a Maltese cross flanked by pomegranates. The cross is Christian, the pomegranates symbolize the Jews, says Lev. And Arab names surround the site. El Mina, the harbor; Tel Melacha, the salty place for the hill north of here: "A Phoenician harbor was once here and salt was extracted in those hills." Lev's hand spans the coastline, and I think how many nations and tribes have claimed this spot—and still claim it.

A legend says that Jesus made a miracle here, says Lev, and that's why this church was built. The books of Matthew and Mark* mention Jesus being asked to heal the daughter of a non-Jewish woman north of Acre. At first he refuses, saying, "I can only help Jews." But the woman persisted. "You help dogs. Am I not as important as a dog?" And so he cured the child. I think of the Nazi signs on shops, NO JEWS OR DOGS ALLOWED, and am glad this story of Christ's goodness is here, inverting and refuting that sign as steadily as the waves hit the rocks beyond the barbed wire fence guarding the mosaic floor.

Since the 1970s, Lev has been going back to Germany to give talks about Jewish life and culture. "Nothing will erase the terrible events that happened, but it is time to build new human bridges," he tells me. "I have been there four times. Once I gave a lecture on biblical plants, once on biblical animals, once on the difference between Israeli and Egyptian beliefs, and this last one was called 'Glaube, Wissen und Gewissen' — 'Belief, Knowledge, and . . . ,'" he gropes for the last word . . . "'Conscience.'" His lectures were filled, he says proudly.

He has also been back to Benheim. He first went in 1969 as part of an Israeli week set up by the city of Stuttgart. Thirty Jews, including ten from Oleh Zion, were invited for an all-expenses-paid trip to their old homeland. He shows me a Schwarzwald newspaper account of the event, and translates:

> In the Café Sonne, we [Germans] had the opportunity to exchange words with the mayor of Oleh Zion. . . . We were welcomed with so much warmth and heartiness that we don't know who we should thank. We had not dared to hope that we would be welcomed in such a friendly manner.

So the legend with a happy ending continues. Cakes were "offered by the Village Council," everyone watched the German

*Matthew 5:21–28; Mark 5:24–40.

TV special on "the sister villages," and "all were delighted," writes the reporter. She mentions the darker past—"For some coming back caused painful memories"—but gives more space to Lev remembering "relations between Jews and those of other faiths as pretty good in the first years of the Nazi Regime." The story of the Nazi Youth leader turning the lights on for the Jews on Shabbat is hinted at in the line "Even the Hitler Youth with which we shared the building respected us," and the article ends with this quote:

> We have finished the past and want to see it as history. This day has been an experience for us and we want to build a bridge over the canyon gap.

Since then, many have crossed the bridge. My Tante Hilde, her sister Thea, and Hans (whose rich voice Inge remembers) have visited Benheim. Herr Stolle, Anna, the Lugers, Mayor Himmel, and Michael and Katherine from Dorn have visited Oleh Zion. And many more. The reunions went well except for a group of Benheim teenagers who spent a miserable week with the teenagers of Oleh Zion. They ignored each other and refused to buy into a happy legend: neither the German version of all Jews escaping nor the Jewish one of Benheim's perfection before Hitler spoiled it.

But the bridge has been repaired. In 2002 Mayor Himmel invited a group from Oleh Zion to come to Benheim as guest speakers for a Day of Remembering. Five agreed to come, expenses paid by the German government, and a crowd of forty or so was expected. Two hundred showed up, Catholic and Protestant, young and old, from all over the Schwarzwald. They had heard the legend of Benheim Jews who escaped Hitler and now live in the Holy Land and they wanted to hear firsthand what these people had to say about their former Heimat—and see who they really are.

In the former synagogue, German Christians listened to

reminiscences of Shabbat candles in the windows and the annual Purim parade on the main street, and everyone singing together in the glee club. They listened to how the burning synagogue ended four hundred years of community and how helpless Jews felt that they couldn't rescue their loved ones—grandparents, parents, aunts, cousins—from the Nazis. And how the old Torah was saved, thanks to the good policeman who took it from the fire. They can see it in the Memorial Room of their new village next to the names of the eighty-seven killed by the Nazis. And though edges are charred and there's a knife slash, the Torah is open, its scrolls revealing the Five Books of Moses as before.

20 | AT MY FATHER'S GRAVE

My father decided to be buried in Oleh Zion, surprising every-one. Instead of choosing Cedar Lawn Cemetery in New Jersey, lying beside his small daughter Hannah and his two brothers and one sister, my father became the pioneer of his dreams. Four months before he died, he bought two plots in the little cemetery where I am standing now, because, as he told my mother, he wanted to be near his former neighbors, people he knew would say the Mourner's Kaddish for him every year. And so we flew his body across the ocean and watched men in blue kibbutz caps and shorts lower his plain pine coffin into the land of Israel.

My father would be 103 today, as I stand over his gravestone where a single red stone lies, placed there by someone in remembrance. Not Tante Hilde, who used to care for the grave. She's dead. Not her sister Thea, now blind and almost deaf in a nearby old age home. It was Hans, Thea tells me. But he is almost ninety, so how much longer for him? The graves, carved with birth dates of 1899, 1901, 1903, increase as steadily as the fields surrounding them decrease, the tall white apartment houses from the town of Nahariya looming closer every year, their solar panels facing the sun.

I say Kaddish for my father as best I can. I know only the last part well. "Oseh Shalom bim romav . . ." Hans knows the whole thing perfectly. Even at his age, I suspect he still has the rich tenor voice that Inge Wolfmann remembers echoing onto the street in Benheim. Was it because of his voice that my father is buried here? Was it Hans he had in mind to sing the prayer for the dead for him every year? Did he not imagine Hans soon beside him in a grave bordering this shrinking field?

This transplanted Schwarzwald world is disappearing as surely as the Byzantine mosaic floor is eroding by the sea just down the road. There is change in the air. New Jewish immigrants, looking for freedom in an established Jewish state, don't care about a "sister village" in Germany or about buried signs from the Order of the Knights of St. John. Even the children of old Benheimers are forgetting their parents' commitments. My cousin Mordechai chooses to live in a tiny private farm outside the village, and Yaron Bern, one of the first born in the "new village," stays in Manhattan. And the young girl with a cell phone, who was sitting on the curb, didn't know where this cemetery is. She may know the whole Kaddish, but what she knows of Benheim is disappearing with each newly dug grave. She is a Sephardic Jewish girl, whose family must have fled from Iraq or Syria or Yemen, and moved to what, for them, is just an Israeli village—one that is a five-minute walk to a new mall with a McDonalds, Ace Hardware, and Toys R Us across the road. *That* she does know, and so does the Ashkenazi boy who was sitting beside her. Maybe he is the great-grandson of a Benheim pioneer, I can't tell.

I try my own silent prayer. *Would you have thought, Dad, that your daughter, once so allergic to Benheim, would spend so many years writing about it?*

I would. A hot dry wind sears the skin. No soft Mediterranean breeze today. *We must all know the story that came before ours, to fit it in somehow.*

Is that why you, Dad, are buried here, and I am asking strangers to tell me what I can only know as legends of my own shaping?

I look for stones to place on his grave, a sign that I have been here. They are hard to find in the fine sand, so I walk into the fields where the earth is red and bring two white stones back to place above the inscription:

My dear man and father and grandfather

Arthur Loewengart

7.6: 1898—in Benheim
2.9: 1973—in New York

This is a land for new immigrants, no matter when they decide they must come.

In my den in New Jersey, I live with fragments of an ancient past: a chipped Greek perfume bottle; two coins from the Jewish revolt of Bar Kochba against the Romans; two-thirds of a Stone Age dish. They sit on the glass shelf, found in the sands and fields when my husband, children, and I spent a year's sabbatical in Israel in 1972, hiking every Saturday to know the land. Most of these treasures are cracked, glued, or still broken, but you can't tell that in their shadows that triple in size from spotlights above them. Their black shapes shimmy whenever someone enters the room at night, as if dancing to an ancient melody I can't hear. But it's in this room that I feel my dad's steel blue eyes and hear his laugh, more than when I look at his photo on our bedroom wall, bald and smiling in a navy blue suit. Or remember a gray slab of stone under the cloudless sky.

13. Jewish cattle dealer with prize bull, circa 1920. *Photo courtesy of Heinz Högerle.*

14. The farmer's daughter who refused to join the girls' Nazi Youth group. This photo was in her red album. *Photo courtesy of Heinz Högerle.*

15. Jewish school class, circa 1880s, when Jews made up half the village of 1,200. *Photo courtesy of Helen Gribetz.*

16. Jewish school class in 1937, when many had already fled Nazi Germany. *Photo courtesy of Maria Gekle and Heinz Högerle.*

17. Building the new village in the sands of Eretz
Israel, 1937. *Photo courtesy of Heinz Högerle.*

18. At my father's grave.

19. Two from the group of Jews who came from Israel, at the mayor's invitation, to take part in the Day of Remembering in the synagogue-turned-church, 2002. *Photo courtesy of Uri Gefen and Heinz Högerle.*

20. Jews and Christians walking through the gates of the Jewish cemetery for a memorial service for the Jews murdered by the Nazis, 2004.

PART FOUR | END POINTS

21 | THE OTHER MIRIAM

She is my namesake, the Miriam who does not use a nickname. She is almost thirty years younger and a head taller than I, lanky and long-necked in an Icelandic sweater and brown corduroys. You'd never know she grew up as an ultra-Orthodox Jew in Zurich, Switzerland, going to what she calls "a very black school." The name comes from the black leggings, black long skirts, and black long sleeves she had to wear to school every day. When she took the trolley car home to her neighborhood, she remembers the Swiss boys yelling "Jewish whore" as she walked to her door. That happened in the 1970s, but her story fits with the graffiti I see sprayed on walls and carved in wooden benches in Zurich twenty years later: *Juden raus! Ausländer raus!* (Jews out! Foreigners out!).

What doesn't fit is that one quarter of Zurich citizens are now married to foreigners, according to Miriam, as we sit drinking coffee on the Bahnhofstrasse. I keep wanting to believe that assimilation breeds tolerance, but keep bumping into the opposite. German Jews were once the most assimilated in Europe, especially in cities, especially at universities. Yet that is where people turned against the Jews most quickly; in tradition-bound Benheim, goodwill lasted much longer.

Miriam and I are meeting to talk about translating my audiotapes from Benheim. My husband and I are on a mini-sabbatical here for a few months, and I've been taking the train two hours to the north to spend time in Benheim. I've been managing with my German, able to make small talk and ask good questions, but I don't always understand the answers. I want Miriam to fill in what I miss. She speaks English fluently from her six years in America, German fluently from her life in Zurich, Hebrew fluently from her "black school," and now Arabic, which she is studying in school. Next month she will go to Israel to live in Jerusalem, she says, and marry an Orthodox man, wear a wig like other Orthodox wives do, observe every Jewish ritual and holiday, and give up Icelandic sweaters and corduroys. She will live in a neighborhood where no one will call her "Jewish whore" but where a car driving down the street on Shabbat may be stoned.

I cannot imagine Miriam in such a closed community. She strikes me as one who will cross borders, no matter which side of them she lives on. Maybe it's because we are both Gemini, even if she needs daily unity of ritual and I need daily change. I shuttle between job and home, a professor in one place, a wife and mom in another. I write on Monday and Wednesday mornings and play tennis in late afternoon. I eat breakfast with a husband who likes wireless technology and spend evenings talking poetry with writer friends. Which is why I cannot imagine myself in the old Benheim where, as my father said, "If someone sneezed, someone down the street said *Gesundheit*." I would have left, as he did.

"What will make your book different from other Holocaust books?" Miriam asks, as Zurich's trolley cars pass both ways. She is eating yogurt; I am eating a croque monsieur (grilled ham and cheese).

"It's not a Holocaust book," I say as I do to everyone who calls it that—although less adamantly than when I started this project. "I'm really more interested in how good people lived through and with Germany's past. And what that has to tell me, us, about our lives today."

"You need to find your Jewish identity before you can understand how to deal with Christians," she tells me with a certainty that makes me think of Rolf.

I bridle. I have been living in a Christian world for over forty years, ever since I left Queens at eighteen. In my high school of four thousand, almost everyone I knew was Jewish (even if a quarter of the school wasn't). But in college, at the University of Michigan, I lived in a quaint little dorm close to campus (that's why I picked it!), and it was filled with Addies and Dennys from Grosse Pointe and Bloomfield Hills, towns that allowed no Jews back then. Only my roommate, Maxine from Grand Rapids, was Jewish. We did have Linda White, an African American who had a single down the hall, and Indra, an Indian in a sari. But I remember everyone else with straight blond hair and plaid kilts, rushing Tri Delt and Kappa sororities. Still, the vibes were good. Addie and Denny snuck us into Grosse Pointe for a weekend, my folks treated everyone to the Pretzel Bell for dinner when they visited, and six months later, in Bombay, India, Indra's parents entertained my father royally. "I like not living on the hill with the other Jews, don't you?" I kept whispering to Maxine. The promise of the American Melting Pot—the one that invited children of Jewish refugees like me to jump in and be American!—was feeling true.

It still feels true. On our street, the neighbor behind me is a former Presbyterian minister, the one to my left attends a Catholic mass on most mornings, and across the way is a Jewish musician married to a Russian/German with a Jewish grandfather. My two children grew up with friends named White, Wright, and Donovan, which didn't bother me, a girl who happily puts boundaries of difference behind her.

I take a bite of my croque monsieur and tell Miriam, "I'm fine in the Christian world. I'm not religious and only go to synagogue on high holy days because I don't want my husband to go alone. He loves the prayers, the sense of community; they lift him up. But I get left behind. It's also how I feel at football games and rallies, when everyone cheers and chants at once."

"But why?" Miriam is surprised.

"Maybe it's the image of ten thousand chanting *Heil* Hitler in unison on a town square. I avoid whatever is aimed at uplifting the collective soul."

"I cannot understand this! My father also escaped Hitler, barely made it to Switzerland. My grandparents were murdered in Auschwitz. With such a past, Judaism gives me a grid of order that channels my spirit, give me self-control. Keeping kosher (she eats no croque monsieurs with ham), saying the prayers, having to leave work early on Friday for the Sabbath—they are acts that remind me every day of who I am." She reminds me of Willy, and the others for whom tradition makes order out of chaos. It's a way of life I've never been drawn to, maybe never needed enough, growing up safely in Queens.

I still see a rebel in Miriam's face, not just in her dress—as if these reminders come with a price. She lacks a well-scrubbed innocence. My first thought is drugs—Zurich is full of them, there's a Needle Park just for addicts—but I am way off. Over coffee, she tells me that she had cancer at fifteen, and just when the treatments were finished and she stopped wanting to die, her favorite aunt got cancer, and for three years she had to watch her die.

"To write this book, you need to find your identity as a Jew," she says again.

I stop trying to defend myself and become an interviewer. "So what does that mean for you?" I ask, thinking whatever she says about order and self-control, she, like me, seems to leave the door of experience open wide enough so no one can shut it by surprise.

"When my good friend was killed in the Sinai, that was too much for me. There is no God! I thought. It was something I didn't feel even with my trouble and when my aunt died. For six months, I turned on all the lights in my house on Shabbat, I rode the tram on Saturdays, I went to parties on Friday night. I even ate pizza with bratwurst. I hate God, I thought, but eventually that stopped." She smiles. No further explanation.

Miriam has many Christian friends, she says. Christian men

have fallen in love with her, but that is a line she has had to draw. She must marry a Jew. I think of how my father used to say, "Marriage is hard enough, why have religion make it harder?" A pragmatic reason I could agree with, and at age twenty-one—by coincidence or his influence, I'm not sure—I married a Jew. And so did my daughter thirty years later, but my son has chosen a Japanese woman whose Shinto religion embraces all others. Which also seems fine. She is lovely, and some part of me even says, "Good! Get this 3,000-year burden off our back!"—but I push that betrayal away, for I need to feel loyal: to family, to history, to all who were murdered for being Jews. But Miriam's commitment is not about loyalty or guilt, but integrity. "I can be a good person wearing corduroy pants. I can be a good person teaching Arab children—I plan to do that once I get to Israel, to help make relations between Jews and Palestinians better. But I cannot be a good person if I intermarry. That would betray myself."

"I can imagine you in the old Benheim—even in your corduroy pants!" I kid, as we drive north to Benheim. She is wearing the same outfit she wore when we first met, while I am wearing a brown skirt and top, very conservative. Miriam wants to meet Herr Stolle and Anna. After hearing them on tape, she has lots of questions to ask. She thinks I have been too easy on them, too cautious, too careful about hurt feelings. One should ask directly what they did in the war and "how they live with the terrible thing their country did." I squirm at her directness, just as I did with Rolf. It's funny how these two, so opposite in background, are so much alike. While I'm being so damn diplomatic.

Maybe Herr Stolle likes a beautiful young woman with serious eyes and a warm smile. Maybe it's because Miriam is the kind of observant Jew he remembers as a child, but the two hit it off immediately. He nods when she says she can't eat bratwurst at the Café Sonne and sips tea while we eat lunch. This is how Jews are supposed to be.

"Of course the Jews must hate that the synagogue is a church," Miriam says without equivocation. "It's absurd for the Protestants to feel justified, a sign of duped self-righteousness." Herr Stolle listens carefully. "They call it a House of God," she continues, "a place built on the graves of the dead, worshipping in a building stolen from the dead. It should have been a memorial."

I'm thinking of all the counterarguments I've heard: It was only seven years after the war and people needed usable spaces. There were no memorials at that time. The other villages had turned the synagogues into parking lots and movie houses. But Herr Stolle keeps quiet, as if awed by a certainty not grounded in blame but in inner faith. *She's not afraid to offend as I am.*

She brings up the murder of Herr Bodenheimer, a Jew supposedly shot in Benheim in 1941. It's a subject Herr Stolle kept sidestepping whenever I mentioned it. Miriam just says, "We heard he was murdered. Is this true?" The blotches appear on Herr Stolle's face, but he doesn't pretend ignorance.

"Mimi has asked me this, and I did some investigating," he says. "He was murdered by some young hoodlums. No one is sure how. He was an old man and they may have beaten him up at night. There was a dispute over who owned the Bodenheimer house, and the next day he was dead. A terrible thing."

"What happened to the murderer?" asks Miriam.

"He went to war, what else?" says Herr Stolle, looking glum. "It shouldn't have happened in Benheim." He shakes his head. "I was not here." Miriam asks where he was, and he says that he was first in France as an aerial photographer, then in Eastern Europe as a foot soldier, in Poland, in Hungary, in Czechoslovakia. Yes, he'd heard about the camps, but never saw them. Yes, he did see Jews—they were digging ditches with Jewish stars on, an image he can't forget. *He never admitted that to me.*

"How do you live with the thought that you did nothing

for the Jews?" Miriam says, just as the proprietor brings us Linzertorte. She has brought Miriam a free piece, thinking she had no money to eat. Miriam smiles, says no thank you. The woman presses her. Please. Until Miriam says simply, "I cannot eat it because I am kosher." I shift uncomfortably. But the proprietor smiles. "Ach, eine Jüedin (Oh, a Jew)," she says brightly. She, too, remembers the Jews and asks Miriam who she is, where she's from, and acts pleased to have her here.

"Every day I wonder what else I could have done," Herr Stolle says after the proprietor leaves, looking directly at Miriam. The man who has deluged me with facts confides to Miriam about feeling tortured by memories of the Benheim Jews who died—and the six million others. The more he works in the archives, he says, the worse it gets. "When I started, I thought I was just recording information, but then names became attached to faces and to their stories. That was very hard to face, but necessary. The past is very painful, hard to keep reliving."

"That is because you always feel on trial," says Miriam. "If you accept your past, your powerlessness at that time, and see what you are doing now—telling it to young people like me—you would feel better."

Herr Stolle nods, looking more relaxed than I've ever seen him. It's as if Miriam has set something in him free. This young Orthodox Miriam, whose family also fled Hitler, is accepting him for who he was and is. It's a gift I have not given him, whether out of fear, lack of language, or lack of empathy, I don't know.

On the way home Miriam tells me how excited she is about this trip. Everything her father had told her about the Germans —how they threw him and his parents out and how he couldn't forgive them for that—was thrown into question by meeting the nice people we met today: people who suffered from the burden of the past, caring people. She tells me she wants to bring the Orthodox Jewish children in Zurich together with a group of German children the same age and get them talking, "so they can see that there are live Jews and Germans who have inherited a past but who are themselves innocent and can start again, better. Right now these young people only see images of the dead. German classes tour the Jewish cemeteries and never meet a live Jew. Jewish youth in Zurich go to German-Jewish cemeteries to see graves of those less lucky than their families. They never meet a live, nice German, so their images are only of evil men. We must build personal ties," she says as if she'll start tomorrow, "the ones that bound the Benheimers together for several centuries, the ones that the future generations must guard more vigilantly next time."

I think what a good person my namesake really is. Like Willy in Baltimore, her faith has made her righteous, but not self-righteous, not intolerant of "other." Her faith has led her to a Jewish identity that reaches across worlds with a warm hand and a smile. One that I too could embrace.

22 | THREE LITTLE GIRLS

Be like a tank filled with love and human hate
cannot hurt you.

Marta Stein, quoting a Christian Science scripture

Marta Stein, a Jew born in Benheim in 1898, did the unthink-
able in those days: she converted. Not because of love, although
there was this Catholic boy she had won a dance contest with,
but because her little sister's life was saved, she felt, by a
Christian Scientist visiting next door. The doctors had offered
no hope—four-year-old Gaby would die—but this woman said,
"There is always hope. Pray with me." The two of them prayed
until, two days later, little Gaby asked for a boiled egg, the special treat of the sick. Fifteen years later, Marta and Gaby were
both Christian Scientists, married to Protestants, and living in
Stuttgart. Gaby stayed in Stuttgart throughout the Hitler years,
protected by her husband, Max, a well-respected businessman.
But Marta, with her three little girls, moved back to her mother's
house in Benheim in 1938, "half because of Hitler, half because
our parents split up," says middle daughter Trudy. They didn't
divorce legally until *after* Hitler, "the one good thing my father
did for us. Otherwise we would have been deported with the
others."

Whereas most *Mischlinge* (the Nazi label for people of mixed descent) hid behind closed shutters or were deported, Marta and her three girls lived openly in Benheim. Their six-year freedom proved lucky for Benheim. When French troops marched toward the village, Marta voluntarily stood in the road with a white flag of truce (actually her white tablecloth), her yellow star, and her passport stamped "Sara" for Jew and told the men in tanks that the villagers had helped her get through the war. "Our mother stopped the village from being destroyed!" her daughters like to say. Others in the village agree, although they also thank the handful of village men who were smart enough to blow up the swastika in the high meadow a few hours before the French arrived.

If I hadn't answered my mother's phone, I wouldn't have known any of this. No one ever said to me: "Talk to the three Stein-Rollsteig girls! They lived in Benheim throughout the war. They went to school there. They passed the swastika on the Denkmal every day!" Marta and her daughters were in no one's story until my father's second cousin from Maine, Ruth Sherman, called my mother when she was coughing badly, so I picked up the receiver.

Ruth was delighted to speak with me, having heard about my project. "Do you know Trudy Merton? She's someone you should meet." Ruth had seen Trudy in Florida the week before. "Trudy grew up in Benheim during Nazi times."

"She did?"

"With her mother and two sisters."

"And they're Jewish?" I asked cautiously. Could Jews have survived in Benheim? *That was a story.*

"Their grandmother was Jewish, born in Benheim, a cousin of your father's." Her voice dropped. "Their mother married a non-Jew and moved to Stuttgart before Hitler." That was why no one mentioned them. They fit into no one's category—but mine: people, neither Jewish nor Catholic, who offer a fresh perspective on Benheim. "Trudy comes to Fort Myers every winter with her husband. Lovely people, both of them. The rest of the year they live in Stuttgart."

She gave me Trudy's phone number, and I called that night. "Come anytime! It will be our great pleasure!" said her husband, Knut, who answered the phone. "And please, stay with us. We have a room ready for you." (They'd already had a phone call from Ruth.) A week later I am on the plane to Fort Myers with five tapes and a tape recorder, thinking, "What if my mother hadn't coughed? Is this how research happens?"

TRUDY

She is waiting with Knut at the Fort Myers Airport, a tall redhead with hair swooping up into a large, 1940s-style bouffant. "Welcome to our second home!" Knut says, grabbing my bag. He is lean, handsome, gray-bearded, and tan. A snowbird with a German accent. "You won't need that here!" Trudy laughs, sweeping my coat off my arm, as we three march through the elderly crowd to a white BMW convertible, top down, of course. They are full of energy, these two. We make a fast getaway, my hair blowing wild while Trudy's mound remains perfectly still, aided only by a thin white veil. *How does she do that?*

They live in a community of white stucco houses, and their house with its pink trim and huge pots of flowers has a honeymoon feel. Which seems right, given that Knut and Trudy created wedding and evening gowns for thirty-seven years until they retired two years ago. "We shipped worldwide, including to the Emperor of Japan!" Trudy tells me with delight. "We were even invited to his ball!" Knut adds with equal gusto.

Inside, everything is muted pink and beige, with many dried flower arrangements, big and small. A picture window overlooks a manmade pond where, Knut says, an occasional alligator appears. "And once, a bald eagle!" Trudy shivers. "It was a huge thing that ate the baby ducks." She hates when animals are killed. It reminds her of when she lived in Benheim and "our chicken, Berta, that we raised and fed, was cooked for Christmas. My mother had no choice, there was so little food then, but I wouldn't eat the meat, only the soup. I still dislike chicken, right?" She looks at Knut.

"I will start the barbecue. Fish you like!" he says, touching her arm before marching off.

Trudy asks me about my father, when he left Germany, and what happened to the rest of my family. And then she and Knut reminisce about how they met in a jazz bar in Stuttgart and how Knut, smitten, had to wrest Trudy away from another boy. "We've been a team ever since," Knut says, while he marinates the fish and she arranges zucchini, fresh stewed tomatoes, corn, and Chinese cellophane noodles on a platter as elegant as in any Martha Stewart photograph.

Elegance. A favorite word of Trudy's as we leaf through their album of wedding gowns. "I want people to feel perfect!" says Trudy, as we look at pages of women in satin and lace with parasols tipped just so. "Like I felt at my grandmother's table in Benheim. It was so elegant. The crystal and Meissen china, the silver candlesticks, and my uncle singing prayers with—What was that on his head, Knut?" Yarmulke, he and I answer. "And she always dressed beautifully. I remember her black fur hat and the matching . . ." Muffler, we both say simultaneously. "Such an elegant woman." She shakes her head, as uninvited memories intrude. "To imagine her shoved into a cow train and dying in a cold barn in Riga. Of typhus.* Or maybe it was gas. My sister Uschi will know. She went to Riga last year and found out everything." Trudy shivers again as she tells me about a photo Uschi found of her grandmother "so thin, her hair disheveled,

---

*Willy Weinberger remembers normal trains except for the guards. (But maybe they were deported at different times. There were three deportations from Benheim.) When I go to Stuttgart four months later to visit Trudy's sisters, I see the photo of Trudy's grandmother looking haggard.

her dark eyes so scared. . . . It was terrible." She hands me a porcelain dish filled with chocolate petit fours. "Please take," she says, "I made them myself."

Elegance is Trudy's talisman against darker days. With Knut's help, she has surrounded herself with what her grandmother lost. He helps her keep it, not just as her partner but as her defender, a Protestant born in Munich, who "when someone makes a wisecrack against Jews," quickly speaks up: "My wife is Jewish!" Her Tante Gaby's late husband did the same as long as he lived, Knut tells me with passion. "No insult to Jews, post-Hitler, can go unchallenged!" (That the women see themselves as Christian Scientists doesn't seem to matter.)

Trudy's grandmother died in Riga, but Uncle Rudolph lived until the liberation and died shortly afterwards. Another uncle escaped to Argentina, and Tante Gaby, now ninety-one, is still living in her house in Stuttgart.

"Have you met Tante Gaby?" Trudy asks.

"I think my parents did once. I have wanted to . . . ," I say.

"She and Max were the ones you Americans visited. They were rich and charming, and she was a beauty, an eye-stopper. My mother was no match for her—and we were so poor," says Trudy, rolling up her white linen napkin to fit into its silver holder. After they moved back to Stuttgart in 1946, Marta's main source of income was making lampshades at home. "My mother was such a fighter, always. And I have that from her." Trudy holds up her fists. "I fought for everything. Right, Knut?" and her long freckled arm scans the beautiful room, as if holding a magic wand.

"I don't know how, but my mother created a safe world for us." It is after dinner and we are walking fast through a mangrove forest to catch the sunset on the beach. Trudy is in four-inch stiletto heels made of Plexiglas. My back would be out in a second with that shoe angle, but Trudy doesn't flinch, doesn't complain, and doesn't wait for the trolley as Knut suggests. "Come on! We can make it!" she says, those heels tapping optimistically on the boardwalk over the swamp. "Of course it helped that everyone liked her!" Trudy is slightly out of breath. "The butcher would give her extra sausage; the farmers let her to go into the fields at night for corn, the neighbors, at night, brought us goat milk. She was kind, and what you give out comes back. Even the local Nazis liked my mother."

Love is reflected in love! her mother always said, and Trudy hears those words still. "They work!" she assures me. Here in Florida, for example, she takes a ninety-year-old man to church every Sunday, and the family can't do enough for her. Also, she invited children of divorcing neighbors over for Sunday barbecues, and now they are forever friends. "My mother tried to see the good in people, and it helped us be lucky. So I do the same." I think of how the survival strategies we absorb in childhood shape us. For me, it was alertness to danger signs and bravery; for Trudy, it was kindness, elegance, and strength.

We reach the beach just as the sun torches the horizon a blazing red, orange, and pink. "Look how lucky we are!" Knut says. Trudy laughs triumphantly, as she shakes the sand out of her glass slippers. If they were mine, I'd still be limping in the mangrove.

Yet fear is beneath her bravado, Trudy confides later as we lie on chaise lounges overlooking the manmade pond. That is why she could never have married a Jew—and warned her children not to. "I was so afraid that if I did, I would be Jewish again. I thought if I marry a . . . a . . . un-Jewish boy, then my children would be a quarter Jewish, and if my daughter marries a non-Jewish boy, no Jewish blood anymore!!" I marvel at her honesty. "So when my daughter met a man, a dentist from Israel, I worried. 'Mother,' she told me, 'if the mother is Jewish, you always stay Jewish!' But I said no. We were, how do they call it, 'Aryan'? It was very important that we had an 'Aryan' father—and that saved us. So I wanted an 'Aryan' husband. It was the fear, you see. It is there."

In Helen Fremont's memoir *After the Long Silence*, she writes about discovering that her grandparents were murdered in Auschwitz. Evidently, her parents were so afraid of being Jewish that in postwar Middle West America, they didn't tell her. Instead, they pretended to be Catholic—and taught their daughters to say the "Hail Mary" in many languages, just in case. Trudy would understand that impulse completely.

USCHI

I am in Stuttgart to meet Trudy's two sisters to see what they remember of their Benheim years—and if their memories match. Uschi, the youngest and closest to my age, invites me to her apartment, a small cozy place full of light, plants, and photos. We hit it off at once. Her sleek silver hair is in a pageboy cut, more mod than Trudy's red bouffant, but the upbeat attitude seems the same. Their mother's aphorisms—Uschi's favorite is *There are no complications unless you make them*—continue to resonate with this daughter, too.

Lately Uschi returns to Benheim to write. "My childhood draws me back," she says. "I felt protected there through a kind of mother love, not only my mother's but the world she believed in." That world included the secret clearing in the forest where they could sit under a rock wall and see the river. Uschi goes back to sit there and work on a memoir called "Village on the Hill," which describes the scene:

Our meadow, we called that spot, and every Sunday for years, I was convinced it would never belong to anybody else. My mother, sisters, and I would start the day early, reading books—sometimes the Holy Scriptures, sometimes fairy tales like the story of the Little Lord who calls his mother *Liebste* (My Love) and melts his grandfather's heart. We three girls would build cabins out of rocks, leaves, and moss, and collect berries to bring to Mother, who sat nearby doing needlepoint or reading her books.

That world also included Rosa, the farmer's wife, who secretly sewed dresses for the girls "with bell-like skirts that would hold up a long time." And Pauline, another farmer, who came when Uschi's mother was sick and was "vigorous and unstoppable. She did not leave until food was on the table for us, the laundry dried, the ironing basket empty, and every single torn piece of clothing mended." And Frau Tehrach, in whose house Uschi always felt welcome "to sit on her lap, her strong arm around me." It was Frau Tehrach, with two children in Hitler's army, who saw Uschi crying in the rain outside of her locked house and called from her window, "Your mother will be back soon, stay with me awhile." And Frau Tehrach who listened to the injustice done to Uschi in math class by a bully who was the son of a big Nazi. He had erased Uschi's correct answer on her chalkboard and put a wrong one, and when she chided him, Teacher Maier overheard and said, "Don't you know you cannot talk in class?" Three raps on her hand, in public, made her cry so hard with indignation that he sent her home.

Such normal memories for a half-Jewish child living in Nazi Germany! It could be *any* child in school, in the forest, visiting neighbors. It could be my father as a boy in 1905, remembering *In Benheim everyone got along!* And Lotte as a girl in 1925, remembering one big happy family! True, Uschi was only three when she came to Benheim in late 1938, and left at age ten, not really old enough to understand what was happening. But she does remember her mother crying for days, her nose a bright red, when her Jewish grandmother and uncle disappeared in 1940. And an angry man yelling out the window at her, "Go away you Jewish bankers!" And the children in the light green house across the street whose fathers only visited occasionally in uniforms—and who weren't allowed to play with them. Herman and his sister Therese, who lived next door, did play with them in the meadow behind their houses, but never inside! Inside was against Nazi law, one more way to isolate the Jews and make people forget them before they were taken away.

And she remembers the pretzel incident at the Denkmal (the plaza in the meadow where the swastika was mounted). It happened during one of the celebrations up there, as she writes in her memoir:

> I was in a circle with other children and my sisters. We moved with the music and then hungrily lined up with everybody else to get some of those delicious pretzels from a huge, tightly filled basket. But before my sisters and I even got near, a woman posted herself between us and the basket and demanded to know our names. My big sisters told her, and she said, "You have to leave!" with no explanation. Without a pretzel, and with the joyful sound of music still in our ears, we walked all the way back to the Geissgasse, where we lived.

Given the widespread brutality of those days, these were small humiliations. The only real violence she remembers involved her older sister Doris. Some boys teased her as a Jew, and after school one took his slingshot and hit her with a stone that knocked out her tooth. After that, their mother kept her daughters close; they wandered less freely but still went to school and to the meadow.

Uschi says she finally avenged her sister—and the whole family—when, almost sixty years later, Benheim had its Day of Remembering in the former synagogue. She was there with her two sisters and Tante Gaby and was asked to speak. *Too bad I didn't know about this beforehand.* "They came from New York and Oleh Zion and talked about Jewish life before Hitler and the trauma of leaving, but I didn't leave. I was there. So I read from my memoir about those who helped us *and* of the boy with the slingshot. Everyone finally heard what he did!" Uschi says happily.

Yet it's the good memories that draw her to the secret clearing. From there she transports herself back in time to the river where they swam all summer, and the snow-frozen path where they sledded in winter and the woods full of berries and mushrooms to pick. Her sister Trudy avoids Benheim, preferring the present to the past. When asked to come to a class reunion, she said no. Uschi says yes. There is an irretrievable warmth in Benheim that Uschi needs, but also something in shadow:

> When I pass [Jewish] houses that once had names associated with them . . . the faces are erased, but something is still there: an image of a bookcase, a grandfather's clock, the sound of its pendulum when it struck the hour, the taste of chicken soup, of sausages filled with tongue meat, of smoked herring, of freshly baked *Berches*, the sparkle of silver chandeliers and burning candles on white tablecloth. (from "Village on the Hill")

I, who never lived in Benheim, seem to need that, too. Like Uschi, I keep trying to shine words on what's hidden—to know where I am.

DORIS

The dark memories of Benheim are strongest for Doris, the oldest daughter, whom I visit in her hospital bed in a rehabilitation home outside of Stuttgart. At sixty-nine, she has had a stroke, but Trudy is sure she wants to talk to me. "It will be good for her. She will have to remember. And she should speak in English." Trudy, with her usual determination, drives us for an hour in heavy traffic so I can meet this sister. "After all, we are *mishpocheh!*" Trudy says, using the Yiddish word for family, a word that I don't expect from a Christian Scientist in Stuttgart. "Your great-grandmother is my great-grandmother's sister! My sister will love meeting you." Doris's husband, Walter, is less enthusiastic about my visit. A tough, silent man, gentle only with his wife, he glares at me. *Because I am Jewish? Because I will make his bedridden wife tired? Because I am stirring up the past?* I back away from him, glad when he disappears.

"School was horrible in Benheim," Doris tells me, the words coming out with painful slowness. "Parents said, 'Why do you play with a Jewish child?' Only Monica Fürle and the Hecht girl could play. We'd go to the fields to pick up corn kernels—and I'd trade them for milk and flour. The others? No." *It's a memory not unlike Kurt Buchman's memory: two powerless, hungry children gleaning almost the same fields.*

Doris's face is sweating. The room is airless, and it's a hot day, but I bring another kind of heat—with my questions. Walter is still out of the room, thank God, because he would not be happy with this.

I am not happy either. Doris is complicating Trudy and Uschi's stories of no real problems in Benheim, which is what I like to hear.

"Some of the boys, they were mean, bad boys. . . ." Doris's good hand goes to her face, touches her mouth, perhaps for the lost tooth, the one the slingshot knocked out. An empty space, filled in now.

"But we had fun anyway. Didn't we?" Trudy says, offering her sister the strawberries we bought at a roadside stand. Doris shakes her head, no. Her hair is matted, a plain brown, and she is very large, with a no-nonsense air that she probably always had. Her manner reflects a life raising five children with Walter in a small village "where only Protestants live and Jews are not mentioned," according to Trudy.

"Remember how we used to make Christmas lights out of wood boxes?" Trudy offers me strawberries. "And the special Christmas cake mother baked?" Doris nods, glumly. "And the funny boarders from Stuttgart that mother took in for money? Remember Dr. Fürst who roasted chestnuts on the stove? *You* figured out how to open them!" Trudy strokes her sister's quiet leg. "Remember, Doris?"

"And then we stole a few!" Doris says, her face lighting up, and the two of them laugh like little girls. Trudy is thrilled. Doris hasn't laughed since her left side became paralyzed three months ago.

"And remember," Trudy is now on a roll, wanting Doris to stay in this old world rather than be trapped in an airless room, "when our sled went into the Neckar and we came home frozen. Our mother had to heat water to defrost the clothes off us." More laughing—as Trudy offers her sister the chocolates we also brought, and Doris takes two, still smiling. Then she becomes serious. Talking with difficulty, she tells me that at age nine, she was her mother's confidante, the one she cried with when their grandmother and uncle were deported, the one she worried with about money when the boarders (all Stuttgart couples in mixed marriages, who felt safer in Benheim) were deported, late in 1944.

The sweat returns. I think that this is too much for her, but Trudy urges her on. "You are doing good!" she says, with that high-energy charm of hers. "You are speaking English."

I ask if the neighbors helped them much, for Doris may be my most reliable source about how Benheimers treated each other back then. She asks for water. "There were ten, maybe twelve, families, without which we wouldn't have survived. They gave us food, extra ration cards, let my mother work in their fields, and came to visit us at night." Trudy gives her a glass. "There were maybe ten others who hated us, the Nazis of the village. The rest didn't care, but they left us alone."

I want to know about "the rest," what exactly they did or did not do. Was it enough to have left them alone—and what does that mean? But Walter comes back, looks at his exhausted wife, and his body language says: GO. He is no one to fool with, not warm like Knut or even as civil as Herr Stolle. Maybe if he smiled, I'd change my mind about this man, but he doesn't, so my Jewish paranoia has kicked in. I say goodbye, thinking that Doris, far more than her two sisters, has married the "other" and lives in a world without her past, for better and worse.

In 1945 Marta did receive deportation papers from the Nazi government. The three girls were to be sent to an orphanage and she, "to the East." To save the family, according to her daughters, their mother biked the sixty kilometers to Stuttgart (amazing given the bombing in those days) and went straight to the authorities. She showed a photo, so their story goes, to the man in charge and said: "If you take me away from my three little girls, they will be *your* responsibility!" The man, knowing the war would soon be over (and that he might need some good deeds for his record), said, "Go home! You are under my protection." *Was it Herr Otz, who Gretl said helped her get Simon out of Dachau?* Six weeks later, a new deportation order arrived, but three days later the war *was* over. A year after that, Marta and her daughters returned to Stuttgart, "so we could get a better education." They saw Tante Gaby and her husband Max regularly, but rarely saw their father. The four of them did go back to Benheim the next summer to vacation in Herr Esslinger's empty house, so their feelings toward the villagers couldn't have been too resentful. Perhaps because their mother and Tante Gaby liked to say: *If you keep hating, the war will never end.*

23 | YES OR NO?

"So was Benheim special or not?" my son Alan asks, right before I leave for one more trip to the village before declaring this book done. It's what I asked when I first heard about the rescued Torah, before the lives of the people I met took over, their stories making my need for a simple judgment recede. Yet here it is again.

I want to say yes. I've met enough former neighbors, Christian and Jewish, who don't hate each other. And collectively, the village did avoid the worst atrocities. No one terrorized the rabbi on the town square as in Konin. No one locked the Jews in the church and burned them as in Jebwabne.* And the river didn't run red with the blood of Jews on Kristallnacht, as one villager from Rhina describes in the movie *Now After All These Years*. There was a sharpness of voice, cold and without remorse, that I hadn't heard in Benheim, from anyone. Rhina, in northern Germany, was a similar size and had the same high percentage of Jews (30–50 percent depending on the year); yet the Nazis won over the village soul. In Benheim, you can't say that so easily.

I have made a list . . .

The policeman saved two Torahs.
The shoemaker kept fixing Jewish shoes and shared his
    ration cards.

*As told in Theo Richmond's *Konin* and Jan Gross's *Neighbors*, two books about other villages during Nazi times, although these are Polish villages.

The barber cut Jewish hair under the sign NO JEWS
ALLOWED HERE.

The farmer's daughter cleaned house, washed, and brought
food to her old Jewish neighbor.

The barber's daughter lent her good raincoat.

The shopkeeper gave food over the back fence at night.

The bus driver kept driving the Jews, one even to
Switzerland.

A farmer had power of attorney over Jewish fields. He gave
them back after the war.

The three nuns kept helping the Jews until the nuns were
transferred. The beloved mayor kept helping the Jews
until he was transferred.

The priest spoke out against what was happening to the
Jews in a sermon. He was reprimanded.

The head of the Hitler Youth Group turned the lights on
and off for the Jewish youth group that met in the same
building on Friday nights.

Someone let the Jewish schoolteacher file an official
complaint about the vandals in the Jewish cemetery.

The Jews kept drinking beer in the *Gasthaus* until 1940 even
though it was forbidden.

Christians paid back debts to Jews even though the law said
they didn't have to.

A farm wife said at the farmers' meeting, "Law or no law, I
will not force Jews to work for me on their Sabbath."

Someone hid the plaque of the Jewish war dead from WWI
in the archives.

At least ten neighbors helped a half-Jewish family survive
for five years. The rest let them be.

Carpenters who fixed the Jewish windows after Kristallnacht
were sent to the Front and didn't come back.

Small acts of defiance. Nothing anyone bragged about. But
I, for one, would like to be able to make a mark beside every

one, announcing, "I would have done that!" And more, yes . . . maybe—if I knew others would join me, not betray me. But how would I know? For decency is often such a solitary act; it's evil that draws a noisy crowd.

"So, was Benheim a special place?" I ask Professor J., as we sit in the meeting room of Benheim's synagogue/church. A Protestant expert on Jewish villages of the Schwarzwald, he should know how Benheim compares to other villages of the Third Reich.

"Yes!" the professor says, rattling off statistics about how only 16 percent of Benheimers voted for Hitler in 1933 and how one-third of Benheim was Jewish then, much more than elsewhere. Familiar stuff. "But the main reason Benheim was special," he pauses to sip his coffee, "was because the Jews were special." Now that's an answer I haven't heard before. The professor points out how well organized the Jews were. "They formed a Zionist group, early on, to go back to the Holy Land. That impressed everyone, even the local Nazis." He praises their honesty in business and their high ethical standards. "Benheim Jews did not tolerate one of their own doing something underhanded. Everyone knew they could be trusted." His praise is getting uncomfortable. "And they had no inferiority complex," the professor emphasizes. "They saw the Christians as equal, maybe even looked down rather than up." I fidget on that one, telling myself he is an academic. This is based on his research, not anti-Semitism.

He makes no mention of the role of decency. In fact, the professor avoids the word, unlike Hannah and Lotte. Before I left the States, I asked them yet again, "Was Benheim special?" and heard "We had no rights and anyone could do anything. The only thing that held them back was their own decency." I tell this to Professor J., who makes no comment. Is it because of his personal history? *He is the right age.* Or are Benheim Jews dreaming and this Christian expert from elsewhere in Wurttemberg knows the truth?

Yes or No?

Professor J. talks of how the Jews were well traveled and brought back new ideas to the village. Fashion. Indoor plumbing. Phone lines. The Christians of Benheim were proud to be seen by the surrounding villages as more modern; so they copied the Jews and appreciated their efforts. The professor talks of very charismatic Jewish leaders such as the schoolteacher Spatz, who spoke for the Jewish community. He helped them push for their own school. The word "push" has a hint of irritation as in his remark about Jews "looking down." But it is soon replaced with amazement at how many Benheim Jews stayed put in the twenties and early thirties. "They were emptying out of Nordstetten and Müringen, and going to the cities, or leaving for America. Only Haiglerloch had as many Jews left."

"But Haigerloch was bigger, wasn't it?" I say. "More like Dorn."

"Yes, yes, that is true," says the professor, less sure of his facts than I expected, as if his scholarship had been written long ago.

He is gray-haired, with a stooped back and bad tremor in his hand. Yet he drove over an hour to meet with me, a nobody in the field. I wrote him saying, "I'm researching a book about Benheim Jews," and here he is. It is as if I, Jewish daughter from America, am needed to fill in the lingering silences before it's too late.

Despite his academic credentials, Professor J., like the villagers, seems to prefer anecdotal story to theory. He becomes most animated describing a game that was played in the Gasthaus Kaiser, where Christian and Jewish men drank beer together. Someone would ask, "Who is the Jew here?" and everyone would say, "Jews have long noses and I see no long noses here." He laughs, I don't. So he explains that this is evidence of everyone in Benheim getting along. *Really?* He goes on to recount in his reasoned voice how Christian boys wanted to see Jewish penises to be sure they were not amputated. *Not exactly stories to prove my Yes or No.*

I mention the Benheim Torah being saved and neighbors bringing soup to the back door at night. "Did such things happen in other villages?" I ask. Yes, he has heard about the Benheim Torah, now in Israel. And about a menorah and banner being saved in Haigerloch. They are in the museum there. But other stories, ones without saved objects, he doesn't know. "Such small acts don't get written down. They are not in the archives."

I'm wondering how many lists of good deeds go unrecorded —even now. In the mixed neighborhoods of Sarajevo, Rwanda, Bethlehem, Baghdad, or Beirut, where "the other" lives next door, did a Hutu spare a Tutsi, did a Muslim dress a Christian's wounds, or an Israeli comfort a Palestinian child? And how often? If we knew the good stories, no matter how small, might more of us find courage to follow suit? Dramatic acts such as the citizens of Le Chambon hiding Jews get retold, but the quiet ones, such as this one in Billings, Montana, only occasionally:

> When a beer bottle was thrown through a glass door of the home of a Jewish resident—spraying glass over the bed of a five-year-old, the people of Billings began posting photocopies of menorahs in their windows to show their support. The hate groups reacted by committing more violent acts. The residents responded by posting more menorahs. After a mass rally in opposition to the hate groups, the violence—and the skinheads—disappeared. (*Salt Lake Tribune*, May 16, 1999)

No major headlines, just a story in a newspaper by a reporter covering a conference on hate crimes. He also mentions a cross-burning on the lawn of an interracial family in Utah, and describes how, when people heard that, they sent dozens of letters of support—and then "a pizza guy showed up at our door with two pizzas," said the African American homeowner, Robyn Henry. "He handed us a card that said, 'We believe that for every act of senseless violence there should be a random act of kindness.'" It wasn't enough to make a difference, and the Henrys moved away.

The new museum in Haigerloch, thirty kilometers from Benheim, is in the old Jewish quarter, tucked into a hillside below the main street. "It was once the synagogue," says my guide, Herr Gurt, who has opened it for me as a favor to Herr Stolle. The museum is ordinarily open on Tuesday and Thursday and this is Wednesday. Badly burned on Kristallnacht, this building was used as a sports gym, a grocery store, and a movie house, before becoming a modern, well-funded museum about the Jewish community that once thrived here. Memorials and museums about the Jews are now springing up all over Germany, but everyone in Benheim told me this one is excellent and "Not to be missed!"

Prayer books, menorahs, and other artifacts are mounted in glass cases. Photos of Jewish families line the walls: what they looked like in Haigerloch years ago and what they look like today in New York, London, Tel Aviv, Montevideo, wherever they are. On one of the many computer screens, I watch an interview with Ruth, now an Israeli, remembering Haigerloch very fondly. She talks of good neighbors and the good life—and how a Christian friend helped her family after Kristallnacht. She says she comes back regularly to visit, brings her children, and says to the camera, head on: "Haigerloch will always be in my blood." On another video, a man named Irwin remembers playing with the non-Jews as a child, no problem. "We all got along before Hitler." Someone else Jewish remembers battles between the kosher and Christian butchers, but "no big problems, really, before Hitler." These Jews are enthusiastic, even more than the Benheimers. Only one old Christian woman in her nineties talks darkly of how the SA demolished the synagogue and attacked the rabbi's house—and how terrible it was. *That didn't happen in Benheim, not as far as I know.*

Herr Gurt is like a lively Herr Stolle, very knowledgeable—and quite forthright. He tells me what is not in these museum rooms: how the Gentiles of Haigerloch were very upset about Kristallnacht and that quite a few protested to the authorities that Christians shouldn't do such things. But a year later, "it was a different story." Sixteen Jewish men were rounded up, beaten terribly for days, and then made to scrub toilets by hand. And everyone looked away.

"What happened?" I ask, astonished at how the moral barometer changed so quickly. How does a community go from outrage to complicity in one year? "Were these Jews from somewhere else, people they didn't know?"

"Oh, they knew them all!" Herr Gurt assures me. He attributes the change to Hitler's speeches after he invaded Poland successfully. His impassioned words "convinced people that the Jews were the cause of all their problems and that Germany lost World War I because of them. He, the Führer, vowed that he would not let that happen again!"

"No one in Haigerloch protested?"

"Not openly. We had a new police chief, a big anti-Semite, and he by then had free rein."

I don't know what to do with this story. I've been thinking gradual, not sudden. I've been thinking that "good" villages stayed good—not really succumbing to Hitler's venom without great trauma. At least not the adults. Yet here was Haigerloch turning "bad" suddenly and without effort. All it took was a military victory, a few speeches, and a sadistic police chief—a man who, my guide says, was later tried for war crimes along with his staff of six. "Unfortunately, they all got off after nine months," he says, pushing his white hair off his forehead.

So this brand-new museum to remember the Jews, much

grander than Benheim's modest exhibits, cannot erase the dark blots in this town, whatever Haigerloch Jews such as Ruth and Irwin remember fondly. And these blots are not on video interviews or mounted on carefully done walls of then and now. The ugliness is not visible. I look again at the displays that had so impressed me, and see only absence.

Before I leave I ask Herr Stolle if anything terrible happened in Benheim. I know Bodenheimer was murdered and no one was arrested. I know Jewish children, like Willy and his brother, were beaten up by classmates. I know Ushi was afraid to walk past the big yellow house where a mean Nazi lived. I know two graves were vandalized in 1941. I know eighty-nine were deported in three roundups, and that people kept the curtains shut. But was there anything else? I need to know the worst, things that Herr Stolle, Anna, and Inge wouldn't do, but what about the Nazi in the yellow house—and the many others I didn't meet? He pauses and says, "There is one thing. . . ." I brace myself for a story that will turn Yes to No on my Benheim scorecard once and for all. "I wasn't here but heard that someone, maybe an official, maybe not, refused to take a Jew to the cemetery in the official funeral wagon. A farmer had to take him in his hay cart." I look to see if he is joking or being ironic about this story of regret. "*Na ja*, that was a terrible thing," he says. "In Benheim, such a thing shouldn't have happened."

Herr Stolle, a man who has convinced himself that he is "just preserving local history," and who has called the deportations "sendings to the East," does not understate this act. He is really ashamed by this local betrayal, as if this small affront, not the eighty-nine or the six million Jews who disappeared beyond the Benheim borders, is the most terrible because it involved people he grew up with, his neighbors. So his village was responsible; it had the power to defy the order and use the official cart. And only one farmer stepped in. I wish there were more. I wish the whole village went to the cemetery together. *That* would have been special. But still . . . Herr Stolle would not have told me the "terrible" story he did if he knew there were others, far worse.

That, I realize, is all I can offer my son Alan when I go home: the only yes I am sure of, delivered by a man I have come to trust.

24 | THE CELEBRATION

For sins against God, the Day of Atonement brings forgiveness. For sins against one's neighbor, the Day of Atonement brings no forgiveness until one has become reconciled with one's neighbor.

Yoma 6–9, Mishnah

1

The air is still, the crows have a muted call, and only a few birds, unseen, sing in the mist blanketing the valley. Yesterday, when we arrived, I had a perfect nineteenth-century view of Benheim from this little pension set into the hillside. No TV antennas. No satellite antennas. Only bright meadows and winding goat paths, the ones my father walked on, heading for the forest. I could picture him, a boy with a stick, a book, and a slice of linzertorte in his pocket.

This morning I picture nothing, not even the bell tower of the Catholic church. Or the golden hen, now on top of the former synagogue. Or the white cross on the hill where the swastika once stood. All I see, through one small patch of blue sky pushing through the mist, is the lemon yellow house of the young Turkish woman, Askar, whom I met yesterday. And bits of her uncles' houses, flanking each side. Forty of her relatives now live in Benheim, many on a street where Hannah and my father once lived.

Askar says she has identified with the Jews ever since she saw a film on the Holocaust in school, and the boy next to her whispered, "You Turks will be next!" The film gave her such nightmares, she never watched another, but she reads books to "understand the Jews. It is all very complicated, much harder than Islam," says this charming woman in Western dress, who speaks fluent German. I wonder if she will come to the celebration today—to honor a past she wasn't part of.

There will be a big crowd, they say, to celebrate the completed restoration of the former synagogue as both church and living memorial, a place where Christians pray and remember the Jews, their former neighbors. I have flown 3,500 miles to see how—if—such a reconciliation is possible. Some Catholics will not be coming until after the Protestant bishop has spoken. And the head rabbi of Stuttgart declined, sending his cantor instead (the rabbi did say he'd come next fall, I was told). And the older Jews from America and Israel aren't coming—not this time. The Day of Remembering, held halfway through the renovation, was enough for them. That was their chance to look back and speak of memories, good and bad. Today is a day of completion, of looking ahead, and the old Jews, pleading frailty, illness, lack of money, declined this invitation. I come in their stead (though they didn't ask me to), and I have brought my husband, Stu, and Carole, who will translate for me. Her best friend Sonya took a 4:00 a.m. train from Frankfurt to see me and to support this ceremony of remembrance. Trudy, Knut, and Uschi are also here, and they have brought their Tante Gaby. So I am armed with an entourage to see what this day brings, as the mists begin to fade and the roll of speeding cars take over from the birds.

2

The others are driving to the synagogue/church to assure we get seats, but I want to walk from the Upper Village, past window boxes of red, pink, yellow, and blue, all in orderly bloom. I find the steep steps that wind down next to rooftops, approaching from above, as if I'm climbing down from the bell tower of the synagogue/church, its golden hen practically beside me. The hen symbolizes "New Church," I'm told, and is mounted as good luck by the Protestants. Somewhere church bells ring on this now cloudless day, and I walk faster, for the bishop is said to start at ten sharp. I already feel the sun's heat on what will be a long day of events: first, the church service; then lunch, brass bands, talks about Jewish history, Jewish music, cakes and coffee; and finally a walk to the Jewish cemetery. It's all in the program printed for the occasion.

3

The inscription, in Hebrew and in German, is still over the doorway: "Here is none other than God's house and here is the gateway to Heaven." And there's a new plaque mounted to one side, at eye level: ZUR ERRINNERUNG UND MAHNUNG (To Remember and Be Forewarned). I take a picture to remember (and to get a full translation later):

> In Benheim, a Jewish community existed until 1939. This building was erected as a synagogue by this community in 1837. During the Night of the Pogrom on November 9 and 10, it was destroyed and burnt. The Torah scroll was saved. It is now in Oleh Zion, which is a community founded by Jewish Benheimers. We remember our fellow Jewish citizens who were victims of the Nazi terror regime and those who lost their home.

Uschi told me over breakfast that after "The Night of the Pogrom" (Kristallnacht), the building was the village eyesore. She remembers a half-burned empty shell where her classmates looked for bits of treasure among the weeds. Her mother told her daughters, "No, no, stay away!" without saying why, and they did. Stories like that are not on this plaque, just as the stone Torah that once stood over the doorway is no longer between the two inscriptions. I saw it, standing straight like a soldier on guard, in an old photograph of the synagogue from my father's days.

4

Crowds pour through the portal, taking me with them. There must be six busloads worth, or more, from all over the Schwarzwald. The society Träger und Förderverein Ehemalige Synagogue Benheim did well. This group of over one hundred has spent five years raising money and social conscience to restore the church in a way that honors the Jewish past—and still moves forward. *Träger* means "to carry" and *Förderverein* means "to promote," and their union, hard to translate, evokes in me an image of Germans carrying the burden of history for all to see. It's why I said yes to Mayor Himmel's invitation:

> Dear Frau Professor Schwartz,
>
> It is my great pleasure to announce that the interior sanctuary of the former synagogue is close to completion after long construction and renovation. . . . On Sunday, June 15, we want to celebrate and invite you to the celebration. We know it's a long trip but we would be delighted if you could come. . . .

"The synagogue is being restored. How can I miss that?" I told family and friends. I pictured a restoration that made the synagogue look like the one I'd seen in Endingen, Switzerland, two hours south. It hadn't been destroyed, because the Swiss had had no Kristallnacht. I called the airlines, delighted. This would be much more meaningful than Haigerloch's fancy museum.

The interior I had imagined in New Jersey does exist—but

only in four giant placards on the synagogue/church's walls. They show the Benheim synagogue that was, and everyone must pass by them to enter the newly restored sanctuary. Some stop to look; others rush inside for a seat. They all know what I did not realize: that inside is the same church I'd been in with Herr Stolle and Rolf. The posters and giant wall cracks are gone. The low ceiling that slices the room in half horizontally does feel higher with its deep new blue color fading into white edges. "It's meant to be Heaven," I hear someone whisper. The decorative motifs, in pink, blue, and green, "are original from the Jews," someone else says: "They were under the old paint." The enormous circular window above the cross "has been totally restored. What a job!" Light floods the room, like a giant sun, making many shield their eyes.

I see my husband with Carole, and wave. They are in a pew close to the front, and a few rows behind them are Uschi, Trudy, Knut, and Tante Gaby. She came despite her nieces' pleas to her: You are ninety-two. It will be hot. Stuttgart is too far away. It's much too long a drive. To me, they had whispered, "She is too unpredictable. You never know what she'll do." Tante Gaby, her face still showing the beauty she was, is the same age as my mother, and, like my mother, she can be charmingly lucid one moment but out of touch the next.

I take my seat, glad to be with friends in this crowded church of three hundred, maybe more. The pews, all new, are packed. Folding chairs have been brought in, all full with people chatting. Carole and Stu are also chatting, but I am studying the cross in front of me. It is plain and graceful, in thin dark wood. No Jesus hangs from it, so no specific narrative blame is mounted here. It could mean anything, really. So could the open book below it. The New Testament probably, but it could as easily be the Old Testament. And the six white candles behind the book, couldn't they just as well be the eight from the menorah? What's the difference, really? I think, as the bishop appears and the church bell rings. Ten times for ten o'clock. Right on time.

5

The bishop is talking about Jacob lying in the fields, using a stone for a pillow after fleeing Esau. His choice of Old Testament over New Testament is welcome, and I relax, looking at the wheel of lights above me. A dozen or more glass globes are mounted on a circle of wood, as if holding hands. I ease into the rhythms of half-understood German words, not unlike listening to Hebrew in synagogue at home. My comfort level surprises me. You are in a church that once was your father's synagogue. Remember that! I scold myself, as the bishop talks on about Jacob.

Jacob looks up at the night sky of stars, like diamonds, and dreams of a ladder going straight to heaven.

(Carole is writing me notes, translating in fragments she will fill out later).

And in his dream, the skies open above him with a magnificent ladder where angels climb up and down. Here is none other than the house of God, And this is the gate to Heaven. In a place where there was no temple, no church, no place of worship, just knowing that God was above him, helped Jacob understand.

A large gold cross around the bishop's neck is swinging from his sudden leaning toward his flock, us, me.

It is unusual that we celebrate a Christian service in a former synagogue. It is unusual that two different religions meet in one place of worship. But it is not surprising that today, the first Sunday to worship after all the renovations, to hear a saying from the Bible, written in German and Hebrew above the gate of this house, a saying from the

Old Testament directed towards both Jews and Christians: Here is none other than God's house and here is the gateway to Heaven.

Many heads nod in agreement. He's made a good segue into reconciling past and present, even if Jacob was under the night sky, not in a synagogue destroyed by the Nazis.

We are asked to rise and sing "Tut Mir Auf Schöne Pforte," and it fills the room. There is no tentativeness, no mumbling. Everyone, except a few like me, sings the words. "It's the same inscription that's above the door outside!" Carole whispers. "The same doorway to heaven." I nod, looking around for Herr Stolle, Inge, and Anna. They must still be at their Catholic mass down the street; but Kurt Buchman, Katherine, and Paul are five rows to the left—and singing with gusto. Trudy, Knut, and Uschi are singing, too, but softly. Only the Jews—Stu, Carole, and I—don't move our lips.

The bishop continues, the cross on his neck, quieter now, except for the dance of sunlight on the gold. He talks about the special relationship between Jews and Christians in Benheim . . . and how we are all God's children and God's house is everywhere. It could hypnotize you, his cross, if you stare at it and count slowly until you are lulled by the promise of good feelings: that Jacob's ladder is for every climber.

More church bells sound, like loud knocks against the windows. It's the Catholic bells this time, one, two, three, four . . . The bishop doesn't miss a beat.

Jews and Christians will continue to live together. Our job is to prevent another tragedy. But even the secret to living together peacefully remains God's secret and we on earth will never solve it.

"Don't leave it to God!" I want to shout at this dignified, gray-haired man whose cross is swinging again. I look away, at the cut red petals strewn on top of the podium like decapitated heads cut from their stems and scattered. God didn't send eighty-nine Jews born in this village to be murdered and save only two. . . .

. . . that Christian faith is rooted in the Jewish faith, even though we differ on the revelation of Jesus Christ . . .

And God didn't exclude a Catholic leader from speaking today. And ignore the Turkish children playing outside, their voices drifting through the windows like smoke, even as you say:

. . . that this house is a symbol of our common ground and our differences. . . .

Mayor Himmel wanted more inclusion today, but a few church leaders felt that inviting "others" would muddy the meaning of the day, and the bishop agreed. I think of Askar, whose son plays with "the German children." Our family is unusual, his mother told me, for the other Turks keep apart. "The Germans are heathens for many, but my family are Allevites. They are more secular, less threatened by the 'other.'" I asked her how she would feel if her son married a Christian. She said that she could live with that even though she herself felt she had to marry a Muslim. "People should be able to stick to their beliefs," she said, wistfully, "and still live under one roof, in the same house." It's her words I hear as we rise for a silent prayer. I pray for all who died, and for the bishop's good intentions, and for Askar's hope for a more tolerant future. And then people are singing "The Twenty-third Psalm," which I know from synagogue, in Hebrew. I don't know the German words, but the rhythms are familiar enough in this House of God with its gateway to heaven.

6

We are downstairs, below the sanctuary, in a meeting room packed with people. Mayor Himmel is welcoming everyone who has supported the restoration of the synagogue. "Thank you to all who have made this day possible: the choir from Dorn, the bakers of all the cakes waiting upstairs . . . " He is a fine man, with less hair than when we first met, but with the same energy and ability to make people believe that good things can be done, according to Uschi, who works with him in the Träger und Förderverein Society. Today's turnout is proof.

Across from him I see the mural of Jesus, Moses, and Elijah, still here. Why did I think that would be gone? I found out its inscription, Matthew 17:1–8, tells how Peter and the disciples were ready to make shelters for all three prophets. But then "the Lord appeared as a bright cloud and said, 'This is my Son, my Beloved, on whom my favor rests; listen to him' . . . And when they raised their eyes they saw no one else, only Jesus."

I turn away. All the Germans—Uschi (Christian Scientist), Mayor Himmel (Protestant), and Herr Stolle (Catholic)—defend its good intentions. The artist, he assures me, is part of an art movement famous for being anti-Nazi. I still hate it. It is where the rescued Torah once was.

"And today we have some very special visitors," the mayor drones, "the cantor from Stuttgart. . . . " Applause. "The Assistant Director of Jewish Affairs in Württemberg. . . ." Applause. "The Swabian band. . . ." Applause. And suddenly I hear my name, that I have come all the way from America, the daughter of a Benheim Jew—and that I will speak. "Did you know that?" whispers Carole. I shake my head no. My husband pokes me in the ribs. Sonya, Knut, and Uschi smile, delighted. "Will you translate for me?" I ask, frantic about what to say. That this is a day of celebration. That there is nothing to celebrate. That there's a good spirit here. That I feel a great loss here. I spot Herr Stolle, leaning against the wall across the room. He nods and I feel calmer somehow, as if I got some necessary permission that he's been withholding. Or so I tell myself.

"But first let me read letters from well-wishers." The mayor reads letters of congratulations from the Benheim Benevolent

Society in New York (Hannah wrote it) and from people in Oleh Zion (Lev wrote it). And then other speeches begin: "Let's learn from the past and never forget it. . . . Let this building support the Jewish-Christian dialogue and the communication of all religions. . . . Let us find peace and inspiration here to reflect on the identical values of the Jewish and Christian religion. . . . Let this building serve as a reminder to all that never again can we allow any form of racial or despicable acts of humankind."

Good words. I make myself stop looking at the mural and start looking at the faces around me. They are benign, smiling, with no scowls in sight. There are Inge and Anna, and six nuns, and young mothers with strollers listening intently to the mayor's words and the reconciliation they promise. These are the kind of people my father and the Jews in New York remember: good people with a good spirit. If only, collectively, they had been more powerful. If only this building could make and keep them so. . . . "And now our speaker, a daughter of Benheim . . . "and I go with Carole to the podium, the mural at my back, to tell everyone how my father, before the Hitler years, had always felt a good spirit in Benheim. And I feel it here today. . . .

7

Midday. The sun beats down and the band plays Swabian polkas and marches. Trombones and horns catch the sunlight, as do the gold buttons on bright red vests. Thirty or forty instruments—it's a full band—fill the air with songs of celebration. I try not to forget the band in a photo I have of the Nazi parade fifty yards from here. That was 1933, this is 2004, and the good people are out today. Visible and engaged. The ones who hate are at home, sulking. They are not eating cakes and tortes and strudel on picnic tables under Coca-Cola umbrellas, the only shade around. They are not members of the Träger und Förderverein Society, to carry forward and promote the memories of what happened, like Herr Stolle, and Kurt Buchman, and Katherine and Paul, and Uschi, all sitting at these picnic tables. Beside me are Erika and Michael, the Stuttgart couple that bought the farmhouse near the Jewish cemetery and helped Herr Stolle publish his manuscript. They have also made an ongoing commitment to publish the newsletter of Träger und Förderverin Society. And they run a seminar series about Christian/Jewish history and plan to publish a book about the Jewish houses of Benheim—with photos and oral histories by neighbors who remember the Jews.

People with no connection to Benheim are also here. Seated opposite me on this picnic table is a high school teacher who teaches the Holocaust twenty kilometers away in a town that never had any Jews. Yet he is a member of the Träger und Förderverein Society and has come today. Why? I ask him. He tells me he became interested, after seeing a Holocaust movie in 1979, in understanding "a force that was so evil. How could that happen in Germany? What does it mean for our society?" And then he went to Israel to see Jews for himself and "I bought a yarmulke from the Orthodox Jews in Mea Sharim and wore it on my head to the hotel. People asked me why I was wearing it, and I said I wanted to feel what it was like to be Jewish."

And there is Sonya, who dedicates so much energy to events like this: to remember and learn. Like Erika and Michael and Mayor Himmel, she is committed to making future generations stop and notice memorials, wherever they are. *Zur Erinnerung und Mahnung.* Remember and Be Forewarned. It's so easy to rush by.

When I told my friend Janet, in America, about the celebration, she was unimpressed. "If it was going to be a memorial or a museum, fine. But to become a church makes me angry." I was surprised. Janet had been hidden by a Christian family in Poland all through the war, so this was not a knee-jerk response of the uninitiated. "I can imagine," she said, "someone saying that this marks the unity of Old and New Testaments. That is worthless. Forget it. They destroyed the Jews who are now gone, period. You can't have your cake and eat it too."

Janet's argument is powerful, but being here, I feel otherwise. If this synagogue were a museum, it would be disconnected from daily life, like the stone memorial in the cemetery or the Haigerloch museum, visited once, maybe twice. Here, people come every Sunday passing the four placards of memorial before they sit in "God's house," praying with neighbors about being good.

8

Inside, a violin and cello are playing. Two teenage boys with yarmulkes are playing Jewish melodies under the wooden cross, sad songs in minor key alternating with a lively Yiddish wedding song. The cantor from Stuttgart brought them to play after his lecture on the history of Jewish synagogues. I thought he would sing, but so far he is silent. The room is three-quarters full, not as packed as before, but respectable. All the old-timers are here now: Inge, the farmer's daughter, listens as if she can hear Hans singing through the open window. Frau Bidner looks as if she is again watching a Jewish wedding where, as a child, she remembered "everyone was kissing and hugging. In our church no one did that, not even at weddings." I see Anna with the Lugers, and Herr Stolle, who has been very quiet. Maybe because the next generation is now in charge, people who don't remember firsthand. Or because the past has moved in close, too close.

I recognize "Dona, Dona" and begin to hum, adding the words in a whisper "How the winds are laughing, they laugh with all their might" to fend off a growing sense of dislocation. Why am I here? And then it starts, like a soft wail: "Kol Nidre," the melody of the highest holy day for Jews, the prayer that voids debts to God so one can start afresh. But can people whose torches destroyed a community start again? Herr Stolle is slumped forward, Anna's eyes are closed. Only Inge sits erect, a farmer's daughter. We all wait for the cantor to start singing, but he stays silent. The mournful strains go on and on without words as this holiest of Jewish prayers is played here for the last time.

9

We are walking up the path to the cemetery, the late afternoon shadows beside us. I am with Uschi in this scattered pilgrimage of Catholics, Protestants, Christian Scientists, and young and old Jews. It is long after five, way behind schedule, this last event. This morning's crowd has dwindled to forty or so, the bishop is gone, the old-timers I know are not in sight. Did they go home, too tired? Or is it because they come here on their own—Anna on her daily walks, Herr Stolle to bring visitors and to clean the branches off the graves? This cemetery is part of their routine, not like the mothers who push strollers behind us. I doubt they've been here before.

Trudy and Knut have taken the car because Tante Gaby can't walk so far. They begged her not to come to the cemetery, that they would take her back to the pension. "Too much for her," Uschi says, sounding worried. "Too much." She means more than old age or the heat of a long day. She means Tante Gaby's bad feelings that she's alive at ninety-two while her mother and brother were deported and died. And worse, they are not buried in these woods, their souls without a resting place.

"Do you know that tree?" Uschi asks. I don't. She points out the initials. AW, 1938. "It was carved by Alfred Weinberger before he left for Palestine." *This is the tree that Anna said the foresters wanted to chop down.* "And up there is where I come . . . to remember." She points to woods above the cemetery where she recaptures, through her writing, the grandmother and uncle who disappeared so suddenly.

I remember . . . how they admired my curls and asked me to show my Bauch (belly), and when I pointed to it with my little fingers, I got a treat. It might have been chocolate, a taste I soon forgot because candy disappeared from our world. "Once the war is over!" everyone promised. . . . But the adults with these treats also disappeared.

Uschi and I have reached the gate, the shadows from the giant conifers taking over as we walk through to the graves. Only shafts of sunlight now, and the wind has picked up, but it feels okay after all this heat. People are gathering in a circle around the cantor, his forehead still damp with sweat. We are down to a hard core of bakers and band players, my contingent and friends, the high school history teacher, mothers with strollers, the man who kept the Sabbath candles lit, Mayor Himmel, Erika and Michael, the Stuttgart contingent, and others I do not recognize. Everyone is standing except for the smallest children and Tante Gaby, seated on the bench beside the stone memorial to "the Victims of Nazi Persecution."

The cantor begins his prayers, his deep, rich voice filling the old woods with the chanting of Hebrew. My father had whispered prayers here and so, I suspect, did the other Jews who came back to honor their ancestors. But today the words ring loud as a bell that could reach the village, drift in through the windows, you never know how far.

Trudy shifts restlessly. She is used to being unnoticed in Benheim. "I like being invisible," she told me as we drove here from Stuttgart yesterday. "Not like Uschi, who has made friends in Benheim. And not like Tante Gaby, who loves being dramatic, the center of attention!" Both nieces still worry about what their aunt might do, which is why Knut is standing behind Tante Gaby.

Suddenly out of the cantor's Hebrew chanting comes German words—Treblinka, Auschwitz, Riga, Lublin, Theriesenstadt, Bergen Belsen. . . . Everyone tenses. This is not your normal prayer to ask God to grant rest and peace to departed souls. This prayer is for all who were murdered in the Holocaust, a special prayer, Uschi whispers. The circle starts to close, shoulders touch, as if to keep all badness out. The wind has shifted, chilly enough for goose bumps, and Tante Gaby on the bench is becoming more and more agitated. "Meine Mutti (My mother) . . ." Her cry echoes through the trees, louder than the cantor's prayer. "Und mein Bruder [And my brother]." It is a wail so loud that the cantor has to stop, as the circle holds its breath. Knut is now beside Gaby, his arms around her, quieting her down. The cantor begins again and the circle sighs in relief, watching Knut, who keeps stroking Gaby's hand. A kind man. We ease back into familiar rhythms, in a minor key that seems right for the coming darkness. And then, like a wave, it comes again: "Meine Mutti . . . " Gaby is standing now, her silver hair catching the last sunlight. "Mein Bruder!" She raises her arms as if to embrace them, while Knut tries to get her back on the bench. I feel the tears I've denied all day, maybe always, for the dark stories of the unburied. They fill the air, Tante Gaby has evoked them, and I, who avoid confronting atrocity whenever possible, cannot escape its consequences here. The sorrow of being Jewish surrounds me. The Holocaust everywhere. I breathe it in, not as part of someone else's story but as my story. And for once I don't resist.

"How could she do such a thing?" Trudy whispers angrily. I look around for Uschi. "She has disappeared," Trudy says. "She couldn't stand it." The cantor continues until it comes again, "Ermordet!! [Murdered]. Lieber Gott, Lieber Gott [Oh my God, my God!]," overpowering his melody. Arms hang limp. Shoulders hunch. We are a circle of grief, the festivities erased by words and wails without decorum on a day of decorum. But unlike Trudy and Uschi, I am glad.

It is good what Tante Gaby did. For after the cantor's last prayer, everyone gathers around her. Strangers hug her. They tell her how sorry they are for her loss—and their loss. Her grief has made the day real; the celebration without her as an anchor would have floated away. I hope "Meine Mutti, mein Bruder" can echo across the valley, reminding everyone that neighbors can disappear while others are home preparing the meal, feeding the baby, stacking wood, and doing all the other chores that took those who came this morning home before the prayers for the murdered began.

What if this last event had started the day, and the bishop had led a long procession to this cemetery this morning, the cantor by his side? (And why not the priest and imam, too!) I hear my pragmatic father saying, Why ask? Such celebrations have never happened and will never happen, but still be glad you are here to celebrate decency wherever it appears. An owl hoots, a few songbirds reply, and I hear his old *In Benheim this . . . In Benheim that . . .* with a new story—as we pass through the gate and head toward the village, the sun gone now, but its light holding for hours.

ACKNOWLEDGMENTS

Many great people and institutions supported this project, and I'm happy to thank them officially . . . at last. First, to members of the Jewish Benevolent Society of the village that put me in touch with over forty people. Also, to my college, Richard Stockton College of New Jersey, for funding research time and some travel costs to the village. And to the MacDowell Writers Colony for providing three weeks of quiet, so needed for getting started on making sense of what I found out.

It was there I met writer Maureen Stanton, who has cheered me on for twelve years with her careful, enthusiastic reading. Many amazing friends also read drafts without reader fatigue: Gail Ullman, Lynn Powell, Penny Dugan, Nancy Sommers, Scotia MacRae, and Madeline Tiger. Thanks also to my advisers who helped put personal observations and experience into a larger historical and sociological context: Suzanne Keller, Gary Gerstl, Carol Rittner, Jutta Cords, Susan Pringsheim, Edith Milton, Vivian Shapiro, Aron Berlinger, Judy Gerson, Eva Gossman, Dorothee Lottmann-Kaeseler, Paul Lyon, Itzhak Sharon, and Jan Colijn. And to friends, and writer friends, who read key chapters: Michael Steinberg, Dustin Beall Smith, Rebecca McClanahan, Nancy Heffernan, Paula Rich, Naomi Rose, Julie Schwartz, and Maxine Winer; and to editor Karen Brazillier; and to Waltraud Pawlak for her on-the-spot translations; and to Barbara Staudacher and Heinz Hoergle for their photographs; and, of course, to all the villagers, wherever they live now.

Several writing groups also helped me out, including two with names: U.S. 1 Writing Cooperative and the Cape May Writers Faculty. Plus, an insightful book club in Michigan that read the nearly completed manuscript. (How often do you hear from readers before a book comes out?) Special thanks to my agent Carol Mann and the staff of University of Nebraska Press, particularly my editor, Ladette Randolph, whose enthusiasm and advice make everything happen. Finally, my daily thanks to Stuart Schwartz, who reads everything first, sometimes before morning coffee, with honesty and authenticity.

Let me also acknowledge the following publications for publishing excerpts of this book when in progress: "Anonymous Translation" in *Florida Review* (Summer 1999); "The Revolving Room" in *Tikkun* 15, no. 4; "Willy of Baltimore" in *River Teeth* (Fall 2006); and "Off the Record" in *The Missouri Review* (Winter 2007).

For additional materials about *Good Neighbors, Bad Times,* including a reading guide, please visit the University of Nebraska Press's Web site at www.nebraskapress.unl.edu.

▌DISCUSSION QUESTIONS

The story of the rescue of the Torah on Kristallnacht becomes the catalyst for the author's search, fifty years later, to find out more about the Benheim Christians who did it, why, and how unusual they were. *What does the author hope she will find and how do her expectations match her discoveries?*

One of the book's epigraphs is, "There is a place that existed before you came to it, closed with the secrets and complexities of history; and there is the place you experience in the present." *Why do you think the author chose it?*

The author says she changed the names of the village and its people to protect the "right to privacy for people who are neither famous nor infamous." *Do you agree with her decision?* In literary nonfiction such as this, with its emphasis on making real people come alive on the page, *how important is it to know the real names of people and of the village?*

Each chapter takes the reader into another living room and another life, remembering the same village before, during, and after the Hitler years. *What happens to the concepts of Truth, Bravery, Loyalty, Betrayal, and Kindness as each person's version of the past and its legacy is revealed?*

The story is told in present tense, as if events were happening right now. *How does this sense of immediacy affect the way that readers experience people and events? Would anything change for you if the story were told in past tense?*

The son of Herr Stolle says that when he found out about the Holocaust at age sixteen, he had huge fights at home. He blamed his parents for not doing more to stop the deportations. *What else could they have done in this small village? What would you have done if you lived there?*

Scholars at the author's college warned, "Don't be naïve! Trust the records, not what people tell you! People are unreliable, contradictory!" *How does the author deal with these caveats—and how true do they turn out to be?*

Like many immigrant children, the author didn't want to know about her parents' foreign past. She was American, "the first Yankee in the family." And that was good enough, at least for half her life. *How do her discoveries about her father's village and its neighbors affect her attitudes about herself as an American? As a Jew? As a good neighbor in today's world?*

What connections do you see between life in this one little village before and during Nazi times and your life in your neighborhood today? What, if anything, can people do to assure that neighbors, wherever they are, can be decent even when political extremists threaten those relationships?

On pages 234-35 there is a list of small acts of kindness that happened during those Nazi years. The author calls them "small acts of defiance." *Do you agree? What would happen if more people committed such acts? Is there a tipping point that can affect a whole community or a whole country?*

Many Benheim Jews now living in America remember a world where "everyone got along before Hitler." Many Benheim Germans remember their Jews "escaping to the Holy Land." *How do we decide how much of such memories is shaped by the need for nostalgia and the urge to tell "good" stories rather than by hard, historic facts?*

On page 141 Willy compares his observations of the other children in pre-Holocaust Germany with what is happening to children today in Palestine. *What other current world examples can you identify that follow this pattern of indoctrination? Why do you think this is perpetuated despite the many examples history provides of the tragic results?*

Of all the examples of how people behaved under threat and constant fear, *which one would best represent your feelings and reactions if you were in such a situation? Which of the Benheimers were the most sympathetic? Why? Which were the least?*

"Elegance is Trudy's talisman against darker days" (225). *What are other talismans in the book? What is Lotte's? Willy's? Herr Stolle's? What is yours? Do you think that one must go through a traumatic experience to acquire a talisman, or is it basic human nature to do so?*

The author's son asks her near the end of the project, "So was Benheim special or not?" *What do you think?*